MONEY AT WORK

MONEY AT WORK

On the Job with Priests,
Poker Players,
and Hedge Fund Traders

Kevin J. Delaney

NEW YORK UNIVERSITY PRESS
New York and London

NEW YORK UNIVERSITY PRESS
New York and London
www.nyupress.org

References to Internet websites (URLs) were accurate at the time of writing.
Neither the author nor New York University Press is responsible for URLs
that may have expired or changed since the manuscript was prepared.

Library of Congress Cataloging-in-Publication Data
Delaney, Kevin J., 1960–
Money at work : on the job with priests, poker players, and hedge fund traders / Kevin J. Delaney.
p. cm.
Includes bibliographical references and index.
ISBN 978-0-8147-2080-6 (cl : alk. paper)
ISBN 978-0-8147-3807-8 (ebook)
ISBN 978-0-8147-6966-9 (ebook)
1. Hedge funds. 2. Fund raising. 3. Money. I. Title.
HG4530.D417 2012
331.7'93--dc23   2011052280

New York University Press books are printed on acid-free paper,
and their binding materials are chosen for strength and durability.
We strive to use environmentally responsible suppliers and materials
to the greatest extent possible in publishing our books.

Manufactured in the United States of America

10 9 8 7 6 5 4 3 2 1

CONTENTS

ACKNOWLEDGMENTS

Since this book makes the point that work shapes who we are, it is tempting to blame all my colleagues for what they have wrought. Instead, I will thank them for their help. I have had support over the years from everyone at Temple University, particularly those with whom I work in the Sociology Department and in the College of Liberal Arts Dean's Office. Susan Herbst, Phil Alperson, Carolyn Adams, and Teresa Soufas have all been supportive deans and great colleagues. Provosts Lisa Staiano-Coico and Richard Englert and university presidents David Adamany and Ann Weaver Hart have been leaders who value faculty research. As evidence of their commitment, this book was aided by a summer research fellowship from Temple University. My longtime colleagues Gretchen Condran and Julia Ericksen have always been available to talk about the big ideas, and Judith Levine pointed me toward several new sources of ideas. The staff at NYU Press, particularly Ilene Kalish, Aiden Amos, and Despina Papazoglou Gimbel helped nurture this book at each step along the way.

I owe gratitude to my colleagues in the field of economic sociology as their ideas and insights inspired this book. The work of Viviana Zelizer and Donald MacKenzie has been particularly important in this regard, and Mark Granovetter and Michael Schwartz have provided me with their intellectual insights for many years. Rich Joslyn, Joe McLaughlin, and Miles Orvell suggested references from outside my own field of study, while Michelle Byng, Mitch Telsey, Daud Watts, and Chris Zuech all shared their networks into particular occupations that I wished to study. Rebecca Alpert and Khalid Blankinship gave me preliminary guidance on some areas of religion with which I was less familiar, and Jared Peifer and Kelly Feighan provided comments on drafts of chapters. Nicole Finnie and Martine Quinn helped transcribe some interviews, and Faye Richardson provided a daily model of strength and dedication. The Delaney and Korman families have always supported me. Susan Korman helped in so many ways, and Rick Eckstein provided the needed diversions.

I give special thanks to all the people who granted me interviews for this book and provided access to their seminars, conferences, and retreats. They were patient with my attempts to figure out a way to study money in their line of work, they talked with me for long periods of time, and they allowed me to hang out and watch them work. The book would not exist without their cooperation and faith in the project.

INTRODUCTION

Thinking about Money

In one way or another, I have been thinking about the issues in this book since I was a young child. I grew up in a rather large working-class family (five children, two parents), and money was always tight. Adding to the money pressures of raising five children was the fact that my mother was viewed by her own parents as "marrying down" when she chose my father. My maternal grandparents worried that my father would not be able to support a family. Reacting to this and to the actual material circumstances of his life, my father became determined to prove to his in-laws (and to the world) that he could have a large family and support them financially. My father had a high school education and a rather poorly paying job with a municipal water district. Yet my parents were committed to sending all five children to Catholic schools, which meant steady and continuous tuition payments for multiple children at any given time. To supplement his earnings at his primary job, my father began taking on additional jobs. He worked as a golf caddy at a country club on weekends and later began working nights as a valet car parker at the same country club. At some points during my childhood, my father actually held down four different jobs: his main job at the water district, caddying on weekends, parking cars at night, and "detailing" cars at the country club in whatever time was left over. As a result, we children saw my father only two weeknights per week (and no weekends at all, typically). My mother, for her part, also worked very hard at home raising our family and trying to make ends meet on the income my father brought into the house.

This meant that money was often very tangible for me as a child. My father would arrive home very late at night from the country club (around 2 a.m. typically), and he would leave a stack of dollar bills on the table (as he was paid solely in tips at his night job). Early the next morning, he would get up for work for his "regular" job, and sometimes the rest of us would be up having breakfast. I remember watching my father count out the dollar bills into separate smaller stacks as my mother verbally recited, almost as if counting along with him, "John's school shoes, Kevin's sneakers, Sharon's school clothes, the washing machine repair bill. . . ." My father's chest seemed to puff out if the stacks were large enough, but there would be palpable tension and significant anxiety if the family's needs were larger than the stacks of bills.

Interestingly, and perhaps not surprisingly, most of my own research has centered on money and finance—and in this way, one could say that the relationship between money and work, the subject at the heart of this book, reaches down from one generation to the next. I have always had an interest in reading about money and related financial matters. Among the thousands of books about money, one commonly finds accounts of money that can align with the one I share here—namely, that events in childhood shape our relationship to money in adulthood. However, as I have grown into an adult and experienced some social mobility and engaged in many different types of work, I have noticed that my own views of money often changed as a result of the work I was doing. In other words, attitudes toward money are not simply set in childhood but rather evolve throughout one's life. For me, it has often been the workplace where I have learned new things about money and where I would find my attitudes toward money changing. For example, when I worked as a highway toll collector, I began to think about money in a very concrete way. I would have thousands of interactions each day with people who handed me dollar bills (this was before the invention of EZ-Pass). I was amazed at how much time toll collectors spent talking to each other about various schemes and scams (both actual and imagined) for stealing money. But I also noticed that they spent almost as much time telling stories about legendary toll collectors from the past who had been caught in these various schemes. I came to believe that these stories were told because we were around so much cash all the time *and* because the daily practices of the job afforded a tremendous amount of time to think and talk about such issues. We could talk across lanes while collecting tolls, but there was also significant downtime in which we sat in the building next to the highway counting out our money and recording it for deposit in a vault. This gave us plenty of time to swap stories, with piles of cash in front of us on a table. I also sensed that the anonymity of the transactions we engaged in over and over again also contributed to a sense of alienation that we felt toward the money we collected. It was easy for a toll collector to imagine that the money really didn't belong to anyone, and who would really miss it? (Of course, we knew very well that it belonged to the state government, and we also knew that someone would indeed miss it, which may be why no one actually did take the money.) We also had a very boring job in which one of the ways to keep your brain active was to think about elaborate ways to get some of the money sitting in front of you in your cash drawer. I think the storytelling that toll collectors engaged in was a way to manage the tension created by being in the constant presence of a lot of cash, and the "cautionary tales" of schemes gone awry served as a kind of socialization and policing mechanism warning colleagues to be careful and to resist easy temptation.

When I worked as a bartender, I thought about money in a somewhat different way. I still was around a lot of cash, but I often talked with other bartenders about how to increase my tips. I became occupied with the question, Why is some money a tip and other money a wage? Again, I think the daily workplace practices of being a bartender contributed to this musing. I worked in a bar where it was common to give the fourth drink to the patron for free. When I served this complimentary drink, it was usually an unspoken signal for the patron to give me a tip since he was getting that round for free. This "system" encouraged some bartenders to try to give the free round on the third drink, rather than the fourth drink, in order to get tipped more frequently. Owners and managers were on the lookout for this, and I know of one bar that made bartenders put a very small plastic cup upside down in front of the patron with each drink served, so there was some "visible proof" of how many drinks had been paid for already.[1] I also noticed that when I worked as a bartender, I always walked around with a lot of cash in my pocket, and I seemed to spend money much more easily with cash burning a hole in my pocket. Since I worked really late hours, I mainly hung around with other bartenders and wait staff who also had a lot of cash available to them. We all lived within what I call in this book the same *money culture*. Money seemed highly discretionary, very immediate, and easy to spend. When we went out after hours, bartenders and servers tipped lavishly in sympathy with their fellow travelers. We had no pension and no health insurance, and this all contributed to a "live for the moment" mentality; and bartenders often talked about how long they would keep going before finding a job with benefits.

A few years later, I worked for a health care consulting firm, and I learned to think in an entirely differently way about money. In this job, I mathematically modeled how to price a prescription drug under patent protection and how to measure the financial return on research and development expenditures. Money became larger in the sheer quantitative terms being discussed but also more abstract (it was now displayed in graphs, spreadsheets, and charts rather than in stacks of bills on a kitchen table or on a bar). Money, as conceived of in this job, had a much longer time horizon (rather than cash burning a hole in a pocket, we were modeling return on investment at least a decade or more into the future). Thinking about my own future savings, learning about different types of investments, comparing the rates of return on my savings, and watching over my 401(k) retirement account seemed much more "natural" in this work setting. When a generic version of a drug was about to come onto the market, manufacturers of the brand-name product sometimes considered raising, rather than lowering, the price of the brand drug in order to wring out whatever profit was left in the brand name. To think about the profit that remains in a brand name was certainly a new way to think about money for me.

When I became a college professor, I thought again in new ways about money, as I was now asking, Is it better to put more of my time into my research or my teaching? Should this decision be based solely on the economic reward for each activity, or should it be based on what I enjoy doing? Later, when I entered university administration and began working with academic budgets, I had to think again in an entirely new way about money: How do you best measure the productivity and value of one academic department against another? How do you develop a budget model that accounts for activities and outcomes that we might desire but are very difficult to measure and put a value on?

In every new job I held, I learned new vocabularies around money and engaged in different daily routines related to money. I learned from others in the profession about how to think about money in that particular money culture. I had different sets of concerns and worries, different emphases and goals, different tools and heuristics for measuring, and a different array of opportunities and constraints. Most of the books I read about how people think about money, however, seemed to overlook these differences and centered either on someone's social class position in childhood (whether they grew up rich or poor) or on someone's psychological adaptation to his or her childhood experiences with money (there are many shelves filled with books to help you discover your "money personality").[2] These did not account for what I was experiencing—that different types of work produced distinct cultures surrounding money, and the type of work I was doing shaped my conception of money.

For a long time, I found it difficult to articulate these ideas, and I strived for a way to conduct research around the notion that the quality and the nature of the work a person does shapes, in some significant and observable ways, the way a person thinks and talks about money. I finally landed on the idea of interviewing and observing people in a wide range of occupations, each of which has money as a central element of work. I hoped that by casting a wide net and looking at very different occupations in comparison to one another would yield interesting insights into how work shapes a person's view of money.

In this book, I focus on the different types of "cognitive work" (efforts to conceive of the meaning of money and work in particular ways) and the different types of "emotion work" (efforts to manage one's emotions about money) that occur in the daily routines of various types of jobs. I show how particular types of cognitive work and emotion work emerge from the structured and patterned relationship of that job to money. By this, I mean that the daily routine of jobs and the accompanying cognitive and emotion work that is needed to perform certain jobs creates specific money cultures. The term "money culture" simply means beliefs and practices about money that are socially transmitted. I show how distinct money cultures develop out of the quotidian practices and socialization experiences that occur at work, and I connect the daily economic practices at work with the money cultures that emerge. A money culture, in turn, socializes newcomers and further reveals and fosters certain practices related to money. Different types of work create particular recurring "cognitive dilemmas" for people around their relationship to, and view of, money (and the many values connected to money). By listening carefully for these cognitive dilemmas, noting their patterns, and understanding how they are resolved (or at least attempted to be resolved), we come to understand more fully how a money culture takes shape.

I hope to introduce a new way of thinking about the relationship between money and work. I want to demonstrate that the work we do plays a very important role in shaping the way we come to think of money, and this often has a spillover into life outside of work. I have come to think of this approach as a *cognitive economic sociology of money and work*. While this phrase is certainly a mouthful, I hope my approach provokes your own thinking about the meaning and impact of money at work.

Across all the chapters in this book, I am interested in understanding a series of issues related to money and finance, including how we think about money, the *cognitive work* and *emotion work* that occurs in different occupations as people learn to conceive of money in distinctive ways; the differing *time horizons* used to think about money in differing types of work; the ways in which people *mark* money for different purposes; the moral assumptions embedded in the language and workplace routines related to money and finance; how ideas about money are encoded in *sacred texts*, *training materials*, or other written materials within each profession; the rhetorical and cognitive responses to the dilemmas and tensions created by particular money cultures at work; and the ways people's conceptions of money gained through work carry over into their family and private lives. Fundamentally, I am interested in how the day-to-day practices of a particular profession or line of work produce, sustain, and legitimate different worldviews of money and finance.

I focus on several organizing themes. First, how do the day-to-day practices of different types of work produce distinctive views of money? For example, how does selling (and the constant pressure to sell) produce certain attitudes and practices around money? How does working as an agent representing someone else's talent in intense financial negotiations lead to a particular view of money and its relationship to talent? How does spending forty hours per week counseling people in credit card debt affect a debt counselor's view of indebtedness and its causes? How does raising funds from high-net-worth individuals and traveling into the world of people with vastly higher incomes than your own affect the way you think about money? How does playing poker for a living or trading in hedge funds produce similar cognitive dilemmas? What are the economic and social sources of the similarities and differences between hedge fund traders and poker players?

Second, how do daily practices produce particular ways that we talk about money, or what might be called *money rhetorics* or *vocabularies of money*? What storytelling devices, cautionary tales, advice giving, and tropes tend to dominate different types of work? How are these ways of talking about money produced and connected to the daily work practices and economic locations of jobs? What cognitive or rhetorical responses arise in response to the *money dilemmas* presented by particular types of work?

Third, how do people *learn* money cultures within occupations? What socializing experiences are important to transmitting particular views of money within professions? Is it done through training programs? Are particular texts or oral or written traditions used to transmit money lessons? Who or what are seen as the guiding influences that produce ways of thinking about money? How do people come to learn the dominant money culture in their particular line of work? Are there *initiation rituals* into occupational money cultures?

Fourth, what happens when people actively try to experiment with money, intentionally flouting conventional ways of thinking about money in their work lives? How does thinking and talking about money change as they play with dominant conventions surrounding money? I explore what happens when individuals try to test the limits of money by altering very basic taken-for-granted characteristics of work and money.

Finally, what does understanding the money cultures created in different types of work tell us about the connections between the economic and the social? How are economic relations embedded in social relations at work, and how do social relations emerge from particular economic locations within the larger economy? How might we think about, and research, the interconnections between the economic and the social?

The book proceeds as follows: In chapter 1, I outline a way to think about money in both structural and cognitive terms. I consider whether money is simply a lubricant for exchange or whether it is an important ritual object in and of itself. For those who are interested in the theoretical backdrop to my thinking about money, this chapter provides some guidance to the way I approach the topic.

In chapter 2, I compare professional poker players with hedge fund traders, looking at the similarities and differences in their work and in the people who engage in this work. I show how structural factors common to these two types of work create similar cognitive dilemmas in managing emotions and balancing risk and aggression. I describe common adaptations or resolutions that poker players and hedge fund traders make to cope with these dilemmas, and I illustrate how certain cultural markers of these cognitive dilemmas are clearly shown in the stories that poker player and hedge fund traders tell about their work.

In chapter 3, I consider two occupations that involve selling things: commission salespeople selling consumer products and sports and entertainment agents selling the talents of their clients. Because of the economic structure of these occupations, and in particular the way people are paid and rewarded, both salespeople and agents must think of their time as money, and they face a fairly stark equation between their sales success and their identity and self-worth. This presents a host of interesting ways that commission salespeople and agents conceive of the connection between time and money. I find that these individuals expend a surprising amount of cognitive and emotional energy adapting the equation of time and money, maintaining a sense of self-worth that isn't completely dependent on sales commissions. I also show how these dilemmas bleed over into similar struggles with the fuzzy boundaries between work and leisure time that are common for many who are engaged in selling.

Chapters 4 and 5 cluster four different occupations that all have in common the crossing of social class boundaries as part of daily work life. I explore how crossing over *into the world of the other* creates its own set of cognitive and emotional dilemmas. In chapter 4, I describe fund raisers and grant givers to understand how people become comfortable in the world of other people's money, including people with substantial amounts of money. In chapter 5, I analyze investment advisors and debt counselors to understand how people give advice to others about how they use money and to understand how that advice differs depending on whether one is advising the well-off or those who are in financial trouble.

In chapter 6, I study religious clergy from a wide array of religious faith traditions. The central goal of this chapter is to understand how and why clergy spend significant time *writing meaning* onto money and resisting the idea that money is simply a way to facilitate transactions. Despite wide varieties across clergy and religious traditions, they are pretty well united on this point, emanating from their foundational belief that money belongs to God. I also show ways in which clergy must straddle the worlds of the sacred and the profane, sometimes trying to bring the two closer together.

Chapter 7 describes a number of people who are deliberately and self-consciously trying to experiment with money through their work. This chapter is meant to explore how far people can alter commonly held conceptions about money through their work. I explore alternative currency systems, in which local people print their own money as a way to promote local economies and local values. I also describe people who experiment with *pricing systems*, allowing people to pay what they think is a fair price, rather than having set prices. I describe other people who are experimenting with pay structures, allowing employees to voluntarily participate in a shared pool designed to reduce income inequality within a firm. In all these cases, people are trying to do new things with money or to use money to make points about social beliefs and social values. Here we come full circle from the view that money is simply a lubricant of social exchange, as these individuals want to do much, much more than this through their use of money. What does experimenting with money in these novel ways tell us about the people engaging in these work experiments, and what does it tell us about the malleability of money itself?

Chapter 8 returns to the central question of how the work we do affects the way we think about money both at work and outside of work. I show that the ways we learn to conceive of money at work also shape who we are as individuals, family members, consumers, and citizens. Finally, a methodological appendix describes the data I used in this study and discusses some of the complexities of studying money at work. I detail the strategies I developed to get people to talk about money as well as my rationale for choosing the particular occupations that I chose to study.

As a child, I watched my father and our entire family react to the ways in which money was earned and entered our household. While I wasn't able to fully understand what was happening, I often felt that money held sway over us, and I sensed that money was connected to work in some profoundly important ways. This book is an attempt to better understand those connections.

1

Money at Work

I was sitting in the office of a hedge fund trader as he struggled to put into words exactly how hedge fund traders think about money. After a few frustrating false starts, he finally said that rather than trying to describe it to me, he would simply tell me a story that would serve as an illustration. So he began:

> We [the partners in the hedge fund] were sitting around the office last week when one of the guys asked me, "What's your number to walk away?" And I said, "I don't know. I haven't really thought about it." And he said, "Oh, come on, you must have thought about it! What is your number?" "I don't know," I said, "ten million? . . . Then, you could relax. . . . You wouldn't have to worry about it." And then he said, "Yeah I used to think that, too [*long pause*]. But I like boats, . . . and now I can't figure it out. But ten [million] isn't it."

Undoubtedly, this kind of talk is part of a tradition of swashbuckling bravado long common on Wall Street.[1] But I think it is more than that. It is also revelatory of the way a person's career and work experiences shape the way he or she conceives of, and talks about, money. I would argue that it is not a coincidence that this sort of talk often happens on Wall Street,[2] in trading rooms, and specifically among hedge fund traders. Even though it is tempting to shrug this off by saying, "This is just the way macho Wall Street guys brag," I think something more profound is happening here that can teach us about the ways in which we learn to conceive of money in very particular ways through the daily routines of work. I also don't think that this kind of money talk predominates simply because of the common assertion that "these guys are just greedy." Of course, there could be *some* truth to this view, but the glib assertion of greediness provides at most a very superficial explanation that I suspect reflects an attempt to trivialize a group of people who inspire jealousy and occasional contempt. I would argue that a better way to understand why this particular view of money and this sort of money talk dominates among hedge fund traders is to think about how this way of talking about money is built into the culture that emerges from the actual structure of the work that hedge fund traders do and the daily work practices in which they engage.

Let's jump to another extreme for just a moment. Shortly after talking with this hedge fund trader about how much money was enough, I interviewed a man who had left his job in commission sales to work for an organization running seminars and retreats on money and spirituality.[3] As we sat in a small coffee shop, I listened carefully to this man who had been leading what he called "reverse mission trips" to Kenya, the goal of which was not to transform others but to transform oneself by working with the world's poor. As he prepared for his seminars and trips, continuing to deepen his own spiritual and religious faith, he became inspired by the biblical story of manna, which carries the message that all will have enough but none will have too much. He began to follow in a long tradition of religious ascetics, coming to the belief that *shedding* money and possessions was crucial to living out his faith. Turning the logic of consumerism completely on its head—not to mention most contemporary definitions of "success"—he described to me the ways in which he *consciously* considered how *low* a salary he could accept as he moved into new types of work. He envisioned his own future as one of "testing the limits," as he put it, of how little money he could survive on and how many material possessions he could do without. Describing the journey from his prior life as a highly compensated salesman, he remarked,

> That [job change] was about a $30,000 income drop, so that was a more significant drop. And it is interesting where thresholds are when we talk about how much is enough and how much do you need. In that jump, I would have been willing to work there for less. . . . I go to places that don't have enough. I just returned to a place in Ethiopia where I lived on potatoes and rice, because I am a vegetarian, and it is subsistence season and the end of a dry season and the beginning of a rainy season; so there are no fruits

and vegetables for me to eat because they have eaten them. . . . And I come home, and I am jarred by the culture here. Part of the jarring is to come back and to go to a grocery store. I come from nothing or one selection to so many. It is just overwhelming.

This man went on to describe to me the long conversations he held with his spouse about how *low* a salary he could accept as he moved down, rather than up, the earnings ladder. His desire was to constantly test new thresholds for giving up money and possessions, but he also wanted to be considerate of his spouse's level of comfort with such dramatic changes.

My interviews with these two people about the connections between money and work produced a kind of cognitive whiplash, as I could not imagine two more starkly different ways of thinking about the question, How much is enough? Here we see one person whose work seems to lead, reasonably enough, to the view that $10 million may not be enough, while another person believes that accepting less money for his work and shedding more and more of his possessions will still leave him with plenty.

Money Culture

Can we come to a deeper understanding of how culture and the economy are intertwined by seeing how conceptions of money are created and revealed through the daily practices, mental cognitions, emotional labor, and worldviews that are generated at work? Is there something about the economic and structural location of work that leads to such distinct ways of conceiving of money? Are there recognizable money cultures created in different kinds of work?[4] I use the term *money culture* to refer to a patterned set of values and beliefs about money that are revealed through symbols, cognitions, belief systems, and storytelling and are socially transmitted to newcomers as part of workplace socialization. Any particular money culture can extend across workplaces because it is rooted in the structural practices of types of work rather than rooted in any single organization or workplace. So if different types of work share similar structural features, we might expect some similarities in the money cultures that emerge from those types of work. By emphasizing the part of culture most closely connected to economic phenomena, economic practices, and economic decision-making, we can see how individuals develop their specific conceptions of money as they work, and this illustrates the interconnections between the structural aspects of work and the cultural attitudes toward money that take root in different types of labor.

One reason why I group certain occupations together within chapters in this book—such as poker players and hedge fund traders in chapter 2 or grant givers and fund raisers in chapter 4—is that I want to demonstrate how key structural economic features that are shared by otherwise different jobs can create similar money cultures in different lines of work. For example, the need to learn how to balance risk and reward when the monetary stakes are high is shared by both poker players and hedge fund traders; the regular crossing of social class boundaries is shared by grant officers and fund raisers. Thus, we might expect that these professions share some elements of a common money culture owing to this structural similarity. A money culture, once established, has a recursive element shaping the individuals as they learn their jobs and make decisions at work. The money culture shapes individuals into particular types of people who in turn further shape and foster the money culture at work.

In this book, I show how the economic structure of particular types of work produce and reproduce specific money cultures that in turn shape and reshape the structure of the job and the individuals holding those jobs. By structure, I mean such things as the compensation system for doing work, the daily work practices required in a job, how money factors into decision-making within a job, how much money is handled at work, how much discretion and control someone has over money, the time horizon by which people think about money, and the nature of the interactions with clients or customers over financial issues. These structural factors produce particular money cultures at work, and we can see elements of the money culture in the patterns of stories people tell, in the attitudes they exhibit, and in the cautionary tales told to new entrants to the field of work.

Structure and culture are never easily separable, of course. Rather, they are blended together in work and interact continuously in an ongoing fashion over long periods of time. Therefore, I can only try to understand a moment in time during this ongoing interactive process. One of the places in which the interplay between culture and structure can be most readily observed is in what I call the *cognitive dilemmas* presented by particular types of work. Each occupation, owing to its structural position in the money economy and the daily practices of work, presents certain recurring and patterned cognitive dilemmas with which people in those positions must grapple. It is in uncovering these dilemmas and then understanding how people try to solve or resolve the dilemmas that we most vividly see the intersection of culture and structure. I use the term *cognitive work* to describe the activities that people engage in as they wrestle with the cognitive dilemmas presented by the role of money in their work activities and through the structural location of their job in the economy. Cognitive work entails efforts to conceive of, and understand, work practices generally and money more specifically. This conception does not arise out of thin air but is shaped by the already-existing culture and structure of the occupation and the workplace. Just as people do *emotion work* to manage their feelings in the workplace, they also do *cognitive work* to conceive of the meaning of money in their job.[5] Cognitive work and emotion work are intertwined in that how one conceives of money can determine the emotion work needed to do a job.

Money Stories

Storytelling can present a window into ways of thinking about money that exist in the workplace and can simultaneously provide a mode of transmission whereby the beliefs of a money culture are transmitted from veterans to newcomers. We can see the interplay between culture and structure by listening to these stories and the narratives that people tell about their work and about their identity as working people. The two stories that open this chapter are reflections of the money cultures in which they are embedded. They tell us much about the way in which work produces certain conceptions of money and also shapes a person's identity. Recent research on economic behavior and its connection to identity have produced some intriguing findings along these lines. Ralph Fevre, in his book *The New Sociology of Economic Behaviour*, summarizes this research, beginning with the foundational insight from Max Weber (among others) that individuals form their identities, including their economic identities, from their group memberships. But as Fevre notes, the research in this field has mainly looked at economic identities in terms of quite large classifications such as social classes or by using large-scale dichotomies such as professionals versus nonprofessionals. He adds, "Economic sociology failed to understand the significance of identity because it treated it mainly as a means to the ends defined by economic rationality."[6] This oversight may be due in part to the point made by David Throsby that economists and economic sociologists have had trouble figuring out the best ways to include culture in their models, although Throsby notes that the cultural context of economic behavior was absolutely crucial to earlier social theorists, ranging from Weber (particularly in *The Protestant Ethic and the Spirit of Capitalism*) to Adam Smith (in his contention that Anglo-Saxon individualism was an important historical influence on the development of capitalism).[7]

The classical theorists tended to be interested in culture at a very macro level, often that of the nation-state.[8] I am interested in a more meso- and micro-level of cultural analysis because I am interested in how particular types of work lead to specific observable money cultures. Work institutions and work experiences are undoubtedly a major force in shaping who we are as individuals. Paul Edwards and Judy Wajcman, in their book *The Politics of Working Life*, succinctly put it, "Who we are is profoundly affected by what we do for a living."[9] Nearly half a century earlier, sociologist Everett Hughes, a pioneer in the sociological study of work, wrote much the same thing in his seminal book, *Men and Their Work*: "A man's [sic] work is as good a clue as any to the course of his life, and to his social being and identity."[10] Interestingly, Hughes follows this statement just a page later with this: "although a man's work may indeed by a good clue to his personal and social fate, it is a clue that leads us—and the individual himself—not by a clear and single track to a known goal, but into a maze of dead-ends and unexpected adventures."[11] This neatly summarizes the complexity of studying work and identity, namely, that work is one of the best clues to someone's social being and identity, but it is, after all, just one clue—and it is a clue that leads invariably to complex and varied outcomes. In other words, what people do in a lifetime of work clearly shapes who they are, but it does not determine who they are. But as Paul Ransome writes in his book *Work, Consumption and Culture,* "By concentrating on the social contexts within which people form and express their sense of identity we are consciously emphasizing . . . that the stuff of which identity is made is at least as much determined by environmental factors as it is by features of personality and psychology."[12]

As Edwards and Wajcman demonstrate, each academic perspective on the role of work in forming identity has yielded interesting insights, but each also has limitations. Psychologists have shown that human personality matters in the selection of work and the satisfaction experienced at work, but human personality alone is not enough to explain the deeper impact that work processes have on us. Sociologists have shown that the social organization of work matters, but structures alone do not determine individuals' reactions to their work experiences. Economists tend to stress the economic rewards for employment, yet those are just one type of reward experienced through work.[13] Each perspective is useful, and it is unreasonable to expect one paradigm to describe, let alone explain, something as complex as work life and identity, as work is a multifaceted phenomenon occurring within organizations that vary considerably one from another.[14]

Mitch Abolafia's study of bond traders is an excellent example of the kind of research that explores this intersection of culture and structure at work. Abolafia described the bond traders that he studied as close approximations to "homo economicus: the highly rational and self-interested decision maker portrayed in economists' models."[15] He demonstrated, however, that rather than reflecting a "natural propensity" of human beings toward this sort of behavior, the role and the character of a bond trader is *structured* and *created* by the culture of bond trading and the structures and rules surrounding trading. For example, he showed that the opportunism common to bond traders actually follows "culturally scripted strategies" such as laying off bonds (using incomplete or misleading information to induce a sale) or showing bids (posting highly visible electronic bids on bonds you already own to create a false sense of the market to potential bidders). These culturally scripted routines are taught to newcomers and passed on as part of workplace socialization, and it is these socialization experiences that help to generate *homo economicus.*[16] New research appearing from both the new economic anthropology and the field known as social studies of finance are assembling ethnographies of workplaces—mainly in the financial sector—that demonstrate how markets and the individuals operating within them are social creations formed through workplace practices and the structural features of work. These studies support the point that financial traders are made as much as they are born, just as financial markets are constructed rather than "natural creations."[17]

These contemporary studies echo the foundational work of Max Weber, who insisted that "economic social action" is fruitfully viewed as a form of social action, distinct from pure "economic action," which to Weber meant only rational utility maximization. We often lose sight of that distinction, treating any kind of action that has an economic element as "economically rational action" that is undertaken simply because it maximizes rational utility. However, the concept of rational utility has expanded to include all sorts of social utilities and social satisfactions. What is economically rational in any situation can often rest on an edifice of social constructs and agreed-on social understandings that are built over significant historical time periods and that may be in existence at any given moment in time but always subject to future change (e.g., regulatory changes, political changes, cultural shifts).

As Richard Swedberg writes, "Weber is careful to spell out exactly what constitutes the basic unit used in economic theory (exclusively rational economic action), in contrast to economic sociology (economic *social* action)."[18] Weber, reflecting the position that economic sociology has a much broader focus of study than economics, saw economic social action as intimately connected to social bonds. As Weber put it, "any act of exchange involving the use of money (sale) is a social action simply because the money used derives its value from its relation to the potential action of others."[19] When Weber turned his analytic eye toward the issue of money, he reflected this foundational position that markets and money cannot be divorced from social ties. As Weber wrote,

> From a sociological point of view, the market represents a coexistence and sequence of rational consociations. . . . The completed barter constitutes a consociation only with the immediate partner. The preparatory dickering,

however, is always a social action (*Gemeinschaftshandeln*) insofar as the potential partners are guided in their offers by the potential action of an indeterminately large group of real or imaginary competitors rather than by their own actions alone. The more this is true, the more does the market constitute social action.[20]

Sociologists have shown that we should not jump to the conclusion that money has become solely a lubricant for exchange and not itself a signifier, carrier, or promoter of social beliefs and societal values. Economic sociologists have been conducting research built on the foundational idea that economic actions and economic relations "spring from social relations," rather than existing as a category completely separate from social action.[21] Mark Granovetter, in his classic article on the embeddedness of economic action, demonstrated the ways in which all human actions, including economic actions, are steeped in social relations, arguing against an extreme "rational actor" or *homo economicus* model in which choices are made regardless of social ties.[22] This view calls for rich, context-dependent studies of how economic actions are enmeshed within social relations and therefore cannot be extricated from the relationships that give rise to economic action.[23]

Viviana Zelizer, in her book *The Social Meanings of Money*, challenges the notion of the complete fungibility of money when she describes "the remarkably various ways in which people identify, classify, organize, use, segregate, manufacture, design, store, and even decorate money as they cope with their multiple social relations." She writes, for example, about the ways that people categorize money as "pin money," "vacation money," "book royalties," or "drug money." There are "honest dollars," and there is "dirty money" (at least until it "gets laundered"). There is "regular income" and "tip income," and if the latter is paid in cash rather than in a paycheck, it seems easier to spend.[24]

While many analysts have assumed that a postmodern world of global finance would stamp out all distinctions surrounding money, bringing it to some "pure form" of electronic capital, Zelizer shows in her recent work, including *Economic Lives* and *The Purchase of Intimacy*, that money continues to be used to mark and demarcate social and family relations, to signify love and hate, and to shape a host of social relationships. As she puts it, money is not "culturally barren" but remains a "ritually meaning-ful object."[25] Zelizer has begun to outline a theory of money traveling in what she calls "circuits," and the defining feature of a money circuit is the distinct set of social relations among individuals in the circuit, the shared economic activities based on those relations, and the shared meanings attached to those activities. In this way, she is making an important move toward a larger theory of *how* money comes to take on the meanings that she outlined in her earlier work, as she points to the importance of social relations in establishing markets.[26] If shared meanings—one of the building blocks of culture—are necessary to make markets work, then it is clear that even the most basic economic processes are deeply embed-ded within social processes. The economic perspective too often wrests money away from social relations, leading to an artificial view of money that attempts to isolate the "economic" from "the social" and "the econ-omy" from "society." The anthropological position stresses the intermesh-ing of the two but sometimes treats money as almost epiphenomenal to culture, underemphasizing the unique characteristics of money that are based on its role as a universal mechanism for exchange.

Money Repertoires

In sociologist Ann Swidler's book *Talk of Love: How Culture Matters*, she demonstrated the ways in which people draw from a set of what she calls "cultural repertoires" that are present in the larger culture and serve to structure the way people think and talk about love. Swidler defines a cultural repertoire as "a set of skills, habits and orientations."[27] She argues that these repertoires provide for, among other things, vocabular-ies people use to talk about something like love that is both ubiquitous and also amorphous. As Swidler shows, repertoires represent "logics" that are often organized around binary oppositions, narratives, homolo-gies, or metaphoric linkages that help to organize ideas.[28] As in the case of love, people draw on available repertoires to make sense of money. While Swidler tended to focus on the repertoires available to an entire society writ large, I focus more on the repertoires specific to certain types of work, recognizing, of course, that these specific repertoires of money are nested within larger repertoires that might characterize an entire society's predilections toward money (e.g., consumerism).[29] Cultural repertoires give you a way to *talk* about complex things such as love and money, but they also provide you with a model for *thinking* about these large-scale phenomena.[30]

Cognitive sociology points toward the importance of understanding the social bases of ways of thinking. For example, Christena Nippert-Eng has shown the value of understanding cognitive categories in the workplace to better understand the field of work and its meaning to those who perform work.[31] Eviatar Zerubavel uses the term "social mindscape" to describe the perceptions and cognitions *shared* by a group of people.[32] I show in this book that people within particular occupations do often come to share very particular "social mindscapes" as they confront the cognitive dilemmas of their jobs, and this shapes the specific ways they come to think about money and finance. This mindscape is linked to the economic location of particular jobs, the everyday work practices implied by that location in the economic structure, the accompanying work socialization that occurs in those jobs, and finally the money cultures that result from different types of work, which in recursive fashion shape workplace practices once again. As Zerubavel puts it, "Mental reality, in short, is deeply embedded in social reality."[33]

In a fascinating study of advertising work, Brian Moeran writes that "advertising people tell stories about accounts, about their agency, and about the industry in which they work as a way of structuring the fleeting moments of their everyday lives."[34] I think perhaps all workers do this. In every workplace I have been in, people spend time telling each other stories that are intended to illustrate important aspects of their job or to socialize newcomers into a particular view of their work or to provide a cautionary tale to themselves or others about their work. These stories frame work in specific ways and thereby serve as heuristic devices for understanding work. As stories, they are also an important part of work culture, transmitting messages to others about how best to understand their work (including to someone like me who is a neophyte seeking to understand what they do and how they think about what they do). These stories, and the ways in which they are constructed and told, allow outsiders a glimpse of how insiders conceive of their work. The stories are interesting both for what they tell and for what they leave out. This makes listening to these stories quite challenging because you have to listen for at least three things: *what* is being said, *how* it is being said, and what is *not* being said.[35]

Most, but not all, of the work I am studying happens within organizations of some sort. Organizations themselves are at once both social and economic institutions (with the two almost always intertwined). Organizations produce and reproduce culture over time, and this culture is partly reproduced through the particular type of work people engage in within the workplace. Organizational theory has often left the study of work behind, focusing instead on the structural aspects of organizations. This risks missing the role of particular types of work in forming organizational cultures.[36] Occupational cultures come to embody particular money cultures, complete with discursive practices, typical modes of action, and disciplinary practices of one sort or another, carrying important meaning systems surrounding money.[37] Clifford Geertz's classic definition of culture as "an historically transmitted pattern of meanings embodied in symbols, a system of inherited conceptions expressed in symbolic forms by means of which men communicate, perpetuate, and develop knowledge about and attitudes toward life" can also be used to describe the money cultures that develop within certain professions and types of work.[38] I am not so much studying workplace culture as I am studying the production of specific pieces of money cultures that are created within particular types of work. These money cultures often reside within larger organizational cultures and contribute to the larger organizational culture, but they are not synonymous with organizational culture. I am interested in how a money culture is reflected by groups of people doing the same types of work—even if that work happens in different organizational settings.[39] It is interesting to find the similarities in how particular money cultures are rooted in the economic location of the work by looking for similar repertoires of economic dilemmas and solutions created by particular types of work.[40]

I seek to understand the complex interrelationships between structure and culture and to underscore the point that money cannot be extricated as something separable from social values, attitudes, consciousness, language, and culture more generally. I intentionally cast my net widely in this book, choosing to interview people in very different types of occupations, each of which represents a different relationship to money.[41] With this design, I am able to describe differences across many occupations while also exploring the ways in which certain professions, which on the surface may appear very different, actually share some underlying structural relationships to money that create similarities in the money culture in different types of work. In particular, I show that people in differing occupations can experience similar cognitive economic dilemmas that arise from the structural location of their job and the similar location in the economy. I ask what it is about those occupations that gives rise to these similarities. Do these similarities reveal something more fundamental about the relationship between the economic and the social and between structure and culture?

As Richard Swedberg points out in *Principles of Economic Sociology,* the concept of culture has not played a large role in economic sociology.[42] Economic sociology has been shaped more by organizational theory and network theory and has thus been interested primarily in structures and cultures only secondarily or as an epiphenomenon of structures. Sociologist Paul DiMaggio suggests that there is much to be gained by understanding the way in which culture influences the economy and vice versa. DiMaggio is careful to argue for a view of culture that is specific and observable so that culture is not defined in such a way that it just appears to be everything. He points to a number of observable and measurable parts of culture that can be studied by sociologists interested in the economy, including "cognitions, values, norms and expressive symbols." He also cites "classifications, scripts and schemas, and cognitive representations" as other possible concepts for research, as well as the more commonly used preferences, attitudes, and opinions.[43] Perhaps not surprisingly, in existing studies of work, it has been common to ask how workplace culture makes people more or less efficient, more or less productive, more or less satisfied, and more or less resistant to organizational change, but it has been less common to ask how work culture shapes the way people think about money.[44]

Zelizer makes a similar point, suggesting that we identify the reciprocal relationships between what we consider culture and what we typify as economic phenomena. The larger and more difficult agenda for understanding the connections between culture and the economy is research that

> tackles the difficult challenge of detecting culture—shared meanings and their representations in objects and practices—in the very social relations we call economic, then integrating culture into explanations of economic phenomena. Examining culture as a dynamic, contingent element of economic processes rather than a mere constraint, the alternative model thus shifts from context to content.[45]

From the very beginning of this research, I decided *not* to interview a random sample of people about their attitudes toward money[46] but rather to deliberately select people working in occupations that I thought might produce interesting money cultures. I chose to study hedge fund traders and poker players, sports and entertainment agents, commission salespeople, financial advisors, grant givers, fund raisers, financial regulators, debt counselors, clergy, and others who work in occupations that I thought might represent particularly interesting interplay between money and work. I chose occupations that have very distinct and potentially interesting locations in the money economy and for which money is a central and important concern in the work. Some people might think it odd to include a priest and a poker player, a debt counselor and a financial advisor, a hedge fund manager and a sports agent in the same book. Yet I have chosen to place these individuals and their careers in counterpoint to reveal something interesting about the relationships between work and money and between the economic locations of jobs and the culture and social relations that emerge.

To be clear, I am *not* attempting to describe a representative sample of Americans and their attitudes toward money. I am aware that different types of "personalities" are likely to enter different types of careers. Accepting this, I seek to uncover what happens at work that shapes the way people think and talk about money at work. My larger goal is to develop, and to illustrate, *a way of thinking* about the connections between work practices and money (specifically) and between work structures and work cultures (more generally).[47] We don't typically think about how people's attitudes about money and finance emerge from the time they spend in particular careers. Instead, we tend to think that we learn our lessons about money in childhood and leave it at that. But this book is an invitation to think in a different way about how people come to their conceptions of money, by looking at how the work we do shapes our ideas about money, how money cultures form at work, and how those cultures influence individuals working in particular occupations. This cognitive economic sociology connects the structural position of work in the economy with learned cognitions about money and finance,[48] provoking novel ways to think about money at work and the role it plays in shaping who we are.

2

Risk and Reward

Hedge Fund Traders and Poker Players

I always thought to myself when I ran trading rooms that you
were maintaining a constant balance between greed and fear.
—Robert Rubin, former U.S. Secretary of the Treasury,
former cochairman of Goldman Sachs, and chair of the
Executive Committee of Citigroup

I was talking with a hedge fund trader just off the trading room in a loft-
style office in Manhattan. He was describing to me how he learned to dissociate his emotions from the monetary implications of the large trades
he was making. Many of the hedge fund traders I talked with described
the importance of learning to discipline themselves, both cognitively and
emotionally, so that they could evaluate each and every trade on its own
merits, irrespective of having a good or bad run of luck and irrespective
of the sums of money that might be at risk (assuming overall firm risk
was being monitored correctly). This is something the average person has
trouble doing, as most individuals are affected by immediate past events

or their sense of future events. This is how one trader described the cognitive process he had learned:

> Let's say you invested $100 and you know you have made $100. And then a trade comes, and you sit down and say, "Should I do this trade?" And what you really should be doing is saying, "Should I do this because I think it is a good trade?" But what will happen with a huge proportion of the population is that they will start saying, "I am [now] playing with house money," which shouldn't come into it at all. It should be only, "Is this a good trade?" And if it is a good trade, you should do it, and if it is not a good trade, you shouldn't do it.

I recalled this conversation a few weeks later as I was sitting in Bobby's Room, the high-stakes poker room inside the Bellagio Casino in Las Vegas. I was there to interview a prominent professional poker player—one of a small handful of women who have risen to the very top of the high-stakes world of professional poker. Owing to the recent popularity of poker on television, she has found herself a bit of a celebrity now, but she has toiled long and hard over many years to develop into a top professional poker player. Sitting in Bobby's Room, we talked at length about how the day-to-day experiences of playing poker had shaped the way she has come to view money. In particular, she described the cognitive processes and mental discipline that she had to learn through her work, a discipline that eventually led her to play in some of the biggest-stake games in Las Vegas:

> You kind of have to dissociate yourself from that aspect of money when you are playing, because they are just chips. So you can't think that you are throwing in $100,000 and then think, "What could that [amount of money] buy you?" Because it buys a lot. So you can't think of it in those terms. It is just impossible to, or you would not take risks and do what you need to do to be a winning player.

Several of the poker players I interviewed used some variant of this statement: "The chips are just our way of keeping score." This signature phrase serves to reinforce the necessary dissociation of the "chips" from the dollar values they represent. Similar to hedge fund traders, dissociation between the monetary value of money and the use of money at work to make trades or to place bets is required to be successful. Poker players and hedge fund traders both need to make wagers based on the odds in front of them, and they cannot be rattled by what has happened in any of the preceding hands or trades or by the size of the wager or trade. And both must learn with experience to become more comfortable with hundreds of thousands of dollars passing through their hands on any given day or night.

But I also wondered whether they were ever completely successful at disciplining their emotions in this way. As Robert Rubin puts it in the epigraph at the start of this chapter, he felt that in running trading floors he was trying to find a balance between greed and fear. This implies that this process of dissociation may not be complete and that perhaps there is not an absence of emotion in hedge fund trading and poker playing but rather an unstable tension between two very strongly held emotions: fear and greed.

Just a Matter of Greed?

What *happens* to people through the daily work that they do that shapes the way they talk, think, and conceive of money? How do the day-to-day practices of particular types of work foster distinct ways of thinking about money, and how do money cultures form in particular types of work? Hedge fund traders and poker players are two interesting examples of how the structural location of a job and the quotidian practices of two different jobs lead to interesting similarities in money thought and money talk. Here we see people exhibiting some highly stylized and patterned ways of thinking and talking about money that emerge from the activities they engage in at work and the money culture that surrounds those activities. What we need to explore is *how* this comes to happen.[1] What is it about a particular job that shapes who we are and how we think and talk about money?

Why do hedge fund traders often engage in conversations about "how much money is enough"? After spending time with hedge fund traders, I think it is too easy to say that because making money is the driving force on Wall Street, conversations about making a lot of money are to be expected. This explains only in the most general way why money talk dominates social interaction on the Street, but it does not really help us understand why talking about money takes on the particular character that it does among hedge fund traders.[2] I am interested in why hedge fund traders invoke the particular form, *How much do you need to walk away?* rather than saying, for example, *How much money do you hope to earn?* I think this particular way of talking about money emerges not simply from the "personalities" attracted to this type of work but from the daily structured *experiences* people have in this job and in the money culture in which it is embedded. In other words, there are specific aspects of hedge fund trading that lead to this conception of money.

The work done by hedge fund traders raises a set of cognitive dilemmas that must be grappled with. First, the temporal nature of the rollercoaster ride endemic to hedge fund trading creates significant emotional stress and leads to recurring conversations about how long the ride can last. People on Wall Street (and it is probably most extreme right now among hedge fund traders) are often asking, "Can I ride this wave to a million [or, often, much more] and get out in time?" The folklore of Wall Street is replete with stories of people who supposedly got out of a market just in time and those who failed to read the signs correctly. Therefore, the concept of *timing* becomes a major cognitive modality through which hedge fund traders think about money and wealth.

This concept of *timing* is deeply woven into the fabric of the work of hedge fund traders and, therefore, also into the rhetoric surrounding work. But the idea of timing is a complex one and is often treated in different—and even contradictory—ways on the Street. For example, there are ways to time the market, but these coexist with warnings that you should never try to time the market. For instance, there are complex models devoted to market timing as well as complex strategies and models devoted to the very opposite—developing the discipline to resist timing the market. Thus, the idea of time and timing are absolutely central to thinking about work and money on the Street, even while remaining always elusive.

Many hedge fund traders, in particular, try to exploit very small mispricings in the market. Using enough leverage, even the most minuscule mispricing can produce millions of dollars in return. However, a pricing discrepancy often narrows and disappears as more traders discover it and rush in with money. As one trader said to me, "Sometimes it is like shooting fish in a barrel." But a particular opportunity won't last very long, so you have to keep searching for novel opportunities to exploit. Thus, one quickly learns in this job that timing is everything.

Adding to the importance of timing, of course, is the stress and adrenaline rush associated with a job in which a *lot* of money is often on the line. Using a great deal of leverage also means that an entire hedge fund firm can come crashing down if the overall risk in a firm is not managed properly. The pressure to make money and to beat the market adds to feelings of exhilaration and exhaustion (emotionally and mentally) so that no one is quite sure how long they can keep going. So hedge fund traders are talking about how long they can ride a particular wave in the market at the same time that they are wondering how long they can keep up the intensity level under significant strain.

Hedge fund traders, however, sometimes chuckle and answer their own question of how much is enough by saying something like, "But most never really do walk away." Usually, they simply invent a new threshold or a new goal that they will have to cross before walking away (as in, "I used to think ten million is it, but not anymore"). Why is this tagline so often added? One can assert that it shows greed, but once again, I think this glib assertion misses a deeper process. I think this conversation is not only about how much money is enough to walk away. And it may not even be *mainly* about how much money is enough. Rather, it is a way that hedge fund traders talk *to one another* about work practice, work discipline, and dealing with the emotions that come along with the rollercoaster ride of markets and trading. In other words, this is partly a process of transmitting the money culture among hedge fund traders.

Hedge Funds

Whether hedge funds as a class are more risky or not is debatable, but I think it is clear that hedge funds are attracting the most aggressive and entrepreneurial talent on the Street because they provide the greatest flexibility and freedom in trading. The term *hedge fund* is a fairly broad one and is generally used to describe a private pool of investment that seeks to generate returns that are not highly correlated with the performance of stocks and bonds. Since hedge funds are more loosely regulated than are other investment pools, it gives traders the opportunity to employ all sorts of trading strategies. In the past decade, the popularity of hedge funds has soared. Estimates are that hedge fund investments exceeded $1 trillion in 2006.[3] By 2007, as much as $1.6 trillion was being managed in hedge funds. Hedge funds experienced a decline during the financial meltdown of 2007, but they have recovered fairly quickly. The number of hedge funds peaked in 2007 at seventy-six hundred such funds. After a decline to about sixty-eight hundred hedge funds in 2009, the decline began to reverse, as the number of new funds started to outpace those going out of existence.[4] There are many different types of hedge funds, and many use significant leverage. Most have very high initial investments (typically $1 million) and charge fairly hefty performance fees (20 percent is typical) in addition to management fees.[5] Many funds use "lock-up commitments" that impose some limits on the speed or amount of withdrawals to try to prevent quick "runs on the fund" should there been a downturn.[6] Gary Weiss, a former *Business Week* reporter, put it this way: "Few areas of financial endeavor have been a subject of so many hoary myths, moronic half-truths, goofy speculation, once-true falsehoods, and knuckleheaded fantasies."[7]

Several well-publicized meltdowns (e.g., Long Term Capital Management, Amaranth, and two of Bear Stearns's mortgage funds) have led many people in the general public to have a fear or distrust of hedge funds. The Wall Street traders who have opened hedge funds tend to find appeal in the complexity of hedge fund trading models, the ability to use leverage, and the trading freedom accorded them in a looser regulatory environment, which they view as even more "entrepreneurial" than other types of trading. Therefore, of all the roller-coaster rides on Wall Street, hedge funds are probably the most adventurous and thrilling (at least until the invention of the next new thing).

I think that when hedge fund traders talk the way they do to one another, they are also communicating something deeper about the risks and rewards of their work and about the type of mental discipline needed to stay in the game. Money, then, takes on some very particular and pointed qualities for hedge fund traders that might be less noticeable in other careers: money embodies temporality, opportunity, high risk, and high reward. To learn to be a trader, you must learn to dissociate your emotions from the value of a trade, while walking the line between greed and fear, ambition and prudence, and trusting your instincts and trusting your quantitative models.

What Do Hedge Fund Traders and Poker Players Have in Common?

To push my argument about the connections between work and money a level deeper, I noticed some other interesting similarities between the way hedge fund traders and poker players talked about the issue of controlling emotions in the face of extreme financial stress. Poker players use the term "going on tilt" to describe what happens when players become so rattled (sometimes caused intentionally by other players but sometimes by a run of incredibly bad luck) that they are no longer able to make sound, rational decisions based on the odds immediately in front of them. A player in this situation is said to have "gone on tilt" and is no longer playing his or her best game because emotions have overtaken rational calculation. This is how a "grinder," or a professional player who "grinds out" a living playing low-stakes poker, put it when I asked him what happens when players have bad luck and let their emotions get hold of them in the wrong way:

> Most people go cuckoo . . . who go on what we call "tilt," which is based on the pinball term of it. . . . [They] overplay hands. Some people underplay hands, they'll lose a big pot, and then they'll decide, "Well, . . . raising with these kings . . . you know, I've raised with . . . I've had kings three times, and I lost all three of them. . . . Now I pick up kings, and I'm going to just call because I don't want to lose any more money than I have to." And of course, that's a recipe for disaster, 'cause now they're allowing more people to come in and beat them. But any time you play a hand differently than you would normally play that hand if things were going well, you're tilting.

Guarding against going on tilt is a challenge not only for the lower-stakes player. Another player I interviewed, who had won the World Series of Poker championship, described the process similarly as he was describing to me his overall strategy for success:

> Where you do have an edge? And poker players have an edge if they are good enough. You have to overcome the luck factor, you have to overcome the rake [the house's take on each hand], and you have to overcome the skill level of your opponents. So when you are playing other top players, you are trying to not go on tilt; the player who has the least tilt prospers the most. You try to at least break even against the pros and clobber everybody else.

Hedge fund traders describe a similar process—one trader called it "having an emotional meltdown." Traders, like poker players, talk about learning the importance of evaluating each and every decision rationally using odds and probabilities and not allowing a prior poor decision or bad run of luck to make you shy away from a risky, but potentially profitable, decision immediately in front of you. Hedge fund traders say they can sometime spot a colleague who is "melting down" due to the pressure of a run of bad trades.[8] Notice how similar this poker player's talk of remaining emotionally disciplined is to the hedge fund trader's description of his emotional task: "I know a number of players who can play really well until they lose a rack of chips, and then they go berserk trying to win it back. Now all of a sudden, they're raising with ace-three off suit because they *deserve* to win the money back." To be a good trader or a good poker player, you must come to embody a learned set of skills that come with experience and with the help of more seasoned colleagues showing you the way. Both poker players and hedge fund traders occupy jobs—or locations in the money economy, if you prefer—in which they are always weighing the odds and always evaluating risk, trying to control their emotions so they continue to make decisions based on the odds. They learn, in the economist's lingo, to make decisions based not on "sunk cost" (as most people do, according to the experiments conducted by behavioral economists) but instead on the odds directly in front of them at that moment. They must do this when the stakes are incredibly high, and there are always unknowns and unexpected events.[9] Combined, these lead to incredible rushes of adrenaline and—no matter how good or careful you are—occasionally tremendous losses that you hope are outweighed in the long run by tremendous gains.

Both hedge fund traders and poker players attempt to discipline themselves into acting logically. So when a particular career offers a chance to see huge financial swings at work, often accompanied by huge swings in personal fortunes, this pressure leads people to think in terms of timing and in terms of maintaining control and discipline while remaining willing to take significant financial risks. Remaining willing to take large risks in the face of this stress contributes to the bravado and swaggering talk. Much like the way young men "bust on" one another to strengthen their masculinity, traders and poker players test one another to sharpen their discipline in the face of stress. In this vein, a top player and I had the following conversation:

POKER PLAYER: I mean, most of the great poker players have been broke. More than once. And so you learn the value of a dollar. Although I wouldn't do thirty pushups just the other day for $2,000.

KEVIN DELANEY: Who offered that?

POKER PLAYER: Phil Ivey. He said, "I just want to see you do them and strain yourself." Here, I am giving you $2,000. And I turned it down. I don't even know why I turned it down, except I just didn't feel like doing them. Even though, you know, I could do thirty pushups, but thirty pushups is probably my limit, so I would really have to strain myself. And it is possible that I would get so strained that I would make different decisions in the poker game—which is worth more than $2,000. Maybe if we were on a golf course and he asked me to do them, then I'd do 'em. But in a poker game, I need my head.

What better example could there be of a poker player weighing up the odds and the risks to her game in response to a test of will from a savvy competitor?[10] Here we see what might be called an example of "workplace socialization," albeit not your typical one. In this scenario, one poker champion is providing another the opportunity to figure out the odds and assess the probabilities, while at the same time trying to throw an opponent off her game. All these are the skills needed to be a great player. Notice also that the player who is challenged to do the pushups not only weighs the odds of successfully completing the task to win $2,000, but she also quickly considers how performing the task might affect her subsequent poker playing, reckoning that while she has a good chance of winning $2,000 in the short run, she might then lose much more in the ensuing game. This is clearly a conditioned form of thinking (weighing up the odds in both the short run and the long run) that comes from the actual experience of working as a poker player. It is no coincidence that the money culture that grows up around poker playing contains lots of testing, bluffing, weighing odds, and thinking about money in highly stylized and unusual ways. While a layperson might think of wagering $2,000 as carelessly throwing around a lot of money or showboating, the poker player who proposes the bet sees it is an "investment" (in throwing another player off her game), while the player who is challenged sees it as a gambit, a bluff, or a form of gamesmanship. I see it also as socialization into the profession and the money culture that results from the structural conditions of the work being done.

Money Discipline

There are other ways in which professional poker players, like hedge fund traders, try to discipline their emotions to limit their chances of losses. One way is through the careful use of a "bankroll," which is a way to segregate poker money from other monies, much the way Zelizer found that people will earmark money for specific purposes.[11] Another way to do this is to play only in lower-stakes games that will serve to slow down the process of winning and losing and help to avoid going on tilt under great emotional strain. One grinder described it this way:

> I mean, the [computer] program [I use] gives me a bankroll tool. You tell it
> your hourly rate, which it knows, your standard deviation, and the amount of
> money you draw out per month, and it tells you what your bankroll require-

ment is. And I don't do that as formally as I used to when I started this thing. I kept all the money separate with no commingling and so on and so forth.

Both hedge fund managers and poker players believe that if they have some advantage, over the long run, they will come out ahead and make money. In both professions, there is a term for this. Poker players call it "having an edge" over an opponent. Hedge fund traders tend to call it "having an informational advantage" (knowing something other traders do not know). Both poker players and hedge fund traders are constantly trying to figure out who has the edge in any particular situation. But it is equally true that in both professions the "long run" can take a long time to arrive, and in between "right now" and "the long run," there can be incredibly jarring bumps in the road, bad runs of luck, mistakes, failure to assess risk properly, and potential losses in the hundreds of thousand or even millions of dollars (for top poker players) and in the hundreds of millions or even billions of dollars (for hedge fund traders).[12]

Where Emotions Enter In

What is also similar in these two jobs is that most poker players and many hedge fund traders (with the exception of the purest quant traders, discussed later) do not fully believe in a completely narrow "rational calculation" as the key to their success. Both traders and card players know that *something* that isn't purely rational, scientific, or calculable is also going on in their work. For poker players, an important part of the game is intuitive—reading other players' emotions. One of the key things that distinguishes a good player from a mediocre player is the ability to "put the other player" on a particular hand, or guess what the other player has. This entails knowing a lot about odds but also intuiting how another player is betting throughout the various rounds of betting within a single hand or over the course of several hands. (For example, particular bets would allow you to "put the other player on a single pair" or even on a single pair of a lower-numbered card.) This ability to "read" another player and guess what hand he or she might be holding comes from a combination of experience, rational calculation, *and* emotional intuition.[13] Thus, poker players *must* use emotion and their emotional intelligence and not simply be calculating machines. This is what makes playing poker so engaging for the very best players. You need to be both mathematically equipped to think quickly about odds and emotionally intuitive in order to read other players. Not many people have the combination of these two abilities at the highest level.

Sociologist Kyle Siler, in a quantitative study of online poker players, found that for smaller-stakes players, there was a negative correlation between the percentage of total hands won and total money won because players would win many small-stakes hands while losing a small number of relatively large bets. This suggests that these smaller-stakes online players (who are likely less experienced than most of the players I studied) are somehow overvaluing winning a hand (without proper regard for the amount won) and thereby winning the battles but losing the war. In my terminology, they are not yet up to the task of balancing rationality with emotion. As Siler puts it, "Adopting risk neutrality to maximize expected value, aggression and appropriate mental accounting, are cognitive burdens on players."[14]

In some analogous ways to poker players, many hedge fund traders use both experience and emotional intuition in their jobs side by side with rational calculation. If, for example, a trader senses that a newly listed bid in the market is really a bid being put up by another trader to create a sense of high demand at a certain price, the trader uses intuition to decide whether he or she believes that bid is a real (or actual) bid. Traders have seen bids that appear and then suddenly disappear on their computer screen. They use this experience to try to sense what is actually happening in the market. They also rely on intuition at times to sense direction in the market. (It should be noted here that not all hedge fund traders do this, and some deliberately reject this idea, holding to mathematical models as a discipline designed to avoid emotion- or intuition-driven trading decisions.) Additionally, hedge fund traders are constantly on the watch for what they call "an informational advantage"—knowing something about the market that others might not know yet.[15] They constantly have to weigh that information as important or not. (Note that I don't say "true or not," because false information is still important if it moves a market.) Since they have to trade in an atmosphere of fairly high uncertainty, they rely on both instinct and information. As one trader put it,

The instinct you obviously can't learn. . . . What traders actually do is make decisions in environments without all information, with uncertainty. So making a rational decision when you don't have all the information, that is my job. That is what a trader does. So if I have to sum up what a trader does, that's it. So you can train for the decision-making process. You can go through game theory and come up with a good decision-maker. You plug the information in to make a decision. And that is why traders always talk about the informational advantage. If everyone has the same information, they will probably all more or less come to the same conclusion. So you are looking for informational advantage.

There is something intrinsic about the nature of the work of poker playing and hedge fund trading that makes the conflict between rationality and emotion an essentially *irreconcilable* tension, in that it will always be there and cannot be fully resolved. James McManus, in his recent book on the history of poker, describes poker players as having "shrewdness, psychological acuity, risk and resource management, and the ability to leverage uncertainty."[16] McManus quotes Andy Block, the professional poker player, as saying, "In poker, you have to put yourself in the shoes of your opponents, get inside their heads and figure out what they're thinking, what their actions means, what they think *your* actions mean."[17] The same description can be applied to hedge fund traders.

It is this endemic tension between rationality/calculability, on the one hand, and emotion/intuition, on the other hand ("having a feel for it," as both professions put it), that makes these professions so attractive to those who enjoy challenge, risk, and the adrenaline rush of uncertainty. But it is also what leads poker players and hedge fund traders to talk the way they do about money. This endemic tension helps create the distinct money culture that we find in these two fields of work. If a person is to be successful at this sort of work, he or she must learn to think about millions of dollars in chips or multimillion-dollar gains and losses (and even megalosses on occasion) as just a way of "keeping score." Talking about money in very cavalier ways helps one to do this, as it continues to create the dissociation between money and its financial value. But this tension between intuition and rational calculation also leads to conversation—and worry—about "going on tilt," while the exhilaration of the roller-coaster ride results in asking, "How long can I keep this up?" It is the structural features of both these jobs—at least as much as the morally laden judgment of "greediness"—that lead to frequent conversations about money and how much is enough. As one trader put it to me, "I don't know if it is all a pure money thing. I read an article once that I thought was very insightful, and I do believe this, since it is my own personal philosophy. Rich is 20 percent more than you made last year [*laughs*]." Is greed at work here? Well, maybe so, if you simply mean the desire to make money. But there is also something much more. The quotidian practices associated with these two jobs produce similar cognitive and rhetorical approaches to money—approaches that stress, encourage, and reinforce temporality, timing, emotional discipline, and the willingness to readily take large financial risks ("to pull the trigger") after quickly assessing the odds in front of you. You know you will sometimes lose and lose very big, yet you hope that you will win big more often than you lose. That is your edge. So while poker players and hedge fund traders are obviously both in it for the money, the nature of their work also demands that they not use money alone as motivation to get them through the most stressful moments in their work lives (e.g., making a huge bet on a trade or going "all in" on a poker hand). Instead, they engage in significant work to control their own emotions while also gauging and manipulating others' emotions. They must simultaneously do the cognitive work to build a mental wall between the value of what they are trading (or betting) and the momentary work they are doing (assessing odds, information, and risk). Put another way, they must both build and break down the barriers between logic and intuition in a very high-stakes environment with incomplete information and in situations when it is not entirely clear whether one should be trusting one's intuition or trying to control it.[18]

The Quest to Tame Emotion

Another group of hedge fund traders believes that they have found the ideal way to avoid going on tilt. The "pure quants" attempt to use scientific and mathematical modeling to completely discipline their emotions, or to put it more accurately, they seek to remove their emotions altogether. I interviewed the founder of a highly successful mathematically based hedge fund who described his approach to trading this way:

> All we do is build models and slavishly follow them. So we come—I come from a scientific background. I was a mathematician for fifteen years, an active scientist. . . . We transitioned by the late '80s into 100 percent model driven and have been there ever since. So that means if you are 100 percent model driven that you don't override the models, that you don't say, "I feel today that the models don't know what is going on, but maybe they will know tomorrow." It means you simply do what they say. And the models have built into them testable, simulatable, statistically significant ideas. So every idea that we get to enhance the model is thoroughly tested—statistical significance, constancy, a whole bunch of things—and then we decide, "Okay, that is an additional feature that should be included."

With this approach, these traders are trying actively and consciously to eliminate instinct and intuition from trading and to find testable indicators that determine their trading. The key here is not having an instinct or feel for the market's direction or knowing, as some traders put it, "when to pull the trigger on a trade" but instead maintaining the discipline *not* to abandon a model in the face of what may just be momentary noise or setbacks. I probed further, asking this person whether there is ever a moment for drawing on instinct about what is happening in the market, and he replied with conviction, "None of that. There is none of that at all. I don't know how to measure it. We know how to measure these things, and that is what we do. And we have been very, very successful doing that." The money culture found at a pure quantitative trading firm is somewhat different from a more trader-driven firm. How do pure quants manage to sidestep some of the culture endemic to Wall Street traders? One way is by trying to hire people who have not been exposed to that culture but rather have been socialized through the training of science. "We don't hire Wall Street guys. So there is no one who has ever said, 'Gee, let's buy pounds. I don't care what the model says. I know pounds are going up,' for whatever reason. I heard this or even 'I have a very good analysis,' whatever. We only hire scientists and always have." For pure quants, then, the challenge is remaining true to the models and the rigorous testing, even when the models are not performing particularly well. One way that quants foster and maintain this type of discipline is by deliberately trying to slow down the speed of Wall Street in order to analyze events. By that, I mean that quants require that a model be tested over long time periods and that adjustments to the models must be tested and discussed in meetings. So I noticed that the quants had a much different sense of time than did other hedge fund traders.

For these quantitative traders, it is very important to think about time as a particular calibration that may need to be measured, and thought about, differently depending on the specific predictor. In other words, for each unit of time prediction, quants want to see how a predictor in the model holds up after as many observations as possible. But the time scale of particular predictors can differ significantly:

> Most things are not clear. . . . So typically, you know, it really depends on the time scale of the prediction. If you have a prediction that predicts the next five minutes—well, there are a lot of five minutes—let's say it is stocks. . . . So if something is not working for a period of several months on a five-minute time scale or a two-minute time scale, then there is overwhelming evidence that it is not a statistical anomaly, I mean, not a statistical fluke. It is like, "Hey, it's just not working!" But if you have a prediction whose time horizon is at the other end of the spectrum—let's say a year—. . . well, you know [*laughs*], it may be a while before you really come to conclude that this is really not going to do so good.

Another important way to discipline against emotion or intuition is to draw workplace analogies not to Wall Street trading but to physical (and other) sciences or to the idea of "uncovering" scientific laws. As another quant put it,

> The universe that we model is not a constant universe. It is not quite like doing physics, where for all practical purposes it is constant. Maybe the gravitational constant is changing, but it is slow compared to humans' lifetime. But here the markets do change. Human beings' behavior does gradually change. But what we found is that those changes are slow, relative to

having a reasonable amount of time to exploit some anomalous feature of
human behavior, which is after all what makes up markets.

This approach leads quants to think about money in a much different way from other hedge fund traders—with much less talk of speed,
intuition, and emotion and also with significantly less swashbuckling.
Instead, one hears the measured language and cognitive processes of the
scientist, particularly one who is in the early stages of discovery. I heard
another scientific analogy provided by a quant, this time to the laws of
nature and weather forecasting. As he put it,

> You are trying to dope out how this amazing set of human interactions
> called the financial markets [works]. . . . We are like early weather forecast-
> ers. We had no notion of the so-called Navier-Stokes equations, which are
> the equations of fluid dynamics that enable one to model fluid flow or gas
> flow. And so today modern weather forecasting puts everything up on a
> big grid, integrates these Navier-Stokes equations, and you can get a pretty
> good forecast. But people could forecast the weather before that. . . . They
> used to say, "Gee, the wind is blowing from the west. I assume that will con-
> tinue for a while. That usually means we are going to get blah, blah," or "It is
> coming from the east, and that usually means. . . ." Well, we are kind of like
> the early weather forecasters.

In the book *My Life as a Quant*, Emmanuel Derman makes a similar
point about the difficulty of modeling when he writes, "Models are only
models, not the thing in itself. We cannot, therefore, expect them to be
truly right. Models are better regarded as a collection of parallel thought
universes you can explore. Each universe should be consistent, but the
actual financial and human world, unlike the world of matter, is going
to be infinitely more complex than any model we make of it."[19] In other
words, quant traders, who are often scientists or mathematicians adopting models from the study of the physical world or the world of probabil-
ity theory, are trying to model a very messy, dynamic reality that is itself
affected by the actions of those who develop and use the models (so the
modelers are affecting the data they are, in fact, modeling, which is generally not true in the study of physics). The pure quants couldn't be further

from the stereotypical image of the swashbuckling trader. Note the caution expressed in this piece of a conversation I had with a quant hedge fund manager:

KD: Do you try to take events into consideration, like in events-driven trading? Do you try to model events?

QUANT: If I knew how, I would. But I don't know how. If you could tell me, "This is a class of stocks ripe for takeover," *and* we could statistically study that and come to some conclusions, then we would put that in as a positive signal.

KD: And you don't say, "It looks like OPEC is successfully controlling output, and therefore we should load up on oil"?

QUANT: No, we wouldn't know how to simulate that in the past. How many examples are there of that in the past? Thousands? No. Two? Maybe.

Contrast this cautious, scientific approach of the quantitative trader with this comment made to me by a hedge fund trader at another firm, describing one mathematician working in his more "trader-driven" firm:

KD: Can you notice a difference between the mathematician [who works in your firm] and the other traders here? Is he the more cerebral, more academic?

HEDGE FUND TRADER: No. . . . I think that what is important about him compared to the other people who I have met who are more "academic" [is that] he kind of had it beaten out of him in this firm, in that there is the theoretical and then there is reality. If you can kind of accept that, that's great. Like we are doing something now where we are working with another company and might possibly look to use some of their trading models. And the guy who has developed the trading models is a professor from an Ivy League university who has never worked in the real world. And we have had a number of conversations with him, and everybody comes back concerned that will we try to get this guy to tweak his model, is he gonna say, "No, it's mine. It's my model"?

Quant traders use the vocabulary and methods of science and mathematics as best they can, using specialized vocabularies and analogies from science and expending efforts to exhaustively model and test. They also try to slow down the rapidity of markets and resist all efforts at timing and intuition-driven trading. Thus, the culture of quant hedge fund trading is quite different from that of other traders: the scientist reigns supreme rather than the swagger of Wall Street.

There is an important caveat to add here. Many quants will still admit that emotion plays a big role in the empirical "observations" that they are sampling and using in their models. In other words, while they are using the tools of science, their observations or "data points" themselves may embody emotion, in the sense that they may represent the collective emotions of groups of traders in historical time periods, particularly during crashes or heightened market stress. If there are emotions in the market (e.g., the emotions of other traders), then these emotional reactions should be built into the historical data and therefore built into the trading models. This presents quants with an interesting conundrum: modeling emotions while remaining unaffected by emotion in their own trading. Economist Robert Schiller describes this phenomenon when he writes about his research into trading behavior during economic crashes:

We investigated the emotional environment at the time of the crash by asking respondents if they experienced "any unusual symptoms of anxiety (difficulty concentrating, sweaty palms, tightness in chest, irritability, or rapid pulse) regarding the stock market." On October 19, 23 percent of U.S. individual investors and 43 percent of U.S. institutional investors said yes. On October 20, 42 percent of Japanese investors answered yes. I find these percentages remarkably high, given that the samples were just random samples of all investors. But the anxiety does not necessarily mean that people were "panicking" or performing badly. It might mean that, in a sense, people were unusually alert and that other matters were brushed aside so that careful investment decisions could be made. From this evidence, we begin to see how popular, intuitive, models of speculative prices informed investor behavior at the time of the crash. The suggestion we get of the causes of the crash is one of people reacting to each other with heightened attention and emotion, trying to fathom what other investors were likely to do, and falling back on intuitive models like models of price reversal or continuation to explain a crash.[20]

Schiller underscores the fact that under times of intense trading stress, traders may be more likely to "fall back on intuitive models," which may mean questioning or abandoning for a period of time models that are less intuitive and moving to those that are more intuitive. When under stress, traders choose heuristic ways of thinking that match their intuitions at that moment.

Consider, as another example, the Black-Scholes formula developed for valuing options and other corporate liabilities and then refined into a model used by traders to indicate when a given derivative is trading outside its expected range (and thereby providing a trading or moneymaking opportunity).[21] The Black-Scholes equation is clearly a sophisticated form of mathematical reasoning and modeling and has proven enormously useful in pricing complex derivatives. The equation and model have been used by many traders to help them make significant amounts of money in trading. However, it is also true that the model has not fully lived up to expectations, and some critics even fault the model—or perhaps more accurately the larger way of thinking that has been inspired by the model—for the meltdown of the hedge fund trading firm Long-Term Capital Management.[22] One reason why the Black-Scholes model remains very useful but still not perfect is that "the model is not an exact account of options prices. Price movements are concentrated further toward the extremes than the assumption of random changes would allow."[23] In other words, while the model might be the very best model we have for options pricing, it might still be somewhat crude.[24] As Roger Lowenstein puts it succinctly, maybe the model is "too tidy for the real world."[25] Recall that quants are modeling collective behaviors in complex markets. Collective emotion may cause traders, as Schiller put it, to "fall back on intuitive models" at certain moments of heightened stress. If so, then a quantitative trading model can only predict this behavior correctly if it has enough historical examples of it and if the collective behavior (even what some people might call panic) operates according to predictable patterns or principles. In other words, the question becomes, can quantitative modelers correctly model panic? Add to this the problem (from a statistical modeling standpoint) that in markets, each observation is not independent of prior observations, as is true, say, with flipping a coin.[26] Traders, and thus the markets themselves, have such things as memories, intuitions, networks of connections with other traders for information gathering, standard operating procedures, and intuitive models to "fall back on."[27]

This brings us back full circle to the conclusion that even in quantitative trading there is still some balancing of rational calculation and intuitive judgment based on experience. In pure quantitative firms, this judgment might enter in, for example, in deciding when to include (or remove) a feature from a quantitative model. After all, one must use a judgment to answer questions such as "When do we have enough data points to consider this a reliable signal in a model?" or "When do we have enough historical back-testing of a signal to include it in a model?" or "How many data points do we need to conclude that a particular signal is adding no predictive value to a model?" The most honest quants admit that there is always the danger that the month after you have removed a signal from a model, it might finally start to work in the way you always thought it should.

The Role of the Cautionary Tale

One thing both quants and nonquant traders have in common with poker players (besides talking about financial risk) is that they all tell "cautionary tales" as part of their money culture. These tales are usually about other hedge fund traders or poker players who had suffered meltdowns or let greed get the best of them. As I listened to them tell these stories, it seemed clear to me that the storytellers had searched for clues as to what went wrong in these situations and then asked themselves if they were properly guarding against such a malfunction in their own firm (hedge fund traders) or in their own game (poker players). Historically, cautionary tales were used in fables and folklore to warn the listener of some danger (e.g., don't cry wolf too many times lest people stop responding). But in my conversations with hedge fund traders, I got the sense that I was not necessarily the intended listener who needed to receive the lesson. Instead, it seemed to me that the tales told by traders and poker players are as much to remind *themselves* as well as their colleagues of a danger. The cautionary tale seems to be told to police oneself and perhaps one's colleagues and partners by reminding oneself not to overstep risk parameters, especially when things seem to be going incredibly well.[28] It is here, more than anywhere else in my conversations with hedge fund traders, that I thought the word "greed" *might* come into play. Here is how one hedge fund trader put it to me:

> There was another recent blowup a couple of weeks ago—and it is still to be laid out in the public what the blow up was, but it's significant. Probably lost, . . . rumor has it, anywhere between 40 percent and 100 percent of their market. . . . So it is a major, major blowup. And what we have heard—and this is secondhand information—is that their prospectus said they could mark their own portfolio,[29] they could make up their own market values of the portfolio. Well, if you are an investor, and you read the prospectus and decide to invest in that . . . ! So I think it needs to be a "buyer beware" attitude.

I found it interesting that when traders talked about meltdowns at other high-profile hedge funds, they did not use the term "greed" but rather talked in terms of the firm's failure to manage risk properly. It is almost as if the desire to make money is simply taken for granted. Here is another typical description from a hedge fund partner and trader:

> It seems like the firm was doing nothing in a mechanical sense that they shouldn't have been doing. What happened was a pure management blunder. They allocated too much of their book to one trader and one set of products, who then put bets on that were too big. But it's not that trader's fault; it's actually the management. They let him do it. They had all the control put in and decided not to put the brake on it.

For poker players, cautionary tales serve a somewhat similar purpose, reminding players not to exceed their bankroll, not to have leaks in their game, not to allow emotion to take over their rational calculation of the odds in each hand. Here is how one poker player put it:

What I don't do, like a lot of my colleagues do, is I don't play beyond my means. I can actually afford to play much bigger cash games now, and I don't do it. It took me a long time to accumulate what I have, and I don't want to risk that. I am not a risk taker. I know that sounds funny. I am a limited risk taker. I won't do anything to put myself in severe financial jeopardy. And I have no gambling leaks. Zero. A lot of people have leaks.[30] It is typical with a lot of poker players, that they will do sports betting, craps, horse races, even slots.

What is a particular challenge for poker players is that they do not really have workplace colleagues in the traditional sense, and they can never be sure whether another player is "messing with them," even in casual conversations away from the game, because one of the key strategies of poker players is to throw others off their game. Sometimes, of course, poker players can share honest conversations with one another about the challenges of their profession, but it may take longer to build that trust with another player. For poker players, tales are often told to get them through runs of bad luck. Cautionary tales also serve one other important function for both traders and poker players. They use them to convince themselves that somehow they or their firm is different and would not get into such dire straits. These cautionary tales, then, seem both to reflect and then to deflect their greatest fears (the firm going down the tubes; going broke), and it was therefore important to all traders and players to assuage those fears by saying, "This cannot happen to me." Of course, the proof of that can only be in the pudding.

The Money Culture of Hedge Fund Traders and Poker Players

The culture of hedge fund trading and poker playing is very much a reflection of the quotidian practices that emerge out of the economic location and the economic processes occurring in these two professions. The central feature of the structural location of these jobs is the irreconcilable tension between rationality/calculation and intuition/emotion/luck that takes place in a setting where large amounts of money are at stake. As I have suggested, in order to manage the tension created by these occupations, both hedge fund traders and poker players engage in numerous methods to manage risk, to dissociate from the actual value of money by trying to limit one's thinking to "chips" and "keeping score," to build and refine statistical models or to venerate intuition, to brag or swashbuckle, and to spin out important cautionary tales to discipline oneself and socialize others. This particular culture is created because a lot of money is at stake, greed (or taking on too much risk) is a constant temptation, and uncertainty abounds as part and parcel of the practices of these professions. One interesting thing about the culture of hedge fund trading rooms, and to a lesser extent poker rooms, is how openly people talk about money, including sometimes personal finance. This can be both refreshing and a bit crass. I think because hedge fund traders and poker players throw around large figures in talking about their trades or bets and because they both engage in cognitive work to make money simply a way of keeping score, many traders and poker players are very open about talking about their personal finances. It is not uncommon to hear a trader simply say aloud, "I just put down a bid on a house, . . . $950K." I also found that traders are often very clear and up-front about the fact that they are there to make money. As a result, in trading rooms and poker rooms, there seem to be far fewer niceties, much less "corporate speak," and much more bold, and even bald, assertions about making and spending money. When traders are discussing their own salaries, there can be a similarity to the way they talk about risk taking in trading. As one trader told me about talking to the partners in the firm about his own compensation prospects,

> My pitch to the partners would be: I don't know what they will pay me this year. We talked about a range when they brought me in, and I think I have blown out their expectations. So I think they are going to pay me a lot. So I would say, "So don't pay me this year. That is my contribution to the partnership." But who knows, if it turns out to be a profit share, it accomplished the same thing for me. And I said to them, "I would like to end it here. I am not trying to do this, build it up to $3 billion [assets under management] and go somewhere else." I am close to done. So as soon as I have enough money in the bank, I'd want to retire. I like doing what I'm doing, but I can't

imagine I'd be doing it in ten years. Ten or twelve years from now, I'd want to be done.

The culture of poker players also includes some of this open talk about personal compensation, finances, and purchases, although I think a bit less so because players are cautious about giving other players an edge over them by revealing too much information about themselves. Since poker players compete directly with one another in a way that hedge fund traders may not (traders do compete indirectly with one another, of course), I found slightly more caution among poker players in revealing information. But in a similar way to traders, poker players are more open than most people are in talking about money because, after all, "it is just money," as they sometimes put it. So I think for both poker players and hedge fund traders, being completely immersed in this particular money culture all the time makes money less of a taboo or stigmatized topic than it is for many other people.

Male Dominance in Trading and Poker Playing

Why hedge fund trading and poker playing are so male dominated is a very interesting question that awaits more targeted research designed to specifically address this issue. However, I would tentatively suggest that there are multiple, reinforcing reasons for the male dominance in these professions. Both of these professions are high risk, high reward, and I don't think it is mere coincidence that both professions are very male dominated *and* described as very competitive and aggressive. I don't mean to be essentialist about this observation at all, as I could certainly imagine an all-female hedge fund (there are none that I know of, but there is an organization representing women who work in the hedge fund industry).[31] However, there may be something about the way this type of work is constructed that reflects and contributes to the aggressive culture that attracts more males than females. It certainly isn't essential that the culture be macho, aggressive, or even male dominated, but many firms are structured in this way as the culture reinscribes and reinforces itself around the macho posturings of traders and poker players. Once a workplace culture takes root, it often replicates itself in small yet significant ways. For example, one trader described the all-male culture at his firm, and it was clear that he had talked about this with his partners:

> We are wary of hiring the first woman, that it will break up this dynamic. It is not hypertestosterone. Guys aren't surfing porn sites. But you know, if someone is on the phone with someone and, you know, they are kind of annoyed, we are flicking rubber bands at them. So it is fun. And it is fun. I will give you a good example. We have one guy who works out of El Paso, Texas. So, one Friday, we bought a pizza and had it in the office [in Manhattan], and he calls and he is saying, "You know, I kinda feel left out. I like pizza." So we FedExed him a slice of pizza, which he got the next day. He said he opened this thing and had no idea what it was!

An older, more patrician manager at a "fund of funds"[32] (who had never himself been a trader) described to me how very young, male hedge fund traders sometimes preen: "Yes, I run into that a lot. Now, keep in mind, I am not the hedge fund manager. I am not sitting here trading. A lot of the guys who are thirty-one are the guys trading. They are the ones who are the cock of the rock, and they are going to be the best trader to ever hit the street." The cultures of hedge fund trading and poker playing are aggressive and might be viewed as "masculine" in this sense, if based on the dominant construction of masculinity as embodying aggression. Some observers have speculated that men are more comfortable taking significant financial risk as compared to women, though it is never clear whether there is real evidence of this or whether this argument privileges biology or gender socialization as the cause of this alleged difference. For hedge fund traders, another factor leading to male dominance is certainly structural, in that many hedge fund traders and analysts work long hours. It is not uncommon to see traders eating dinner at a firm or talking or emailing someone on the Asian trading desk at off-hours. There is also some travel and some entertaining required. It can be hard to manage family responsibilities with these work demands (unless you pay for significant amounts of child care or have a partner who handles these duties). This is likely to be a more significant barrier to women than to men. Some traders do work late into the night (one described working until 11 p.m. several days per week). Poker players have the benefit of having some discretion over their time. However, the most active games usually happen at night. As one poker player told me, "You have a better chance of waking up a poker player by phone at two in the afternoon than you do by phoning at two in the morning."

An additional structural factor leading to male dominance in hedge fund firms may be what is sometimes called the "pipeline" effect, with women running into barriers and being excluded at several different stages in the pipeline. Many of those who start their own hedge funds do so after leaving a larger house with a group of their buddies. This tends to be a group of risk-taking men who did well enough at a larger fund or as part of a trading desk at a large wire house. They strike out, usually with other guys they have become close with who want to be partners in their own fund. If you go further back in this pipeline, many of these traders got their original experience through early internships working on the floor of the New York Stock Exchange (NYSE) as broker-dealers, and the floor of the NYSE is a very male-dominated culture. Over time, women who do enter the business of trading may get weeded out at each step along the way through combinations of barriers, structural bias, individual or family choice, comfort level, mentoring, and a host of other factors. So by the time you get to a group of traders who begin talking about striking out on their own to form their own fund, there may be very few, if any, women left in the room. Similarly for poker players, many men start out playing poker with friends and then begin trying their hand at card rooms, and so there is a much broader pipeline of males. So like gender segregation processes in many occupations, segregation may result from structure and culture as well as the interplay and mutual reinforcement between the two that lead to this male dominance.[33] Poker players, however, can have more flexible work hours, and this is seen as a benefit by female players.[34]

It is also interesting to consider how the culture of hedge fund trading *results* from the relative absence of women and how that culture might be altered if there were more women among the ranks of hedge fund traders. How would this alter the work done by Robert Rubin, quoted at the outset of this chapter, saying that his main job was to try to balance greed and fear? While some men might speculate that the presence of women would dampen their risk-taking behavior, my guess is that it might dampen some of the high jinks but could also provide a useful corrective in finding the balance between greed and fear, risk and reward, trading instincts and modeling. If successful trading truly involves all these human faculties, one could argue that having a more diverse array of humans in the trading room might produce better results in the long run.[35]

High-Stakes Balancing Act

To succeed as a hedge fund trader or a poker player, one must balance greed and fear, as Robert Rubin put it, or perhaps more accurately, one must balance aggression and caution. This balancing act creates a constant tension, particularly when the financial stakes are so high and the speed of action so fast. The money culture that develops in hedge fund trading and poker playing reflects attempts to deal with this tension while at the same time socializing and initiating new entrants into the field.

Jonah Lehrer, in his book *How We Decide*, argues that as neuroscientists begin understanding the way the brain works in making decisions, it is becoming clearer that often the best decisions are ones that blend rational calculation and cognition with intuition, feelings, and what some people call "gut instinct." Another key to a good decision, Lehrer posits, comes in understanding in which situations rational calculation is likely to produce a better result and in which situations we ought to trust in intuition.[36] What is so interesting about this new approach developing in the field of neuroscience is that it mirrors some of the wisdom generated by individuals who never saw any brain-imaging scans.[37] In other words, what poker players and hedge fund traders may be doing results from the structural position they occupy (never knowing all the information to make a completely rational calculation, combined with a great deal of intuitive expertise gained through experience in similar settings), and this structural situation produces the internal cognitive wrestling match that neuroscientists can only now see on a sophisticated fMRI (functional Magnetic Resonance Imaging) machine. I would argue that it is the nature of these jobs that lends itself to the particular cognitive and emotional responses that are common among poker players and hedge fund traders.[38] In this sense, a very particularized money culture emerges in these professions that reflects common cognitive solutions to the tension created by this type of work. This money culture includes the use of specialized vocabularies in an attempt to monitor failures and to maintain the balance between fear and greed, aggression and caution ("going on tilt," "melting down"); the development and reliance on quantitative modeling as one attempt to remove as much emotion as possible or, alternatively, the elevation (and indeed veneration) of trading intuition; and even the sometimes over-the-top swashbuckling talk and behavior. Hedge fund traders and poker players hone and test the abilities that are needed to do their jobs, as well as test one another (as in other initiation rituals) through proposition betting, cautionary tales, and other storytelling. All of these are commonly used to create and pass on lessons about the need to balance aggression and caution. Their particular form may sometimes be masculinist, sexist, and even misogynistic, as it is developed largely by men under the pressurized environment of large amounts of money being at stake.[39] Greed and fear may indeed be ancient universal human emotions; and here money becomes the "ritually meaningful object" for their expression and irreconcilable tension, and this could simply be another reincarnation of this process.[40] In a historical study of the emergence of the finance profession, Marieke de Goede writes,

> In the eighteenth and nineteenth centuries, the lack of a conceptual distinction between "finance," "gambling," and "speculation" increasingly became an obstacle to the respectability of trading in stocks, shares, and credit certificates. A separation between gambling and finance became thinkable only through a prolonged political, cultural, and legal struggle surrounding the meanings and boundaries of "the financial sphere" and the character and behavior of "financial man."[41]

De Goede suggests that modern financial traders emerged from the realm of gambling and speculation through a long historical struggle that demarcated the area of finance as cognitively and then legally separate from "gambling," developed a regulatory structure that distinguished respectable trading from wild-eyed speculation (a separation that is episodically threatened), and created a more positive image of "the financial man." I think that some of the similarities in the social organization and norms that emerge in the money cultures of hedge fund trading and poker playing are tied to the ways in which people have continued to figure out uses for money that are tied to both the ancient (betting and gambling) and the postmodern (electronic trading and finance). While hedge fund traders and poker players may continue to be accused of being greedy, understanding the complexity of their money cultures shows that viewing them solely in terms of individual attributes is simplistic. It is the structure of their work that gives rise to their highly stylized money cultures.

3

When Time Is Money

Commission Salespeople and

Sports and Entertainment Agents

He feels the pressure of [his] reputation every time he drives
to work, every time he chases a number through yet another
change of seasons. This year, he's chasing the biggest number
he's ever faced, and every month he gets a little closer to it—
though not quite close enough.
                                        —David Dorsey, *The Force*

What is it like to be under the constant pressure to sell? How do salespeople structure their own thinking, as well as the way they spend their
work time, in response to the pressure of sales quotas? How do they cope
with the stress of their income being so heavily dependent on their sales
success? In this chapter, I detail the cognitive and emotional work that
salespeople undertake around issues of time and money and show how
these issues bleed into other dilemmas that arise between work space and
private space. Salespeople face what might be called problems of fuzzy
boundaries. They must navigate a set of porous boundaries between time
and money, work time and leisure time, and work space and private space
and between their very own identities and the products that they are
selling, as this selling involves not only selling products but also selling
oneself. This leads salespeople to a type of emotion work that can blend

and blur identity and success as they become measured by, and encoded through, money.[1]

The occupation of salesperson is one of the largest occupations in the United States. The 2000 U.S. Census listed about 14.6 million people in "sales and related occupations" (with an additional twenty million in office and administrative support jobs, many of whom work in support of sales). There is an incredibly wide variety of sales positions, from the on-the-road salesperson hawking products to the new Internet salespeople who wear out computer keyboards rather than shoe leather. Trying to capture the array of salespeople is obviously folly; so in this chapter, I focus primarily on people selling food and beverage products, residential real estate, and clients' talents as entertainers, athletes, or writers. I chose these specializations partly because of the connections I have in each industry but also because I wanted to include salespeople from a well-established, mature industry with a good amount of travel and customer contact and fairly "concrete" products (food and beverage sales), others who sell a product that involves a certain amount of "emotional value" and in a somewhat less stable industry (real estate), and finally some who are selling something much less concrete and tangible—the embodied talents of their clients (sports, entertainment, and literary agents). I hope that this variety of salespeople can provide at least some window into the ways in which selling shapes the way one thinks about money and finance, by providing enough different types of selling to give a sense of what cognitive and emotional work might be endemic to sales more generally and in what ways the specific "product" being sold may affect notions of money and work.[2]

In addition to being part of a very popular occupation, "the salesman" has long been an iconic figure in literature and popular culture. From Willy Loman in Arthur Miller's *Death of a Salesman* through the shady, fast-talking "land deal" salesmen in David Mamet's *Glengarry, Glen Ross*, the figure of the salesman (now anachronistic, as many women have entered sales) has been used to embody the unbounded promise and significant pitfalls of the world of business.[3] There is simply something about the salesman that captures our imagination. Perhaps it is the alleged freedom of "life on the road"; or perhaps it is the raw capitalism that seems to be embodied in the work of the salesman (Marx might have called the work of the salesman "transforming a commodity into money"); or perhaps our fascination comes from the fact that people in sales are also "selling themselves" to some degree, and that is an interesting process to observe. Whatever it is, the image of the salesperson continues to fascinate.

"I Am in Sales"

One of the most common responses to the prosaic question "What do you do?" is "I'm in sales." However, life in the world of selling has changed quite a bit since the days of Willy Loman, and our stereotypes have not always kept pace with those changes. Sales is no longer a highly male-dominated profession, as many women have entered sales and in some industries have come to dominate the profession, such as in real estate sales. Today, selling can be done on the Internet or through video conferencing sometimes as easily as it can be done in the customer's office or home. No longer do salespeople have to pull off the road to use a pay phone; they can be wired in twenty-four hours a day, seven days a week (some salespeople I interviewed wore headsets while driving because they conduct so much business on the phone as they drive). The modern occupation of sales has become more diverse and varied.

Despite this variety, one of the first things you notice about people in commission sales is how often they all seem to talk about time and how often time and money get linked in conversation. This seems to emerge from their daily practices, including, of course, their compensation system, as well as from the cognitive processing of their work lives in relation to those daily practices. In many interviews, when I asked questions about money, the conversation often very quickly turned toward time, as exemplified in each of these quotations from four different salespeople:

> I am a sales guy. I tell people I am in the "time-stealing business" more than the sales business. I think you have to steal time from your suppliers to get their time, to bring to the table your persuasive ability. . . . My job is to represent my brands while at the same time get to my brokers and steal time from them.

The "moms and pops" that I sell to are the most time-consuming. And if you look at it from the customer side, the customer where you are making the most money is not necessarily the one where you are spending the most time.

I am always grateful for it [a customer's time]. Even if someone looks at your product, and it doesn't work out for him, and they are not going to use it, you always thank them for the time they spent looking at your product.

My bosses are always like, "Do more, do more." But there just isn't that much time in a day. My customers are always appreciative, but they don't realize how much time I take out of my day to, maybe, pick something up for them. You try to remind them, but you don't want to sound like a prick. . . . So you have to stroke them, stroke them, then pull the chain every once in a while.

The Alchemy of Time and Money

It is not hard to understand why the aphorism "time is money" feels almost, but not quite, literal to people working in sales. Most of those whom I interviewed are paid either substantially or entirely on commission. Thus, their earnings only come when they make a sale, and making a sale usually requires some expenditure of their time. In other words, their compensation system works to connect time and money because when time spent with a customer results in a sale, their time actually does turn into money. However, there is also the possibility that a salesperson can spend a lot of time with a client and not make a sale. Here, time was "wasted." However, one can never know this in advance. Sometimes a salesperson has to invest a lot of time over a long period to eventually become a supplier to that client. Here, time that seems to be "wasted" actually became time that was "invested" because it eventually led to a payoff. Salespeople can never be sure if they are "wasting" time or "investing" time because they do not know the outcome. So for salespeople, time and money become closely related because they are always thinking about the proper allocation of their time.

One might think that someone paid on an hourly basis would equate time with money, as the equation is so straightforward in this case: if a person earns $10 per hour and works thirty hours, they earn $300. Here, time is directly equated with money in a very straightforward and linear way. However, hourly workers don't seem to talk about time and money nearly as often as do salespeople, and I think the reason for this is the discretion in "spending time" that is afforded to salespeople, combined with the significant uncertainty over whether particular expenditures of time will actually translate into money. There is not much point in an hourly worker talking about time, because there is little to talk about. Put in x amount of time, get y amount of money. So while it may seem counterintuitive, it is actually the *uncertainty* over the equation "time equals money" that leads salespeople to think so often about their time and money.[4] As one salesperson said,

A couple bad weeks can ruin your mood and put you down in the dumps. You are literally riding a roller coaster. Some people handle it very well and are very focused. Some people let it get to them a little bit more, have hard times, and get frustrated, whatever it may be. There have been times when I have been in bad moods because things just don't work out. You might not be able to get hold of as many people, or some people may not be interested, whatever the situation may be. Then there are times where you find a new client who is great to work with, and it is fantastic. Yeah, it is a roller coaster.

I believe that eventually when you get out of your comfort zone, you are going to start to get a little bit stronger as a person. So I like to think that when I first came here, I was bewildered and dumbfounded and didn't know what to expect. But now, yeah, I'm having a bad week, but I can't control it; let's keep going, let's go forward, do what we gotta do to get through the week and make sure we are taking care of all the work that we are gonna get done.

I knew when things were slow, and you felt like crap. I had one friend of mine, what he would do is once he set his goal, he would start setting up trades for the next month but hold them back; he literally had the tickets taped under his desk. At eight o'clock the first day of the following month, if he wanted to make $100,000 that month, he would put in $40,000 in commissions, and then he would just back off. So he was costing himself maybe $300,000 a year. So he was paying $300,000 a year to feel good twelve days a year. . . . It is all mood! It is a terrible mood thing. What happened was I was so driven that I would be selling a $5,000 or $10,000 bond, the smallest staple we could. I would be there at 4:30 still working. If we were having the Christmas party in the office, I would be yelling to people to "Shut up! I am still working!" I was driven.

Thus, the calculus of time and money is never simple for salespeople. Time does not simply equal money; sometimes it does, sometimes it doesn't. For example, salespeople often invest a considerable amount of time at the beginning of a relationship with a client, without knowing whether that investment will eventually pay off. So this "sunk cost" of time could potentially lead to a large monetary payoff that will extend over many years or decades in the event that a person becomes a steady, long-term customer—akin to investing in an annuity that pays off "over time"—or it could lead to little or nothing at all. This uncertainty contributes to the constant questioning, both by sales managers and by salespeople themselves, about whether they are spending their time in the most beneficial way in purely monetary terms. Add to this the fact that salespeople don't always spend the most time on the customer who ends up buying the most, as some customers are more "high maintenance" than others. Statements by several salespeople illustrate the constant struggle over how to spend time:

There is a class of customers who I visit when I want to, but I don't need to go there on a regular basis. In our business, 80 percent of your income comes from 20 percent of your customers. But I am still calling on that other 80 percent, and my days get swallowed up by some of those people.

You need to look at this a couple of times a year because you need to know that 30 percent of your living comes from this supplier, and you aren't spending any time with that supplier because you get that squeaky-wheel syndrome, where the one who bothers you the most is the one you spend time on, and that is not necessarily who you want to be working with. It is the same with customers. Certain customers are time-consuming. And if you look at your customer side, where you are making the most money is not necessarily who you are spending the most time with.

You have a certain number of hours that the office is open; you call it opportunity time. . . . If someone walks in, you are meeting a total stranger, and you have to convince them to work with you. So there is a lot of spinning your wheels. So one day I just said, "I would rather have my time back. I'd rather have that time for me than sitting in the office."

Making the equation between time and money even more complicated for salespeople is that they are also trying to build friendly relationships with clients that are not only monetary but also have elements of long-term friendships (as with the fund raisers described in chapter 4, these relationships can come very close to actual friendships and can last longer than many friendships). Sometimes salespeople talk about how much they enjoy "spending time" with certain clients, but it may not be the client who generates the greatest commission. So as salespeople "spend their time," they have to think about whether they are allocating time to a client because they enjoy that time or because that time will pay off monetarily, even if they do not enjoy it. Some clients who are more enjoyable to spend time with, or who give salespeople more ego gratification, may not provide the largest sales, while other clients, who are not enjoyable in the least to spend time with, might create large commissions. So salespeople also have to add these considerations into the calculation. This creates cognitive and emotional tension for salespeople as they are pulled to spend time with someone whose company they enjoy but are forced to ask themselves if doing so is really a waste of time.

As I show later in this chapter, many salespeople say they are "selling themselves" as much as they are selling a product. By that, they mean that they are selling their personality, their trustworthiness, their work ethic, or their ability to get things done. So there can be a form of ego gratification that comes from some customers (who may stroke the salesperson with compliments). This ego gratification is also worth something to the salesperson, who often puts his or her ego on the line, sometimes getting it bruised. This calculus of time equals money just keeps getting more and more complicated, as a salesperson's time can pay off in sales commissions, in enjoyment, in ego gratification, or in any combination of those three. I think this is why salespeople can never fully solve the equation time equals money, nor can they ever satisfactorily answer the question "Am I spending my time wisely?"

KD: So do you think about how you are doing on a weekly basis? Do you check each week?

SALESPERSON: Daily! Daily! As far as I know, I probably made $30 today and spent $35 on gas. One of my customers bought me lunch, and then I left a $10 tip, so I am losing money today. But then it may come Thursday, and I make $200. Tuesdays [today] are often bad days. I have another customer I usually make money on, but they are on "stop" because another restaurant they own hasn't paid, so they can't order.[5]

Contests, Trips, Carrots, and Sticks

Salespeople link time and money not only because they are paid on commission but also because their employers create a particular money culture that encourages them to think this way. One way in which sales organizations do this is through the use of constant contests. There are many games and sales contests that are engineered to create the incentive and pressure to sell more. In some sales organizations (such as Xerox, as described in David Dorsey's book *The Force*, quoted in the epigraph at the beginning of this chapter), there is a yearly contest to "make trip," which means that if you make a yearly sales goal, you get to go on an exotic and expensive company trip. "Making trip" is seen as important both for getting the "all expenses paid" trip and also because it provides bragging rights and an ego gratification. Nested within this year-long quest to make trip are monthly contests such as the ones described by one salesperson I interviewed ("chemical of the month," "fresh fish of the month"). Prizes for these contests might be a digital camera, a savings bond, or an MP3 player. Three different salespeople described their reactions to these contests:

We have about seven contests going right now. Chemical of the month; steak of the month; 12-for-12, where you win something if you sell twelve different items over twelve weeks. You win prizes like cash, trips; it really is an endless amount of stuff. I just won a trip to New Zealand. It was based on who the division VP thought did the best job on a new brand of wine from New Zealand that really caught fire. They have a trip each year if you meet a goal based on gross commissions earned.

It is a retreat with my friends and an opportunity to hang out with them. And it is like a pat on the back. They give you things: open bar, massages, really good speakers—the last one was the first blind person to climb Mt. Everest, and he was brilliantly inspirational. They put on fireworks; you eat lobster, filet mignon. And see, this is so silly in the big scheme of things, but you go back to your room each night, and there is a present on your bed. It can be a jacket, a bathrobe. This year it was a suitcase, a blanket another night, a T-shirt, a beautiful scarf, a bouquet. But to me, it's the biggest fun: you are stumbling into your room at night and you yell, "AAAAHHH!!" And you grab it and unwrap it. There is this big bow on it. I love that! And, you know, probably the cost of all that, bought in bulk, is maybe $400 to $500 per person, but there is just something extremely fun about that, and it probably motivates me more.

KD: Were you always driven, even as a kid?
SALESPERSON: No, I was a lazy, fat bum. I was a bum, and then I got driven because I was offered this opportunity. I stepped into shit, and I loved it so much. . . . It was when I got in that atmosphere, it kicked in. I fell into the perfect job. I had the aptitude for it, and I liked it, and it just fit.

When the carrot doesn't work, there is always the stick. While not quite a public flogging, many sales organizations figure out ways to make it quite clear which salesperson is "bringing up the rear" or not carrying his or her weight. Some sales managers will post publicly all the salespeople in a division, ranked by their sales numbers. Other salespeople told me that they will receive an automated group voice mail from their sales manager every Sunday evening, publicly naming the leading salespeople in the group that week or those who met their sales goals (and it is painfully clear to everyone who is *not* named in the message).

> We get numbers that show where you are at, and those come out every week. They are posted so everyone can see how they are doing. It can be a great motivator. Certainly if you are competitive, it can be a great motivator to drive your activity.

> You are part of a team of seven people. Each Sunday, you get a voice mail that says, "So-and-so was up this much, and leading the pack was Patricia with $10,000. If you don't hear your name on that voice mail, you know you were down.

> It was the game. It didn't matter. I told you, if I cared about the money, I would have kept track of my run. It didn't matter what I made. I just wanted to make more than this other top salesman or that other top salesman. And it didn't really bother me if I didn't, but I just wanted to do the best I could. And don't forget that the atmosphere in the office—what's another word for atmosphere?—they were always encouraging you. I used to get a pat on the back and a handshake from my office manager when I made $10,000 gross in a day, but if I made $7,000 and worked my ass off, he wouldn't shake my hand. So there was a structural pressure from the organization. And I didn't really care about the guy's handshake.

Both the carrot and the stick can take an emotional and physical toll on salespeople, as they learn to cope with the pressures of spiraling sales goals. Most of the salespeople I spoke with had come to some terms with this pressure as they gained experience in the sales business. However, there were a few that continued to show some form of resistance to the pressure:

> My bosses would take issue with my persona. They want you to push more, push what will get them their bonus. To them, all I am is a number. They don't care if I like my job or not. All they care about is that I make them look good. They say, "I want you to be successful," and that is so they can be

successful. And that is fine. That is their job. They don't care if my name is Tom or John, as long as the numbers are there.

Look at this: they put up the list from 1 to 100 of the brokers. They don't put up the money, but they put up the list. I was always number 1, 2, or 3. I said, "Wait a minute, I don't like that list. I don't mind that I am number 1, but I feel bad for these guys at the bottom. What are you trying to do? Are you trying to embarrass them to do better? Don't you think everyone is going to try to do the best that they can?" I was revered because I was always up there. [But] I didn't think it was right.

My problem and the reason why they don't really love me in the company is that I am not a materialist! I don't need a big apartment. I don't need a big car. I don't need a lot of clothes. I don't need anything, and I have never been that acquisitive an individual. My needs are simple and easily met. . . . [But] they want you to have the biggest house you can possibly buy, to have the biggest mortgage hanging over your head like the Sword of Damocles, so that you wake up every morning saying, "How the hell am I going to make enough money to pay for this?!"

Even though I found some small pockets of resistance, at the end of the day most salespeople embraced their profession and saw it as an exciting challenge and a game worth playing:

How do you get the person [the customer] to say yes? At the end of the day, you have to get the person to say yes. So the question is what will you do to get that person to say yes? Will you lie? Will you shave the truth? Will you just tell the truth? Will you be extra belligerent? Will you just keep calling them? It is a zero-sum game; you have to get the person to say yes.

What's the word—you are not in a confidence game, but you are in a duel with the person. And the only way to win the duel is to have them say yes and buy the thing from you.

Or consider this exchange I had with a food salesman:

SALESMAN: You don't want to ruin your relationships with your customers, but you don't want to piss off your bosses either. Sometimes it costs me money out of my own pocket to keep everybody happy.

KD: How so?

SALESMAN: If I haven't sold something that I needed to sell, and I don't want to get that phone call, "Why haven't you sold this?" then I just buy it. I pay with cash in my pocket. I just give it to the customer: "Here, you might like this kitchen degreaser." It might cost me $50 a case. I do give myself a very good price on it [*laughs*]. I'd rather spend the $50 on it than listen to that voice mail.

KD: Do managers know you do this?

SALESMAN: Yeah, one told me to do it: "Just buy it. I need to qualify for this, hit this number. I'll give you half," he says. . . . And then he never does! [*laughs*]

Money Culture as a Structured Equation

This constant equating of time and money in all its variations, then, is organized into the very structure of work through things like the compensation scheme and related practices of quotas, sales contests, and the myriad of subtle (and not-so-subtle) congratulatory symbols given to sales leaders and embarrassments meted out to sales laggards. All of this creates an aggressive money culture that keeps the sales machine moving forward by keeping the salesperson's eyes squarely focused on the prize of increasing sales. Most salespeople come to take on this challenge (if they don't leave the sales game entirely) and undertake the cognitive and emotional work to shape the pressures of this particular money culture into a suitable way of living and working. Although some salespeople say they were a born sales(wo)man, it is the way in which the sales job is constructed within the money culture of the sales organization that shapes the salesperson in this unrelenting quest to turn time into money.

Moving in tandem with the difficulties of calculating the proper relationship between time and money is a second problem faced by salespeople: the fuzzy boundary between work and home.[6] This problem seems particularly acute for salespeople who don't spend time in a traditional office setting. Because most salespeople work in and from different locales—their car, their own home, their customer's office, and hotels while on the road—the boundary between work space and private space is often very unclear. This is how one salesman described his routine at the end of his day:

> I will stay in the car in my driveway and talk on the phone. It's easier than going into the house, with all the distractions. One time my son called me on the cell from his room when I was in the driveway to the house. He said it was easier to reach me that way!
>
> This consultant [the firm had hired] viewed the office as the hub of the business. Well, it is not. This is a sales company, a transactional place. The transaction place—the customer's door—is the hub of the business. So I clashed with the clerical management team in the office. These clerical people were running the show. They could tell you how it should be done for your customer. So I was being dictated to, in terms of customer service—how my customers could order samples, how much lead time was needed. I have customers who will call and ask for unrealistic things, but if I can do it, I do it!

The salesperson must confront these questions: Where is the hub of work? Is it the office? The customer's workplace? The car? The telephone? The home? While the work space is often unclear, so too are work hours. Many report taking calls before and after what people typically think of as normal work hours. Cell phones and the globalization of work have increased this confusion over the boundaries between work time and leisure time, as many salespeople take calls at almost any time and any place and from any time zone (often including in the middle of my own interviews with them). The cell phone, of course, has given the salesperson more freedom in some sense (to be at a child's soccer game, for example) but also more constraint in not being fully present (to conduct business at a child's soccer game means not paying attention to the child's game). Combining with, and increasing, this confusion over the boundaries between work and leisure space and between work and leisure time is another confusion, created by the actual interactions salespeople have with their clients, which can sound like friendships at times (similar to the fund raisers discussed in chapter 4). Because much of the sales relationship involves talking, including talking about family life or leisure interests to build a relationship with a client, sales calls on the phone can at times sound similar to a call to a friend or family member. Salespeople are also breaking boundaries in another sense. They intrude into a customer's place of business and steal a customer's time. So salespeople must also be sensitive to the boundaries of others' work and time.

> In sales, you approach someone at their work. They usually don't want to be there. They don't want to be working. Either you are a break in their day, or you are a nuisance. . . . You have to walk in, knowing that what you are doing is right, to overcome the initial resistance. That is why I don't like sales. Because the things I am selling are not always the right thing, but I am making them think it is.

It might be said that for people in sales professions, boundaries of all sorts are both blurry and porous. In my many conversations with salespeople, it was not uncommon to move from discussions of the time and money dilemma to some of the dilemmas of time at work and time at home. Several salespeople made the point that this cognitive dilemma had caused significant conflict with spouses or other family members who had trouble seeing, let alone understanding, these fuzzy boundaries.

> My wife is the type where she came home with a load of groceries the other day, and it was around five o'clock, and, you know, when you are working at home, I was at my desk. I usually work until about a quarter to six. I was not quite finished, and I got a call from a guy from California who I had been playing phone tag with all week. So I called him back. Well, she was furious that I was making a call to someone [rather than helping unload the groceries] and, as she said, "yukking it up." Well, I yuk it up for a living!

The concept of "movement" also came up often in my interviews with salespeople. As they put it, salespeople are almost always "on the move." Many become comfortable driving while talking on cell phones, glancing at orders, and jotting down notes on a pad of paper. They move rapidly among customers troubleshooting problems, as they are often the link between the customer and the home office and production staff. Many of the product salespeople I spoke with talked about the sense of constant movement in their jobs. Several indicated that if they were not moving, they felt like they were wasting their time. While no one said it directly, I got the impression that for salespeople, being on the move meant they felt like they were earning money or doing the things they needed to do to turn their time into money. Several told me how much they hated meetings, both because they felt like meetings were a "waste of time" (if time is money and movement is money, sitting in a meeting does not appear to equate to money—at least in any way they can discern) and also because they simply had trouble "sitting through meetings." Several salespeople joked about having ADD or ADHD (attention deficit disorder or attention deficit hyperactivity disorder), saying they could never do an office job that required them to "sit still." I was initially surprised by the fact that more than one commission salesperson jokingly said to me, without any particular prompting, "I think I have ADHD." They were using this common phrase that exists in our culture to describe the feeling of needing to keep moving all the time. I think one of the major attractions about selling for the people who do it is this constant sense of movement—physical movement in a car or plane as well as cognitive/mental movement in bouncing quickly from one problem to the next, resolving issues that need quick and immediate attention.[7]

> I get buzzed when I am in the car. If I don't get in the car in the morning, I spin my wheels during the day. I do a lot of things, but at the end of the day, I cannot figure out what I have done. . . . Whereas if I am on the road, I can say, "Just let me know if there are any important emails."

> I find that if I stay home, I am absolutely, totally bored. I have high energy, and most people can't keep up with me. . . . My son had ADD, attention deficit disorder. . . . I actually think he might have gotten it from me, because I think I have some forms of it. But I have learned how to deal with it. What I learned is how to delegate. So anything that causes me stress, I plug a person in who can do that.

I have no idea whether commission salespeople are actually more likely to have attention deficit disorder than other people are, but it is interesting to think about why commission salespeople allude to the disorder. It is reasonable to wonder if people with ADHD find their way into sales positions because of the adrenalin rush and the constant movement. But it is also worth raising the possibility that some types of work actually *induce* feelings akin to ADHD. In other words, when you are in commission sales, you ride an emotional roller coaster, juggle dozens of client problems at once, move around constantly, and can rarely focus on a single problem in isolation for any significant amount of time. Many people who were to spend a month working in commission sales might also find themselves saying, "This job makes me feel like I have ADHD!"

Selling Talent, Selling People

While product salespeople are selling something concrete, agents sell something much more intangible: their clients' talents. Yet I found that some dilemmas of time and money are perhaps even more pronounced for literary, entertainment, and sports agents,[8] who are indeed selling a product on commission, but in this case the product is the embodied talents of their clients.[9] For agents, we also now add the ego issues embodied in the product (i.e., the client) into the equation between time and money, as well as adding another very large dose of the unknown in the ephemeral and elusive judgment of "talent." Agents invest huge amounts of time (often measured in years) in their clients without knowing whether there will be any monetary payoff at all from the invested time. For example, music agents can spend endless hours listening to submitted recordings and going out at night to see different bands in clubs as they sift through the masses of talented people to find the ones they believe might be worth representing. Even after this intensive sifting process, usually fewer than 10 percent (and often many fewer) of the individuals or groups that an agent chooses to take on will ever produce any monetary return at all for the agent. The reason why agents are willing to do this, of course, is that there is the potential for one of those clients to really hit it big, leading to a very large payday.

Agents learn to think about the investment of time that they put into clients (many of whom never pay off in any economic return at all) as they dream of—and plan for—the bonanza of representing someone who hits it big. They are willing to put in a significant amount of unremunerated time in the belief that this is required to find the one talent who does hit it big. Agents also have to learn how to think about, measure, and calculate the worth of a person's talent in contract negotiations. How do you "sell" another person's talent or potential to someone? How do you determine how much money that is worth?[10]

Similar to product salespeople, it is the structural position in the economy that shapes the way an agent has to think about time and its connection to money. This calculation is even trickier for agents than it is for salespeople of more traditional products. First, agents have to learn how to find and select talent. Many told me that as they gained experience in their field, they had to become much more selective about how they allocate their time. They become more and more discriminating in their taste for signing artists. However, there still is no scientific formula for knowing when a talent (whether a writer or a musician) will ever "make it."

> We get five or six [musical] submissions a day; it's about fifteen hundred to two thousand per year of people who want us to represent them. . . . We've got to be cautious about who we're taking on, because we could easily be the busiest people in town not making any money. So we have to be very selective. . . . And so, of the say two thousand submissions that we get per year, we'll maybe take on four, five tops. And of the five we take on, maybe one gets a deal. Maybe two if we are lucky.

> You have the opportunity to get rich, you know? You do a deal for a guy who goes out and sells five million records and gets on a world tour and, you know, starts doing a whole bunch, . . . you know, does a Reebok deal and gets his own clothing line, and all of all sudden you're making a million bucks a year.

> That's the difference between lawyers and literary agents, for example. The agent, you know, can work six months and get nothing, . . . or you can work, you know, for half an hour, and somebody picks up the phone and says,

"I'm going to make a movie [out of this book], and I will pay you a million dollars."

We really can't afford to take a book that we don't think will command a $50,000 advance. Our overhead is higher than the agent with a little loft on a side street. . . . But this is an enthusiasm business; it's driven by enthusiasm. Because it is not a science; . . . the rule of thumb in publishing is that only 10 percent of the entire list earns out his advance. And in the agency, probably only 10 percent earn out the advance. . . . So it isn't a science; it is really a small percentage that drives the business.

A Matter of Taste?

An additional issue that is quite important for agents (but less so for other types of commission salespeople)[11] is learning to separate their own personal taste from their judgment about the potential for commercial success. Because agents deal with aesthetic judgments, and they are often musicians or writers themselves with strongly held artistic tastes, they find themselves needing to make aesthetic judgments and commercial judgments, which sometimes overlap but often may not. As a top literary agent put it, "Well, we are making two judgments. We're making an aesthetic judgment: . . . this is not very good; this is promising; this is wonderful, and we don't care if we lose money on this because we are going to be proud of this till the day we die. We can only afford to take a few of those." A music agent talked about the similarities in business arrangements across different types of music: "We have classical, we do jazz, we do punk, we do rock, we do foreign music, we have clients who do Bhangra music from India, we have rappers and rap producers from Japan—all across genres; it doesn't matter. . . . It's not difficult to switch gears from a classical deal to a rap deal to a country deal. The people are different in attitudes, but the deals are very similar." However, this same agent explained that when it comes to aesthetic judgment, as opposed to the commercial structuring of a deal, an agent can feel more comfortable in certain genres than in others. His experience as a musician, however, helps him to evaluate genres with which he may be less familiar:

It definitely helped that I was a musician because even at the age of thirty-five, when I started in the rap game, I was able to learn a brand-new genre of music for me. . . . I just said, "Why should I not pay attention to this? It's vibrant, it's very popular, and people involved are willing to experiment. It's just a different rhythm." So I applied the same analysis I would apply to a rock, classical, or jazz act. I analyze the rhythm, the harmony, the melody, what they are saying lyrically, how it is mixed, the quality of the production, the quality of the musical performance. And I was able to learn the music and delineate what's good and what's not good.

I found that agents differ on how comfortable they feel in making judgments about different genres. Some prefer to stick with one or two areas of expertise, while others believe they can develop an ability to move across a wide array of genres. Contrast these two different approaches:

I can tell you what I don't understand artistically well enough to talk about it intelligently. I don't understand hip-hop music on the creative level that I understand other types of music. Other than that, I have a reasonable ability to distinguish good from bad just because of my own background as a musician. I will have some reference points where I can say. But with hip-hop or really hard-core rap or really heavy metal, I'm out of my element. I will typically not get involved and shop that material. I'm not a good advocate for it.

The judging is somewhat more than just separating the wheat from the chaff. So, for example, I get many, many demos each week. I think I am able to discern those who have a shot at least at going on and doing well. But it is not really my call. If someone is interested, I want to negotiate the best for them. I don't have to like every single genre of music. I don't have to like every single sport. I don't have to like every book that gets published. I don't have to like every movie that I work on.

As a whole, music and literary agents do tend to end up having specialty areas within music or literature, either by choice or because they simply develop a reputation for one particular genre and then attract more clients in that specialty area. This does not mean they won't represent people outside that specialty, as they often do; it simply means that they become known for their expertise in a certain style of music (e.g., rap, jazz, or classical) or a certain type of literature (e.g., celebrity biography or historical fiction) or a particular sport (e.g., football, basketball, or boxing).

Product Dilemmas

Perhaps another way to understand the nature of the work that salespeople do is to say that the product they are selling raises specific dilemmas for them as they attempt to turn their time into money. As we have seen in the music and publishing industries, aesthetic judgment and specialization by genre are important to selling the product. For sports agents, the dilemma of product is that the embodied physical and mental talents of an individual player are sold, and if the player is gifted, he or she may achieve significant success at a very young age. This raises unique issues, as described by two sports agents:

> There is—you can call it psychological hand-holding. There is a certain degree of reality to the Jerry Maguire syndrome. Some of it, of course, with Tom Cruise and Cuba Gooding, Jr., was for effect in the movie. And there is a lot more to it than just "Show me the money!" But there is a difficulty with young men and women, many of whom have not had that kind of dollars, suddenly focusing on large dollars and the effects it has on them. Some handle it well, some don't.

> And these young men and women who are blessed with a God-given talent and can make a great deal of money, it becomes very important to them to see to it that—and it is hard for them to realize, because they think this will go on forever—but if they can conserve and be a little more conservative, you can provide very much for your family in the future in the years to come.

Sports agents spend significant time educating their young clients about the business realities and possibilities in sports. In this way, agents are both selling their product and educating and socializing their product at the same time. One of the dangers for a sports agent comes when the athlete's expectations exceed reality. The agent must worry that players will change agents if they believe they can do better with another agent. As one longtime agent told me when I asked him what elements went into structuring a deal,

> It is more than just experience; it is also research, and then there is what we call "comparables." Again, going back to the National Football League, the players are somewhat slotted. That means within the framework of where they are drafted and where in that round they are drafted, there is a range. There are pieces of it that are contractual, but the majority is just experience. What then happens is that agents and attorneys can be creative and develop other nuances and other areas where dollars can come from incentives or bonuses or whatever, and there is where your negotiating comes in. But in reality, if you are honest with your client, a seventh-round draft pick in the NFL is not going to get the money of a first-round pick no matter how good he thinks he is. . . . You get a lot of young guys come in here, and they think they are going to work hard and they will be the exception, play into their late thirties. And they have a career-ending disability. Or you might have a platinum record, and the next time you put out a record, the public doesn't accept it, and it bombs.

Similarly, music agents have to encourage their clients but also manage their expectations:

AGENT: I always say to all of my clients that everyone who walks in this office is a superstar.

KD: Me, too?

AGENT: Yeah, you are a superstar. The problem is that sometimes you are not recognized by the rest of the world as a superstar. The dollars and the royalty rates and the album sales are a function of geography, timing, and what is going on. You get a feel with experience. A lot of time it is what the traffic will bear. Give me a rap group or a rock-and-roll group when there are three or four major labels bidding. That is one thing. But if you have someone who is lucky to get a deal, and there is one little company willing to do something, [then] you can't command the dollars of a major.

There is a lot of emotion work, then, that sports and entertainment agents must do, both in relation to their clients and also in relation to themselves, because there are many times when a significant amount of work is done with little payoff. One agent, who had been in the business for several decades, described how he learned to manage this emotion work:

> There is a lot of emotion attached to it. I guess when I was young, I used to think, "If I am good at what I do, and I am ethical and straight, why would I ever lose a client?" The reality is that's the nature of creativity. . . . I have had some clients who I have had for over three decades, yet at the same time, you can't satisfy everybody. Sometimes, people don't make it. It is not necessarily your fault, but there is always blame to be attached. Yes, there are certain times where I have seen wonderful things happen, and you get elated; and there are times when terrible things happen, and you get depressed. I try, and it is not always easy, because I am supposed to be objective and keep an even keel. So I try not to have as many mountains and valleys.

In the food and beverage industry, the product implies a very different set of constraints and challenges. Food and drink products are somewhat more interchangeable than celebrity talent is, and they don't talk back. So for people selling food and beverage products, they have a different problem; they must struggle to distinguish their product from that of their competitors. Price, of course, is one such distinction for product salespeople and becomes an increasingly important one when there is a downturn in the economy. However, salespeople want to avoid constantly spiraling downward pressure on price that squeezes their profit margins and squeezes commissions, so they often would prefer to show that their product is superior to the competitors', rather than cheaper. One way to do this, of course, is to focus on the quality of ingredients. But because ingredients are not often visible in a product, salespeople in the food and beverage industry are often alleging that the competition is using inferior ingredients to those in their own products. This spawns an entire discussion of trust and money that is particularly salient for sales-people in this industry:

> Many times you are trying to say that your product is an exact duplicate of another product [that is more expensive]. One of the suppliers is tamper-ing, he is putting in corn syrup, and he is not selling them malts. Malt is a forty-five-cent item; he is adding eighteen-cent corn syrup. It sweetens it, it makes it taste better, but it is not malts. I take the samples, send them to the company that I represent; they send them to an outside lab to get a third-party evaluation of what they are buying. It takes months and months. Then we show them, "You are buying 80 percent corn syrup and getting raked over the coals by this company. You need to correct this." They are at risk because they then [in turn] supply to major manufacturers and are at risk getting caught not selling the right ingredients.

> I sell Mexican chili flakes, and I have to certify that there is no Sudan Red in that [a cheaper substitute]. That is a $150 test. [Using Sudan Red] shows you are using a cheaper chili and putting a red coating on it.

> What we are selling, first of all, is our trusted relationship that we are capa-ble and we will deliver the results they expect. They trust us to deliver.

> There are legendary rumors in this industry about what people did with wine, putting air into wine bottles using hypodermic needles! But I do think the industry has changed a great deal. I came into it at the end of the old days, when it was the Wild West! The "bag men" were legendary, com-ing around with bags of cash. If you bought this, here's a bag of cash. We were called "Missionary Men," because we went around all day buying peo-ple drinks. That has changed.

The product provides a different and particularly vexing problem for sports and entertainment agents because the product they are selling is embodied in a human being. Many of their clients are young, artistic or athletic, focused very narrowly on their particular area of talent, and often not well schooled in the complexities of business.

What you need to be successful as an entertainment lawyer or agent is you need to be a people person. You need to be able to deal with the artistic temperament and to explain to an artist in very simplistic but accurate terms what the business deal is that they are about to sign or that they have signed. . . . At the same time, you need to be able to translate the artist's view of the world to the business people. Creative people have very little money but lots of talent. Business people have money and no talent. You put them together; hopefully you combine the two, and you have money and the talent necessary to create a project that is commercially successful.

Dollars, yes, dollars are definitely issues! A lot of times musicians, once they begin to receive publicity, they make the cardinal error of believing their own hype and saying, "Well, I am in the newspaper, I am getting good reviews, my video is being played on BET or MTV. I should be getting a million dollars." . . . And they get very emotional about that, and you have to explain to them that the way their deal works is that for the past year, or year and a half, the company has been investing in them, and the current amount is six hundred thousand or seven or eight hundred thousand, and only when that is paid back do they start to receive royalties.

There are a lot of kids who are street thugs or hoodlums with a gift for gab and the ability to express in rhymes what they have experienced, and even Caucasian kids in the suburbs are willing to buy that, and it gives them street credibility. . . . And the record business is a cash business; it's always been one that's rather easy, if someone puts their mind to it, to launder money through a concert or through record sales on the street, T-shirt sales, things of that nature. As a result, you know, you have a lot of slimy people on the edges of our business taking in a lot of cash flowing around the business.

I think you run into a lot of people who have sort of a lofty aesthetic contempt for business. You have to have a real interest and compassion for the people you are working with because mostly what they do is they go into a room by themselves for nine months, and they give something that other people take away from them. . . . And the book comes out, and it is a failure—and that is what happens more often than not—so you need to have a certain capacity for compassion.

Agents must deal with an unusually complicated time-equals-money alchemy because they invest huge amounts of time in clients, many of whom never pay off. Any monetary payoffs that do come often come only after years of investment of time. This makes it very difficult to know if you are spending your time wisely each day. On the other hand, agents have the potential for a very large payday should one of their clients hit it big. So agents dream of hitting the home run much more often than do other salespeople. They must become comfortable with the idea that they need to be willing to invest their time and never get paid, in the hope that it will all balance out in the end if they do hit the jackpot one day. As two agents put it to me,

> You have the opportunity to get rich, you know? You do a deal for a guy who goes out and sells five million records and goes on a world tour and starts doing a whole bunch of, you know, does a deal with Reebok and gets his own clothing line. All of a sudden, you are making a million bucks a year. . . . It's like prospecting; that's exactly what it is. We're out here digging around in the dirt, hoping to come across a nice golden nugget. Being an entrepreneur, you have this great opportunity, you know. Like "I've been poor, but I've never been rich." You know, "I'd love to give it a shot." . . . My business model is different; it is stay alive long enough to get a good payday . . . You know, you want to stay in the game to grab that ring.

> We don't make huge gobs of money, but there is the potential for huge gobs of money. If we've got a percentage on a client, and the client becomes the next JLo or the next, you know, whoever, and we have a percentage deal, we can do extremely well, very quickly. And I've been waiting for years. It's being in the right position to take advantage of deals and to know how to do the deal . . . I feel that I have the wisdom and experience now that if it happens, I will know exactly what to do.

Whether you are selling wine, food, houses, or people, the product you are selling creates the particular challenges you face in turning time into money. For salespeople in the food business, the challenge might be proving that your commodity is superior to that of a competitor; for a real estate agent, it might be transforming a house into the embodied dreams of a home and all that represents to a client; for a sports or entertainment agent, it is the challenge of selling the individual client to a corporation while carefully shaping that client's expectations and behaviors. Here again, we see that the equation for turning time into money grows ever more complicated. Agents have to spend significant time molding their clients:

It's not easy to deal with this kind of stuff. I am emotional myself, being an artist, and I understand how they feel. It may just be business to the record company, but to [a recording artist] it is real life. Those songs are her babies, and they came from the heavens above, through her brain and through her voice onto a piece of tape. And it's very, very hard to understand that one's better than another or one's more commercial than another or one's no good. So, yeah, it is difficult, and I have to use all my powers of persuasion, and I can say, "Look, I'm a musician, too, and I know where you are coming from on this." . . . A lot of times it requires that you convince them to take a step back, and I say, "Let's take the emotion out of this for a minute, and let's look at this as a business deal for a minute, and then we'll go back to it from the artistic point of view."

You have to remember that musicians, artists, athletes, . . . they are blessed with talent and are often very successful at a young age, much younger than the normal amount of maturity to handle a mid- to high-six-figure salary. You've got people with very little life experience, who often come from poor backgrounds, who have never budgeted, never understood a checking account; they are used to going to check-cashing places, not a bank. They don't understand retirement accounts, investments. I remember taking a [boxing] world champion to the bank and opening IRAs for him and his wife. . . . He was the best in his weight class in the world. He knew how to throw a left hook and was completely unafraid in the ring. Out of the ring, he was at sea, like having a boat without a rudder.

You know, it's ironic because I do view the amount of money changing hands in these contracts differently. Typically, if I'm working for a corporate client, the amount of money changing hands is significantly larger, but it is not in and of itself as critical to [the corporation] as it is to an artist for his or her first few big contracts. And the other thing is I view dollars and cents differently because I know that, you know, a $10,000 check to an artist who has never made more than fifteen a year for her artistic pursuits is going to be very important, and it's going to change her finances. . . . I do think about it differently, as clients become more established. . . . I said to one girl when she signed her contract, "Alright, you're now the CEO of the business of you. And you know, you should not take this check as license to go out and piss it away. You know, what's set aside, a certain portion of it is just a completely discretionary lump, but the rest of it—get making some money for you at something else. Start providing for when you can't do this anymore; you know, let's do some tax planning. . . . You now have to manage your money like a grown-up."

The Perfect Suit

As well as representing the product, salespeople (of all stripes) are also selling *themselves*—not only in being personable or friendly but also in building trust with customers and clients. As one salesperson succinctly put it, "Sales is about trust. It they trust you, if they like you, they will buy from you. If they don't, they won't." Notice that he says that customers must trust you and *like you*. Thus, the salesperson must sell him- or herself as well as selling the product. One way that salespeople establish trust is by convincing the customer that they will deliver on promises made and, most importantly, come through for the customer in a jam. By the salesperson's going the extra mile, the customer may view the action as a "favor" that carries an unspoken assumption of reciprocity. Since the salesperson has gone out of his or her way for the customer, the salesperson will expect good treatment, including perhaps receiving a favor in return (again, this is usually unspoken). As one salesman put it,

> Let's say they forget to order something; they say, "I need five cases of potatoes." I have to load it in my car and bring it there. A lot of guys won't deliver the potatoes unless they take something else—the chemical of the month, a degreaser—that we are pushing [in a sales contest]. "I'll take you

the potatoes if you buy this." I don't like to do this, and I won't do it. But with my guys [customers], they may do me a favor if I do them a favor.

You have to show support for your clients. Like I took my brother out to dinner [at a client's restaurant], and he did a ten-course tasting menu for us. We had a handful of drinks. It cost $140, but it was worth $200. My client might think I am banging him on price, so I want to show him I am willing to spend money at his place. And I stroke him: "This is really good, fantastic, a great time. I made a joke, of course, saying, "Hey, I didn't sell you scallops!"

When salespeople are constantly selling themselves as well as their product, the ego becomes invested in the transaction: "If I am selling myself, and you reject my product, are you rejecting me?" That is the emotional trip wire for many salespeople, and they must get used to this feeling of rejection. One way of doing so is to try to separate the "self" from the sale, but this is clearly not possible if you are selling the trust a person has in you. Thus, salespeople take both hits and boosts to their ego and must try to maintain an even keel by managing their emotions. This is easier said than done because salespeople often have to "pump themselves up" to get a sale; therefore, it is not easy to manage a letdown if you need to pump up the emotions to bring energy and enthusiasm to the sales call. One cannot simply turn on emotion to try to get the sale and instantly block it off if the sale does not occur. I listened as one relatively young salesperson explained the ways in which he was trying to cope with the emotional roller coaster. Notice how money plays a large role even in the emotional management as he tells me about his wristwatch:

I bought this watch because I quit my prior sales job. I went against the grain. I wasn't happy for a long time there, and people said, "Quit. Quit." And I had nothing lined up, but I quit. And people were shocked and said, "How could you quit without a security blanket?" But to sort of prove it to myself, go out and buy something that you can't really afford. It was sort of like rewarding myself for doing something hard, for taking control of a bad situation. [*He shows me the wrist watch he is wearing and points at it*]. $2,500; that's a plasma TV. I am wearing a plasma TV on my wrist. I was feeling down. I just quit my job. So I bought [the watch] to show confidence in myself. . . . The most important part is the self-esteem boost—that I can afford successful things. Successful people have nice things. You have the nice car, the nice TV; you have a nice watch, so you must be doing something right. . . . [*Pointing at the watch*] This is what makes me feel good about myself.[12]

Another salesperson expressed similar feelings, this time about a suit:

The confidence you feel in a perfect suit, when you don't have to worry about it, when you get exactly what you want, and you're not thinking about it. You are just proud in it and convey that to other people. . . . I thought I would spend $200 to $300 on a suit, and I ended up paying $900. My wife was showing me how to shop, and it was a great experience. And it is true that when I wear that suit, I feel like a million dollars. It is perfect. It is flawless. Perfect. There is *nothing* wrong with that suit. . . . But it is not about showing off to them. It is about showing off to yourself. You want to feel confident in yourself, and that projects onto other people, and they believe you. They trust you. Because you believe it, they believe it.[13]

Thorstein Veblen famously described conspicuous consumption as one way in which "the leisure class" would use status markers to distinguish themselves from those below them in the social hierarchy.[14] But in the sales profession, with identity and self-esteem on the line, salespeople cope by buying things that help them feel confident and self-assured in the face of potential assaults on the ego. For salespeople, they have to get up the courage, self-confidence, and enthusiasm to try to sell a product. But in selling the product, salespeople know they are also selling themselves, helping others feel confident and happy buying from them. Thus, you have to radiate confidence. If you fail to make a sale, you cannot help but wonder if something is wrong with *you*. I think the reason that the salesperson just quoted talks so much about his suit is because that suit gives him the confidence to keep trying to sell himself and his product. His statement, said with an almost palpable sense of relief, "When you don't have to worry about it" implies that his perfect suit gives him one less thing to worry over, one less chink in the armor surrounding the ego;

and if he feels good in a perfect suit, he will sell product. And if he doesn't sell product, it won't be because of a bad suit.

This same desire to secure the ego may be why there are so many popular business books about selling. They often help salespeople feel better, feel more in control and most importantly help them get up the next morning to jump back into the fray of selling. For salespeople, success is measured by making sales, and the fluctuation in income can easily be felt as a failure of the self. A realtor and a food salesperson described the emotional strain in these ways,

> Yeah, in a lean year, I would be frustrated, I would be disappointed that my earnings were off. And then you can come to a point in the road where we call it "I'm listless." You have no listings! And when you are new in the business and insecure, you never know if you will ever get another listing. And you can have two months go by, with no deals, and in that period of time, you do start to think, "Maybe I have just burned out in this business. What is wrong with *me*?"

> It's not perfect. If it was perfect, I would whistle coming into work every day. There are some days you absolutely love it, and then there are some days that you just can't stand it. Because you really put a lot of time in and a lot of effort in, and when things don't go well, you question yourself, which sometimes isn't really fair to yourself. There are some times that I just literally can't stand it. And then there are some days that I can't be happier.

The Making of a Consumer

Spending one's life in commission sales also seems to affect the way a salesperson thinks about spending his or her own money. Similar to the bartender or waitress who tips very well when off from work, many salespeople told me that they like to buy and try new products and they believe that being an active consumer and buying other salespeople's products is important to keeping the national economy going. Similar to the poker players who don't feel particularly troubled by giving someone a $100 tip, salespeople seem to have the constant selling rub off on them in their personal lives, making them active and engaged consumers in their off-hours. Salespeople also know from their own business practice that price is a bit malleable, but to my surprise several told me that they don't dicker much over price (as I would have expected) because they sympathize with the salesperson and know "they need to make a living too."

Every morning I have my routine. I get into the office, plug in, and start updating my computer, buy coffee, go to the vending machine, get a breakfast thing. Got a car wash today. That was $9. My car gets extremely filthy. It's green. A half hour afterwards, it's dirty again. You gotta tip the car-wash guys. Ten guys wash your car; you gotta give them a couple of bucks. $15 at the dry cleaner. You go through it quickly. If I want to go play golf somewhere expensive and it costs $110 to play one round of golf in four hours, I can justify that to myself and say, "I do this once every couple of weeks, and I usually play at cheap places. I'm worth it." Like, we are going to Arizona [on vacation], and I'm gonna play wherever I want to play. If it's $200, $300, I'm never gonna be able to play these courses again anytime soon. . . . So it's an experience to me.

When I went out [last week], I spent $140. . . . I wasn't expecting to spend that much, but the chef comes out, and he says, "I'm gonna do this, and I'm gonna do that." And we have a few expensive glasses of wine, and suddenly the bill is a little more than I expected.

I like to try new things, like if there is a new flavored beverage. I figure it keeps the economy going, right?

On the whole, I found that most salespeople seemed more free-wheeling about spending their own money than were people in most of the other occupations I studied. Many of them held the view that "consumption makes the world go round." I think that is because so much of their day is spent right in the heart of capitalism: selling. So they have a keen interest in "products," and they have great sympathy with people selling products. While they want a good price on an item, they also seemed cognizant that the salesperson is probably making his or her living based on the profit margins and resultant commissions. Salespeople were similar in this regard to poker players, in that they were very comfortable dealing with money, and in some ways money comes to lose some of its meaning or mystique precisely because they are dealing with it constantly. In the same way that poker players come to say, "Money is just our way of keeping score," salespeople can come to value "making the sale" and the afterglow that comes from successfully selling oneself, more than valuing the actual money involved. For salespeople, money becomes recognition of how hard they have worked, an endorsement of how much they are trusted, and a measure of gratitude for going that extra mile for their customer. Time is money; the problem is in figuring out how the equation works.

4

Other People's Money

Fund Raisers and Grant Givers

He need not come from the provinces in literal fact, his social class may constitute his province. . . . The story of the Young Man from the Provinces is thus a strange one. . . . From it we have learned most of what we know about modern society, about class and its strange rituals, about power and influence, and about money, the hard fluent fact in which modern society has its being.

—Lionel Trilling, "The Princess Casamassima"

Lionel Trilling in the opening epigraph to this chapter described Henry James's *The Princess Casamassima* as a classic example of a literary trope he called "the tale of the young man from the provinces." These sorts of stories describe a person from the countryside traveling into the big city, delighting in what he discovers there. Perhaps more profoundly, they also reveal what the young man from the provinces *learns about himself* from crossing boundaries.[1] However, as Trilling points out, the frontier that is crossed in these types of stories is just as often the boundary of *social class* as it is the rural/urban divide. From both a literary and a sociological standpoint, the idea of transgressing social class boundaries has long fascinated us because it puts to the test some of the loftier ideas behind the great American experiment—the idea that we can be a society in which social class boundaries are not as strong as they might have once been in the European context. The crossing of social class boundaries taps into promises of meritocracy, fairness, and equality that have characterized much of the writing about modernity.[2] However, a wealth of sociological research has shown that many Americans live, go to school, marry, socialize, and worship in economically segregated settings and that sustained and intimate crossing of social class boundaries may not be quite as commonplace as people think.

What happens, then, when a young man or young woman "from the provinces" begins to rub elbows with the very rich as an essential part of his or her job? Conversely, what happens when upper-middle-class, well-educated professionals spend much of their work time with people in dire financial straits? When crossing social class boundary lines is a quotidian part of someone's work life, does it affect the way he or she thinks about money? Does it lead to sympathy, empathy, and intimate connection with others from a different social class, or does it lead to stereotype, judgment, and condemnation? In other words, if someone's job entails regularly working with others who have either "so very much" or "simply not enough," does it shape the way that person thinks about money and its role in the world? What types of cognitive and emotional work must people do in these types of positions to make sense of money and to understand inequality in financial circumstances? How do the differing structural arrangements of these jobs shape the particular money cultures that are formed at work such as this?

More generally, how do you become comfortable talking about *other people's money*—particularly when the "other people" may be in a very different financial circumstance from your own? Over the course of the next two chapters, I examine money cultures that develop in jobs in which people work with other people's money. In this chapter, I describe the money cultures created around fund raising and grant giving to illustrate dilemmas that are created when your job is to ask for money or to dole it out. In the following chapter, I describe the money cultures that surround two other occupations in which people work with other people's money by giving advice about how to use money: investment advisors and debt counselors. In all four of these occupations, people not only learn to feel comfortable talking about other people's money, they also routinely cross social class boundaries as part of their jobs, working with people who may have much more or much less than they have.

Here again, much like poker players and hedge fund traders, the occupations of fund raising and grant giving share some crucial structural features with one another in that the incumbents are called on to frequently move across financial boundaries and to deal, more or less comfortably, with other people's money. Thus, these occupations demonstrate how a shared structural location in the economy creates similarities in the cognitive and emotional work necessary to stay on an even keel while doing these jobs. Yet these jobs also have key structural differences that produce observable and patterned distinctions in the money cultures produced in the two lines of work. These jobs, like all those in this book, underscore the connections between structure and culture as well as the complex intertwining of the realms of the economic and the social.

Fund-Raising Boot Camp

While it may take some time in one's career to rise to the level of principal gift officer (the person who is allowed to solicit from the wealthiest clients), even novice fund raisers can find themselves at events with the very rich, while they themselves have modest incomes and little experience in such settings. But before fund raisers (or development professionals, as they are sometimes called) can become principal gift officers, they experience a socialization process in which they learn a particular money culture, complete with its own specialized vocabulary and very particular way of thinking about money.

I was curious as to how a person gains the comfort level required to talk to people with significant wealth and eventually to ask them for money, so I sought out an opportunity to gain some quick lessons by attending a "fund-raising boot camp."[3] This boot camp was a weekend retreat and conference for those who were new to the fund-raising game. It is generally regarded by the profession as one of the very best training grounds for new fund raisers.[4] During the boot camp, I joined about a hundred other novices as we learned a new lingo, ways to measure someone's "giving capacity," how to "make the ask," and how to properly "steward a gift" once it is secured. But along with all this, I found that we were most importantly learning a new way to think about money. Perhaps the phrase "boot camp" accurately conveyed the event, since a boot camp can involve the stripping down of one identity and replacing it with a new one.

The fund-raising boot camp set the stage for learning a new money culture by quickly reorienting our thinking about money. This process began by handing each of us a fake one-million-dollar bill at the opening event. Our teachers and mentors asked each of us to write on the back of the bill what we would do with this money if we suddenly were given a million dollars. Most of us wrote about the good and beneficial things we would do with the money, ranging from helping out immediate loved ones (e.g., "pay my child's college tuition" or "buy my mother a house") to larger philanthropic causes (e.g., "donate half to the American Cancer Society"). This exercise put us in a generous mood and allowed us to see what good can come of money if used properly. It also was an exercise in thinking about "other people's money," since this really was not our own money but money that had been given to us. The exercise also served to divorce people from thinking only in terms of immediate needs (because it was so much money) and led us to inventory in our minds all the possible uses for the one million dollars we had unexpectedly been given. I think it is fair to say that it would have seemed crass in such a setting to write on the back of the bill, "Buy myself a Lamborghini" or "Head to the nearest casino!" Needless to say, no one in attendance wrote anything like that on their money.

One of the first important lessons you learn as a novice fund raiser is that you don't ask someone for money right away. In fact, you may not even mention money for several meetings with a prospect. Rather, you must first "build a relationship" with a potential donor and try to discern his or her interests so that you can then try to connect the prospect's own passions to some activity or goal that exists, or could be reasonably created, within your own organization and its mission. This process happens well before talking about dollars. So, for example, if you are trying to raise money for a college or university, it helps first to know whether the person is passionate about writing, the field hockey team, helping students who come from limited financial means, or funding new research on Alzheimer's disease.

Talking to potential donors can be a very pleasant experience, particularly if their connection to your institution is a strong and positive one. However, one of the crucial cognitive challenges that fund raisers confront (consciously or unconsciously) is understanding and interpreting the scope, authenticity, and boundaries of their relationships with donors as they get to know them. Is this an economic relationship or a social relationship? Is this a mutually beneficial relationship, an instrumental relationship, or a manipulative relationship? Are we friends?

Fund raisers learn how to navigate these dilemmas in different ways. A few (and my sense is this is a minority of fund raisers) do come to see the relationships with donors as friendships—friendships that may center on the shared mission of the organization (e.g., the alma mater, the cancer treatment center) but then move out to other shared interests (e.g., family, golf, attending weddings and funerals). Fund raisers can on occasion become sounding boards for donors who are thinking about changing jobs, going through a divorce, or seeking advice about getting their children through a bumpy point in their lives.

More frequently, fund raisers recognize that there are—and probably should be—boundaries or limits drawn around these relationships that make them distinct from friendships. These fund raisers prefer to see the relationship as a somewhat more formal and more professional one and therefore say that the word *friendship* is inappropriate to describe the connection. These fund raisers liken it more to a long-term salesperson-customer relationship, in which over time you come to know each other fairly well and the relationship can be tinged with a very close personal connection but remains centered on the instrumental connection. As one fund raiser put it to me, while pondering his career at his current university,

In ten years, I have developed some pretty strong relationships with alumni and donors. Are they my friends? That is a really interesting question. Because if I leave [my university] tomorrow, do I expect to keep up the relationships with those people? Probably not. So I tend not to think of them as friends. But I do have colleagues who go to bar mitzvahs and to christenings and to weddings. And that is trouble: crossing that friendship line. Your judgment is changed and how you approach the individual. It is now different—and some good, but I could argue, not as good.

As this fund raiser indicates, drawing linguistic and cognitive distinctions between "donors" and "friends" can be easier said than done. One reason for this is that fund raisers sometimes conduct their business in social or family settings—meeting in restaurants, visiting a potential donor's primary home or vacation home, going out for a ride on a boat, or playing golf. Once you are in a person's home, you have transgressed the work/home boundary, and it is not uncommon for a fund raiser to look at and talk about family photos in the home, to attend the wedding of a donor's son or daughter, to tour the cancer center where the donor's spouse was treated, or to tour the college campus where the donor went to school as a young person. These activities and the settings in which they take place all blur the line between "business" and "social." Add to this the fact that donors often make gifts that express or reflect their own personal lives, for example, honoring a loved one who has died by funding research on a particular disease. Often the conversations that lead to gifts involve topics that are not typical in professional relationships: college days, fraternity or sorority activities, current hobbies and interests, the health of loved ones, addiction, family loss, or heartache.

One of the things that fund raisers quickly learn is to ask questions about a potential donor's life and then to "sit back and listen," as fund raisers often put it to me in my interviews with them. Fund raisers try to learn as much as they can about a person's life, and a good fund raiser learns to always be listening for ways to connect the donor's interests with activities occurring at the fund raiser's institution. Given all this, it is no wonder, then, that the relationship between a fund raiser and a donor can have elements that are quite similar to a friendship.

This blurred boundary may be more common in relationships than we think.[5] We often cannot neatly separate the economic world from the social world or the work world from the private world, as these are inextricably linked. My point here is that in the case of fund raisers we see a more extreme or pointed version of the blurred boundary between an instrumental relationship and a friendship, rather than a completely different class or category of relationship altogether. What is somewhat unique about a fund raiser's job, though, is that he or she might go to a meeting at someone's home already armed with information that the prospect has a net worth estimated at six million dollars, has earned his or her fortune by manufacturing doors for industrial use in a family business, owns a pleasure boat, is enthusiastic about deep-sea fishing and race walking, has three grown children (one of whom also attended the alma mater and majored in anthropology), and believes passionately that liberal arts education is the best preparation for the business world. When the fund raiser enters the home, sees photographs of the children, and asks, "Is this Michelle, who also went to your alma mater?" it isn't necessarily clear whether this question is of social interest and personal concern or simply a piece of the economic relationship moving toward asking for a financial gift.

For the good fund raiser, it is indeed both. They learn (though a few told me that this just "came naturally")[6] to be genuinely interested in the donor (and his or her family) while simultaneously being able to think about connecting with the person in order to solicit a "gift" (the preferred term for a donation to the institution). This simultaneity—of holding both personal interest and instrumental economic interest together within the same interaction—is a key attribute of a successful fund raiser and contributes to the blurriness of the relationship between fund raiser and potential donor. To push the argument a bit further: if the answer to the question "Is this Michelle, who also went to your alma mater?" happens to be "Yes, that is Michele, but she really hated it there," most fund raisers would probably not initially think (as would a friend, absent the economic relationship), "What a shame for Michelle. Did she find happiness elsewhere?" Rather, the fund raiser learns to immediately think, "Hmmm, that's bad for my goal of soliciting a gift," to pause for a brief recovery from being thrown for a loop, and then to say, "I wonder how we might work to make your alma mater a better place for students like Michelle? What is it that she did not like about it?" It is in these crucial and pivotal moments that a friendship circumscribed within a larger economic relationship shifts ever so subtly (if done well) toward a more clearly instrumental goal, and the friendship portion suddenly appears much more limited and (if not done well) wholly inauthentic.[7] Note that an element of concern—however small or however instrumental—still remains, in the sense that the successful fund raiser genuinely wishes to know what went wrong for Michelle and how the situation could be improved for other students.

Having said this, it is interesting to look at the issue of blurred boundaries from another angle. In what we consider our more "genuine" friendships, are there not also elements of instrumental calculation? This question is clearly beyond the scope of this book, but I pose it to signal that because the fund-raiser/donor relationship can reveal a sometimes crass instrumentality nestled within a relationship tinged with elements of empathy and concern does not mean that ordinary friendships are not themselves tinged with elements of instrumental calculation (how often are we told to use our friends to network to find a new job?). Thus, the role of the fund raiser may evidence a difference in degree and balance (between instrumental and altruistic/empathetic concerns), rather than a difference in kind, between the relationships that I am describing and what we usually refer to as more "authentic" friendships.[8]

Blurred Boundaries in a Money Culture

All of this difficult cognitive and emotional work surrounding blurred boundaries happens within the context of a structured money culture. One of the ways that fund raisers deal with the tensions created by forming relationships around the desire to solicit money is to create elaborate organizational systems that help to structure that relationship and to keep it on track toward the goals of the larger fund-raising operation of the organization. These systems might be considered methods of trying to shape and tame unwieldy and messy personal relationships within organizational routines. So, for example, many fund-raising operations have complex tracking mechanisms that keep abreast of the number of contacts between a fund raiser and a potential donor. Each time a fund raiser has contact with a donor, this is recorded in a database, and notes are written about the meeting, often including the topics that were discussed and potential follow-up actions to be taken. Sharing some similarities to early forms of "scientific management" in industrial work, the various tasks involved in fund raising are broken down into their constituent parts so that they can be measured and monitored.[9] Compensation systems and bonuses can even be tied into this measuring system. It is typically considered unethical to tie bonuses directly to the amount of money a fund raiser brings into the organization. This in and of itself is an interesting contrast to the commission salesperson, who also can be friends with a client yet is paid according to how much business is brought in from that client. It says something important about the money culture of fund raising that the profession itself sees tying an individual's pay directly to the amount of money solicited as detrimental to the over-arching goals and image of fund raising. Here again, we see an intertwining of the social and the economic and the tie between work structure and money culture. The fund-raising profession relies on the generally agreed-on notion that the relationship between a donor and an institution is not a crass economic relationship and that what is being solicited is a gift or a donation for the common good (with the implied tax implications that are, of course, also crucial here) and not a purchase or sale with something being provided in return or a donation given in order to increase the salary of a commissioned fund raiser. If a fund raiser's pay is tied too closely to the amount of money brought in, this could threaten the tax status of a donation, but equally important, it could threaten the heart and soul of the relationship as well as the shared understanding of what is going on here: the solicitation of a gift.

It is common, however, to design performance goals that include things such as "scheduling x number of donor contacts" as a performance goal and then tying such measures to performance reviews, bonus schemes, and the like. Notice that compensation is more often tied to the effort of solicitation and the process of fund raising rather than to the dollar amount brought in. This serves to make compensation at least one step removed in a cognitive sense as well as a literal sense from the relationship of dollars brought in to salary paid. Additionally, the culture of fund raising stresses that fund raising is a team effort that can unfold over several years or even decades on the road to a major gift, and giving one individual credit and direct compensation for the gift undermines that concept. Note, though, that the same probably could be said of a salesperson, yet the culture of sales insists on the more direct incentive of sales leading to commission. This suggests that the money culture around product sales is less concerned with creating a separation between selling and commission and indeed wishes to keep the nexus as tightly linked as possible.

Through the complex organizational tracking systems commonly used in fund raising, donors are envisioned as being "brought through" the steps in a well-thought-out process geared toward eventually "making the ask" for a gift. The process begins with the research necessary to uncover the donor in the first place; then a donor's "giving capacity" is estimated; then there are various contacts and meetings to gauge and engage the individual's interests and "giving inclination"; and then finally an "ask" is made. If the ask is successful and a donation is made, then the stewardship process ensures that the gift is properly acknowledged and that follow-ups are made (e.g., having a scholarship recipient write a letter of thanks to the donor) to inform the donor of the impact of his or her gift. This system keeps the process on track and attempts to rationalize and measure the process to allow for measures of achievement of various sorts for the larger organization in which fund raising is embedded. It also helps to systematize what could be a somewhat unwieldy and blurry relationship, and it helps the larger operation coordinate its overall fundraising work, making sure multiple fund raisers are not working at cross-purposes, with each trying to gain face time with an important donor.

For an outsider, these systems seem interesting or even somewhat odd, as they are applied not to an industrial manufacturing process but to what is essentially human-to-human contact that can sometimes look a bit like a friendship. But what the tracking systems allow is a way to monitor the development of contacts leading to the solicitation of a gift. It makes sure that continual steps are followed in the building of that relationship. It also helps—or at least tries to help—maintain a clear boundary between friendship and the professional relationship formed for the purposes of fund raising. It is the rare individual who would chart all their meetings with a friend or a romantic interest in such a systematized way. By entering notes about meetings into the tracking system, the fund raiser is continually reminded (by the actual cognitive process of entering information that others will see) of the ultimate purpose of the social interactions he or she has with a donor, interactions that might otherwise appear to be mere socializing. Going to a college basketball or football game with a donor can feel like just a fun night out until the next morning when you are typing your notes into a computer tracking system for your supervisors to review at the next staff meeting. Several fund raisers told me that there are even ways to embed cautionary warning flags to other fund raisers about potential donors who, for example, might drink too much: "Best to meet with this donor at the workplace."

Many fund raisers have a name for this overall process: "moves management," which reflects the idea that each "move" in the donor-cultivation process is managed and charted. A "move" can take many different forms, including sending the potential donor a birthday card or a note following up on a meeting, which serves to summarize the discussion of a donor's interest.[10] In this way, donors are viewed as "moving along" a process toward giving a gift. Some fund raisers define "moves management" as a system of managing relationships—an interesting turn of phrase that indicates that this relationship is one that is managed, systematized, and rationalized toward a particular goal.

I also think, however, that these systems not only chart and rationalize the process but also help to focus fund raisers on pressing the process forward by giving them the cognitive tools to assist them in conceiving of their job and the role of money in their job in a particular way. In other words, this helps to shape the money culture of fund raising. By presenting what fund raisers are doing in their work as a method of undertaking each step in a systematic donor process, it helps fund raisers feel more comfortable with getting from someone information that may be of a deeply personal nature when the goal is the instrumental one of soliciting a gift. With fund raisers breaking the steps down and entering information in tracking programs, each step along the way feels important, concrete, rationalized, essential, and fitting a larger organizational framework. Even if a fund raiser does not get a gift, he or she has contributed to the store of information in the database that will help a future fund raiser gain a gift. Viewed in this way, these systems send cognitive signals that help to rationalize an emotionally laden human process of interaction. This rationalization of the process not only helps to make the process of gaining gifts more successful (even if only in the sense that it prevents donors from falling through the cracks and provides centralized and shared information), but it also helps the fund raiser stay engaged and positive about a process that could otherwise feel amorphous, confusing, frustrating, or distasteful. The rules and systems, in other words, help to do the cognitive work of framing money and human interactions in a positive and instrumental way rather than in a complex, contradictory, and messy way. This helps to create a money culture in fund raising that transforms the fuzzy human interactions the fund raiser has in a very particular and stylized way—as part of a larger rationalized, logical, and acceptable process—and, like all cultural systems, gives fund raisers the cognitive tools to conceive of the process in a certain way. The culture, complete with its systems, rules, procedures, specialized vocabularies, and socially shaped cognitions about money and donors, provides a solid and ongoing socialization for newcomers. This is how a fund-raising professional with vast experience put it to me:

> I think there are some people who are clearly with the process, but I've worked with volunteers who have been very uncomfortable with the process initially and who have become very good fund raisers ultimately. You know, people say, "I just don't like to ask people for money." . . . But if I've had an opportunity to get him in front of a prospect and work through the process, over time, I have, you know, been able to sort of change that, and the person has felt, you know, much more comfortable with being able to ask. I break it down very simply. . . . "What's the worst, the worst thing that could happen to you?" You know, this is what I tell my staff or if I'm dealing with training: "What's the worst?" I mean, the worst thing [someone] could say to you: "No, I'm sorry, not a priority for me." "Not the right timing for me." "I'm sorry it's too much money." So what do you come away with? You come away with more information with that donor. Maybe it's timing, which would be, "Okay, today's not good, but two years from now, would that be better?" Maybe, maybe not. But you generally can walk away with more information. And the worst case would be, "No, absolutely not." "I hate you." "I will never give you money." "Don't ever come to me again." So what have you done for yourself? You've just relieved some time off your plate, because we can close the door on that prospect, could put him or her to sleep and then move on to someone else and stop wasting time

with that person. So when you go about it that way, then it becomes [less frightening].

When I asked fund-raising professionals what characteristics they most looked for in employees, this was typical of the many responses I heard:

> When we look at major gift fund raisers, we think first and foremost we need people who are skilled at relationship building. We look for those who are good listeners, who display empathy and understanding and then have strong communications skills. Always at the top of my list—and you can't teach this—is impeccable integrity that always comes off. And number two, I started on the listening skills, relationship-building skills, empathy, and communication skills.

Gaining Comfort around Other People's Money

The dilemma for veteran fund raisers is how to help new fund raisers become comfortable around other people's money. How do you make sure that novices get the message that although these relationships have strong elements of friendships, they are clearly not friendships? The systems I have described help to do this through organizational framing and routines. But, as in other professions, storytelling is another important addition to formal training and organizational systems. I found that cautionary tales are often told by higher-level fund raisers to new entrants to pass on the subtleties of working with other people's money. One apocryphal story commonly told to new fund raisers is the story of the novice who kept taking friends out to eat and recording those as prospect lunches and subsequently got in trouble for doing so. In this story, a distinction is underscored that even though going out to lunch with someone can feel like lunch with a friend, business must be the main feature of the meeting. I would argue, though, that another point driven home by this cautionary tale is an early signaling of the difficulties of the cognitive dilemma of the blurred distinction between friendship and fund-raising relationships. At some fund-raising lunch meetings, business is intentionally disguised, or very much under the radar, as you discuss family, friends, interests, and old times at the alma mater. Often, a sea-soned fund raiser deliberately chooses to avoid discussion of donations or money in early meetings because the initial goal may be simply to find out areas of interest for the potential donor. It should not be surprising, then, that some novice fund raisers who are being mentored by a veteran become a bit confused about what is going on. Cautionary tales shared after lunch are intended to insist that even though this lunch looked just like a friendly lunch you might have with a friend, it is not that.

An additional cognitive and emotional dilemma that is faced by fund raisers (and probably by any boundary crosser who spends time with people who have much more money than they do) is the trappings of seduction. Spending time with the rich or famous can be a difficult emo-tional task for some individuals, particularly because of the way this time is spent. For example, a young fund raiser may end up in a social setting with someone vastly wealthier than they are. The meeting could even happen in the wealthy person's home. The conversation can create an almost artificial sense of friendship and equality. The conversation, by its very nature, tends to be somewhat simplistic (as in, "What was the key to your success?" "Well, hard work and a bit of luck."). It can become very easy for the young fund raiser to think, "That could be me." This is how one fund raiser described the problem that many novices encounter:

> A lot of these people are in their twenties, just coming into the field, and pretty early on have to come to terms with the fact that you are going to spend a lot of time in other people's worlds. And other people's worlds tend to have nicer houses, bigger cars, and bigger boats. And then you get back off the plane, into your smaller car and into your house. And you have to come to terms with that. If you are an envious kind of person, that can be hard.

This boundary-crossing problem occasionally causes significant trou-ble for a fund raiser who may fail to see the social class boundary and trip over it. As one senior fund raiser put it to me,

> I think it is hard for young people in this business. You are exposed to it [wealth] in such a big way. The people we work with tend to take us in, treat us as friends. Do I dress nicer than most of my friends? Do I try to be mindful

of conversation topics that will be interesting to someone at that level? Yeah, absolutely. But I think you are exposed to it in such a big way when you are in your early twenties or midtwenties, and you are starting to see people branch off into various paths—some on the more money-oriented path—and you are in higher ed, working for a nonprofit; you are on the other path. . . . So [you are dealing with this] just when you are trying to figure all that out. . . . I have about four or five friends at other institutions, and we talk a lot about this.

One early-career fund raiser, who subsequent to my interview left the fund-raising profession, put it this way,

The problem with development is you dress really nicely; you have to look good and present yourself well. You have to be an impressive and charismatic person to a certain extent. And you have to hobnob with the high and the mighty and the wealthy. You yourself are not high and mighty *nor* wealthy. But you might start thinking that you are. And here you have this job, which is basically moneygrubbing, but you would like to think of it as something that is really, really glamorous. So you want to think, "Look at me. I am this glamorous mover and shaker." And you are not.

Another fund raiser commented on the same issue, outlining some of the ways to manage the cognitive challenge of rubbing elbows across significant social class boundaries: "Yeah, we have a comfortable life, but we are talking with people that have like four houses, a boat, and all the pieces. . . . You have to be okay with it, or you have to know how to manage it and compartmentalize it. . . . Otherwise it does get frustrating." In a different context, R. Foster Winans described the same danger of seduction in his book *Trading Secrets: Seduction and Scandal at the Wall Street Journal*. Winans was a coauthor of the *Journal*'s "Heard on the Street" column and came to know several young and wealthy Wall Street traders. Crossing social class boundaries and traveling in the world of the "other" played a part in activating his own desires for a better financial life than was possible on the salary of a newspaper reporter. He ended up involved in a scheme to leak his stories in advance of publication to allow stock trading on news that could move the market the next day.[11] Because there wasn't a money culture at the newspaper that provided support and lessons in managing the cognitive dilemmas created by the kind of boundary crossing he was doing, he tried to deal with it on his own and ended up making some serious mistakes as a young man.

Cultivating Prospects

What about the person on the other side of the giving relationship? Potential donors, of course, vary in their own level of sophistication and knowledge of the "cultivation process." Most high-wealth individuals are approached so often for major gifts that they are quite familiar with it, even if they don't use the same terminology as the fund-raising professionals do. As one high-level professional put it to me,

> When people first become acquainted with major gift efforts and what we're trying to do, the initial reaction is, "Oh, my stars! Aren't donors aware of the fact that you're cultivating them in hopes of, . . . in anticipation of consideration of the major gifts?" And the answer is, "Of course." But what you find out after a while is that implementation is everything, and it needs to be done well and in a sophisticated way. And when it is, it's . . . it's not a surprise to donors that you're building a relationship in the hopes that it leads to something further. In fact, after a while, donors begin to trust the process and feel comfortable about you and how you're doing it. So implementation does become everything. We were at a seminar, and we were interviewing a philanthropist, a Q and A—a lot of fund raisers in the room. And one of the fund raisers asked, "Are you aware of the fact that you're being cultivated?" His response, "Well, that's a term I think you use in fund raising; it's not a term I use, but of course." He said, "I run a business and try to involve customers and potential customers, and I think that's the same thing." And he said, "Now let me make something clear: I accept an invitation because I like the organization or the people inviting me, but that doesn't mean I'm going to make a major gift. I'll make that decision when I get there. Of course, I'm aware of the fact that you're trying to cultivate those relationships in the hopes of support follow-ups."

This suggests to me that a socialization process of sorts is also occurring for the potential donor, who also learns the process of solicitation by going through it with a gift officer. Both the gift officer and the potential donor are taking part in an elaborate dance, and like most dances, it is at its best when the partners do not appear to be paying too much attention to how they are moving their feet.

A Culture of Philanthropy

Spending your career as a fund raiser transmits lessons that get carried over into home or private life. Almost every fund raiser I talked with had learned and absorbed a particular money culture from their work, sometimes referring to it as a "culture of philanthropy" that made them very conscious about their own philanthropic giving. Several used the phrase "having a giving plan" to describe their attempt to plan thoughtfully about their own generosity. Through their work, fund raisers gain an intense consciousness about philanthropy and giving that in turn structures the way they see the world. I have no way to measure whether fund raisers give a greater percentage of their income to charitable causes, but I would be surprised if this was not the case.

Interestingly, several fund raisers joked to me about being themselves the "object" or "target" of others' fund raising. For example, one senior fund raiser described being solicited by his alma mater in this way:

> We give to [an environmental foundation]. My wife has [a chronic disease], and so we give for that, and we give at church and the junior league. It is kind of fun being on the other side [getting solicited] and seeing how the person approaches it. . . . [When I get solicited from my alma mater], we tease each other. You know, she will make an ask, and I will say, "That's your best?! I'm insulted!"

Another fund raiser commented that because of the work she does, she pays particular attention to the quality of interactions with the charities that she actively supports. Like the sales professionals who are fascinated by how other products are marketed, the fund raisers like to see how others do it:

> I also have really been paying attention—because I am here—to how organizations treat me and how organizations might treat me differently from

[my organization], how the university treats me versus my favorite [char-
ity] and how they steward me. [With my favorite charity], their stewardship is just so good. I mean, I don't give that much money to them, but you
get an immediate email back. Then a few days later, you get an email from
the teacher. Then about three months later, you get thank-you notes from
the kids and pictures of them using whatever it is that you bought for them.
I am going to give to them for the rest of my life!

Moreover, several of the fund raisers (like the grant givers to be discussed next) mentioned talking with their own children about the importance of giving to others, and one mentioned using a "piggy-bank system"
with her children, in which one coin from allowance goes to a bank for
long-term saving, one coin goes in a bank for charitable giving, and one
coin can be spent on something the child wishes to buy immediately.
Here we see again how lessons learned from a particular money culture in
the workplace extend into home life.

Grant Givers

People who evaluate and award grants cross into two worlds that might
be very different from their own. On the one hand, they cross social class
boundaries as they meet and come to know very wealthy donors and
board members. On the other hand, some also spend time with recipients
of grants, who can sometimes be very poor. Although not quite Robin
Hoods, they do ask from the rich and give to the poor. The job can cause
a kind of social class whiplash, as grant givers move from a meeting with
the very wealthy to a meeting with the very poor in the course of a single
day. As a result, grant officers sometimes feel like they have one foot on
a firm dock and the other on a boat that is beginning to float away. But
the work can also be invigorating, as it offers that elusive opportunity to
make a difference, which many grant givers cite as the main reason they
entered their occupation. A major cognitive and emotional challenge for
grant givers, then, is to learn to straddle the worlds of the wealthy and the
poor: "I think about a typical day, [like] today, when you start out with a
meeting in Chestnut Hill or Bryn Mawr [two relatively wealthy commu-
nities] and end with a meeting in Kensington [a poorer neighborhood].

And I will be in Kensington later today. I feel like I am very sensitive to class issues because they are in my face all the time."

Interestingly, two grant givers made the point that straddling these two worlds led them to see that there are stereotypical views of both the poor and the rich that are not quite fair. One put it this way:

> This might sound really funny or really bizarre, but I have actually seen the way wealthy people suffer from having a lot of money. . . . You know, I have seen a lot of screwed-up lives: people who have never been able to focus on a career or [have] a direction because they have so many options and no need to do that. And it takes a toll, a psychological toll. I have also seen people, especially on the left, suffer from a kind of—there is this slogan: "Eat the Rich"—we try to bring one or two people onto the funding board who are wealthy, and we do that for institutional reasons, because we know that their contribution will usually increase, but they have to listen to a fair amount of "hate the rich."

The opportunity to see the process of stereotyping working in both directions is one that is fairly unique and structured into the job of grant givers—at least the ones who work on both sides of the class divide. One of these grant givers talked of how this shaped her identity:

> How have I personally navigated this? I like to think that I speak up about it when it is called for. I have not always spoken up for it. I like to think in every single instance I—whether I am encountering people who have stereotypical views of wealthy people or stereotypical views of working-class or poor people—that I challenge that. I know I haven't challenged it in every case, but I do feel like I am in a good position to do that because people trust me.

Worthy Causes

A second challenge for grant givers is trying to make decisions among a variety of very worthy causes. How does one decide if an AIDS education program is more deserving of money than the city's mural arts program? How do you choose between funding breast cancer research and an excellent after-school mentoring program for teens living in poverty? All of these are worthy causes, yet decisions need to be made. As one foundation director who had come from the for-profit world told me in describing the difference in the cultures he encountered,

> In the for-profit world, you worry about revenues, expenses, bottom line. In the grant-making world, in the philanthropic world, there is an expense: it's a grant. The return on that investment is not in dollars and cents; it is in outcomes. It's measured in the results of the investments. So the differential as opposed to worrying about the bottom line is, "Am I going to make an impact, and am I going to change some set of circumstances for the better?" That's a very different reality.

One way to handle the difficulties of comparing one worthy cause against another is to build a good portion of the decision into the institutionalized screening practices of the organization. This serves to routinize decision-making by building it into standardized operating procedures. One way that many philanthropic organizations do this is by selecting a small number of areas in which to specialize. One foundation might choose to focus, for example, on community development and maternal health, while another might choose basic literacy programs and cancer research. The decision to specialize in particular areas shuts off the need to make individual judgments across so many differing causes, as they are simply ruled out by the decision to specialize. This also serves all the agencies and foundations collectively because they can then parcel out the world of needs, divvying up responsibility, so to speak, among granting agencies and foundations. One foundation professional put it this way: "Say a nursing home wants us to give them money, but it is not a great fit [for our mission and goals]. Sometimes they understand that, and sometimes they don't. We might try to support them in other ways: say they have a fund-raiser gala, we would buy tickets to that. . . . My job, which is challenging, is to try to stay as focused and on target as I can."

This does not always work so neatly, of course. As some philanthropic areas become "hot," large foundations may change direction and move in to that area. Another problem with decision by specialization is that for some of the for-profit companies that have their own foundations, a decision by specialization can be overruled for important customers or clients of the for-profit company. So, for example, if a large bank has a foundation that specializes in after-school and literacy programs yet has a very important client who has a pet charity involving the detection and treatment of colon cancer, the foundation may come under some pressure to make a contribution in that area to preserve its business relationship with the key client. Once this happens, of course, it can cause problems for the grant officers who have turned down other health-related requests using decision by specialization as the reason for deflecting the request, only to be found later breaking this rule in the case of the important client.

Once areas of specialization have been carved out, grant givers can then make advance decisions about what percentage of their overall granting budget will be channeled into each area. Here, then, comes a second way to routinize decision-making, or what might be called decision by budget allotment. This acts as another aid to grants giver in making heart-wrenching decisions between particular grants (e.g., they can say they cannot fund a particular request because they have allotted 20 percent of the total budget to this area, and this grant would eat up the entire amount).

Finally, for the grant proposals that make it past both the decision by specialization and the decision by budget allotment, most agencies and foundations employ scoring rubrics developed to help make more refined choices among proposals.[12] They might rate the requesting organization's capacity to deliver the particular service and its economic stability, as well as judge its performance in prior grants, using various assessment techniques. None of this is neat or straightforward, however, because in the world of nonprofits, worthy requests often come in from organizations that need the very grants to build their basic organizational capacities. They may even need a grant just to develop their own organizational capability to perform an assessment. There aren't always many nonprofits applying for grants that have great stability, solid backroom operations, and long track records. This has become a particularly difficult issue to navigate because philanthropy is changing to require more and more assessments and proof of outcomes that borrow from business models that can be quite antithetical or simply unfamiliar to the agencies and organizations most in need. One grant giver described her efforts to deal with this dilemma:

> We would get things with, like, three different fonts used. When I got there, there was a one-page form [to report on the results of the grant], and it was real bull. But it was reflective of an attitude of thirty years ago that a one-page form that tells us how you spent the money, you know, and give us a paragraph about how you spent the money and give us the budget. We changed that four of five years ago, so there are questions in it like, "Tell us what you have learned about social change as a result of working on this project. Tell us the positive things, the negative things." And in parentheses it says, "Honest answers will be appreciated more than uniformly positive ones." Some groups write two paragraphs, some actually write, like, two single-spaced pages, which on a $5,000 grant is a lot. We say, "When you get this grant, start a file, and throw everything related to this grant into a file and submit it to us at the end—more of a portfolio."

Venture Philanthropy

Other grant givers described a real sea change occurring in their world as younger people bring their business models as well as their wealth into the philanthropic world:

> There are venture capitalists that want to get in and get out in five years. Well, now there is a "venture philanthropy" approach: I want to get in with a grant, put everything into it, treat it like venture capital, and I want to see it happen in five years. So there is this visible presence of folks wanting to see things and not wait around.

> We watched first hospitals adopt business practices and then higher education and now nonprofits and foundations. And you know, you could see it by about 1995 or '96, and I have written about this and spoken about it at foundation meetings, . . . that nonprofits and foundations have ceded their traditional role and their useful role in society by becoming enthralled with business models. What happened during the high-tech bubble of the mid-'90s is that foundations became completely enthralled with the "New Phi-

lanthropists," who were taking business models and applying them. . . . I am aware that my tone of voice is changing, and this really aggravates me. . . . Foundations become enthralled with anyone who was doing philanthropy in the Silicon Valley and Seattle, and they were touting these new models with businesspeople making lots of money and saying, "I am going to run a foundation in a hands-on way, and through this foundation, I am going to become involved in your nonprofit."

Because many needy neighborhood groups and community organizations cannot always live up to the new requirements coming from the venture philanthropists, funding agencies have tried to build relationships over time with their grantees, so that they can help them build their capacity, nurture the organizations along, and see the signs of visible growth and stability. Meeting these requirements and shouldering these responsibilities come with some misgivings: "I think underlying the whole discussion are some very classist assumptions—that you can't trust poor people or working-class people. . . . We are trying to figure out, how do we evaluate ourselves, how do we evaluate our own grant making? And whether we are doing what we say we want to do. And that may result in some changes to our reporting system, I don't know."

Spillovers into Family Life

Several grant givers mentioned to me that they enjoy spending time at events that celebrate the difference a grant has made in poorer communities. What I found most interesting, however, is that grant givers also say that doing so gives them the opportunity for their own children to see and spend time with children of much more limited financial means than their own. Several grant givers also mentioned that they often end up having dinner-table conversations about poverty and inequality that emerge from their day at work. Thus, the job of grant giver, because of the opportunity for boundary crossing, provides for an interesting experience for the entire family related to issues of financial (and other) inequality in the United States. Because of the boundary crossings that occur at work, the routine dinner-table question "How was your day at work?" gives grant givers the opportunity to discuss the issue of inequality in very direct ways with their own families. However, these opportunities come with additional dilemmas. While grant officers overtly (and sometimes didactically) articulate to their own children that all children are the same, they also simultaneously reference poor children to impress on their own children an appreciation for their more fortunate circumstances. This is an unexpected (although perhaps understandable, given their work) use of the poor by grant givers to provide a context of appreciation that becomes part of their daily family practices.

It is grant givers' specific social and economic location in the economy and the particular money culture in which they are embedded that affords them the experience of moving across social class boundaries, presenting important and compelling dilemmas of inequality that are confronted within their family life. In other words, the structure of the job of grant givers gives them the opportunity to discuss openly with their children issues of inequality. Yet grant givers are also constrained in what they can do about social class inequality. They can feel good about providing a grant, but fundamentally, the class boundary and much of the structural inequality remains; and grant givers confront this issue more directly than most other people do. So while they desire to believe that all children are created equally, their job shows them directly that this is not true, in the sense that the circumstances of some of the children they meet are so vastly different from their own children's circumstances and opportunities. So, at best, grant givers do their work, try to make what difference they can, and tell their own children that they should appreciate what they have. Similar to some other helping professions, their work attempts to mitigate inequality, but it can rarely change the structure in a major way. So they take solace in knowing they are making some positive contribution, and they say that their job allows them to feel appreciation and gratitude for their own fortunate circumstances.

One grant giver described it this way:

We give back to groups and people in need that don't have what you have and what your family has.... Or we can help provide arts to everybody and equal education to everybody, because thing are not equal. Unfortunately, what you may have is not the case with every child, and we want to make sure every child gets a fair chance. [*KD*: Do you say that to people?] Actually to my own kids.

Another grant giver expressed the difficulties involved in crossing this class divide and its impact on her family:

I come home after going to a school in North Philadelphia, and I tell my kids the story. "Guess who I met today?" And I had the experience of seeing a child who maybe got their first book that they could bring home with them. I tell them to let them know what a great experience it was but also to remind them of what we do have. And I think we—many people—are blind to that because they don't have the opportunity to see what I see. I am not faulting them—well, some people I fault—but for a lot of people, it is just not there, it is not top of mind, so they aren't even made aware of it.

One grant giver brought a particular program that her foundation was supporting into her own child's school, describing it this way:

I was able to bring a program into my daughter's elementary school where they bring children from a suburban school and a city school [together] as partners. And then they stay with that school all year, and they go back and forth between the two schools to kind of get to know one another. And each kid has one partner the whole time, and they email each other and write each other and do workshops while they are together. And I was able to do it in my daughter's classroom. . . . So they can see that this is what these kids are like: "They are different but not really that different from me, but they have to deal with a lot of different things." We were funding this, and I asked, "Could I request that it be at my school, so I can actually see it going on?" I was the parent sponsor of it. I had to do some talking to get the principal to commit to it. . . . There was a lot of skepticism.

Grant givers often believe their job has a fundamental impact on how their families relate to money:

Oh, yeah. I always say, I don't bring my work home as far as stressing over it and taking time away from them, but I do bring home what I have learned about what we have and what other people don't have. And I do share with [my children] my experiences, and I have even brought them to things to kind of show them what the challenges are and how I am trying to help. And they understand it enough at different levels. It's cool that you give money away, and it is cool that you are helping this child by giving them a book to read. So I think it is sometimes hard for them to measure exactly what I am doing, but I think they respect that my job is something where I am helping people, and I think that makes them feel good and makes me feel good.

Even when grant givers are thinking about their own successes and their own financial situation, they often compare both up *and* down the class hierarchy in a way that aligns with the work they do:

My peers who graduated from law school with me are now partners in law firms, and that is the choice they made. And of course, they are earning $600,000 or $1 million a year. And I was never interested in the for-profit sector. . . . I am finding that is my attitude toward money, now working with foundations, I am kind of jaded: $50,000 is nothing as a grant, $20,000 is nothing. Maybe when I was a young twenty-four-year-old lawyer, and I heard, "Oh, [you] got a $50,000 grant," my eyes would have popped. I think now that is a really small grant. Working with the United Nations and its enormous budget, I sort of now have this skewed concept of money.

You know, working with poor people, I know what a poor person makes. I know what I make. I know what a partner in a law firm makes. I feel like I am at the low end, comparing myself to my cohort of private attorneys, but then I have to remind myself that I didn't choose that route. And I am certainly making more than a family of four earning $12,000 a year.

Money Culture and Other People's Money

When people work with other people's money and cross boundaries as a routine part of work, they develop an interesting money culture through work. The first and most obvious structural characteristic of these jobs is that individuals directly confront social class differences in their work, making inequality difficult to ignore. Particular types of cognitive and emotional work are common in these jobs, as boundary crossers struggle to make sense of these inequalities. Important features of the money culture developed in these jobs result from the desire to minimize the uncomfortable feelings that arise from these social class boundary crossings. Grant givers, who move both up and down the social class hierarchy, most pointedly confront inequality in people's financial circumstances in the widely differing opportunities that even the youngest of children confront in our society. The money culture that develops around this job embodies a shared discourse that describes this emotionally laden experience as one of being able to make a difference. At the same time, grant givers talk of using these experiences to teach their own children that they are very fortunate—in other words, to give them an appreciative standpoint for their own lives. So, one might say, they use the poor as a reference point to teach their own children a sense of appreciation rather than entitlement. This is at the same time understandable and tragic.

Fund raisers must gain a different form of comfort, moving up the social class hierarchy and sometimes being around a lot of other people's money. To help them cope with this crossing and avoid the seduction that could get in the way of doing their job properly, they are immersed in organizational routines and storytelling designed to keep them pressing the fund-raising process forward while reminding them of the instrumental nature of a relationship that can sometimes appear to be a friendship. Individuals who work with other people's money inevitably also work with other people's lives, because discussions about money are often discussions of everything money represents. These jobs illustrate that the dynamism and particular contour of a money culture reflect the core structural dilemmas that people in a given occupation face on a daily basis. Like other jobs and their associated money cultures, the specific culture formed when working with other people's money helps individuals in these occupations make sense out of what it is they are doing and manage the emotions they experience while doing it.

5

Advice and Counsel

Investment Advisors and Debt Counselors

If you can count your money, you don't have a billion dollars.
—J. Paul Getty

If you have debt, I'm willing to bet that general clutter is a problem for you too.
—Suze Orman

What sort of money cultures form when one's job is to advise people on how to manage their money? Similar to the fund raisers and grant givers described in the previous chapter, financial advisors and debt counselors become comfortable talking about other people's money but also find that they become enmeshed within a host of other issues in their clients' lives. For example, one financial advisor whom I interviewed described refereeing among three heirs who were arguing over their parents' significant fortune. A debt counselor described sorting through the unpaid bills that a client had tearfully brought in a crumpled paper bag to a counseling appointment. It was very obvious that these unpaid bills and the accompanying feelings of shame revealed much more than the person's financial state of affairs. By analyzing investment advisors and debt counselors, we see the similarities and differences that emerge in a money culture when someone is giving advice to the well-heeled or to those in dire financial straits. These jobs also give us another opportunity to explore how the structure of a particular occupation helps to produce the money culture surrounding it.

While those who work in these occupations are called on to give financial advice, they cannot help but give other types of advice, since money represents so many other things. Although on the surface they are the ones giving the financial lessons, a range of lessons about money actually cross back and forth between advisor and client, as I found that investment advisors and debt counselors draw lessons from their work experiences as often as they offer advice to their clients.

Financial Advice

Financial advisors struggle at the beginning of their careers to build a client base, experiencing the emotional roller coaster of good and bad financial stretches, as their pay is often heavily based on commission. The initial job socialization of a financial advisor includes hour upon hour of formal training about various financial products as well as formal and informal socialization in managing one's emotions while struggling to attract clients. Added to this socialization is on-the-job education that simply comes from talking to an array of clients and potential clients who are in widely differing financial circumstances. These daily interactions allow financial advisors the chance, like Scrooge in Charles Dickens's *A Christmas Carol*, to see the "ghost of Christmas yet to come" in time to alter their own financial trajectory.[1] Here is how one advisor reflected on his first few years in the business:

KD: Did having this job affect the way you began to think about money?

FINANCIAL ADVISOR: Oh, immensely. You don't see all the effects that savings can do for you until you work with people. I work with people who are just getting out of school, people who are right around retirement. . . . So I see a wide variety of people with all different situations. . . . But you don't realize how much the effects of not saving in the past can really affect you. You can't take back time, unfortunately. . . . From my own perspective, I am going to do whatever I can to save for myself and my future family.

Given this reality, a major challenge for investment advisors, much like for commission salespeople, is maintaining (or perhaps manipulating) their own emotional state as their incomes swing wildly, particularly in the beginning of their career. What makes this challenge even more intense as compared to commission salespeople is that investment advisors have to handle these swings within a daily workplace routine of meeting clients with differing financial circumstances and talking about the importance of money. While you are trying to maintain an even keel for yourself in months where you make very little money, you are simultaneously meeting with clients who sometimes have significant net worth. I suspect that an important factor in career turnover in the early years for financial advisors has to do with the difficulties of enduring days in which they make little money while talking about the importance of money all day long.

A novice advisor is likely to spend hours cold calling for clients and making little progress. Newcomers described strategies to manage the psychological toll this could take on them.[2] Seasoned managers sometimes suggested cognitive techniques they could employ to manage their emotions and "stay in the game." One of these was to focus on measurable goals other than commission, such as making a certain number of telephone calls each day. This goal is achievable and immediately measurable and helps to shift one's focus away from a successful call that earns a commission (which you have less control over) to simply a numerical goal of the number of calls you make (which you have control over). Newcomers are taught to adopt the cognitive logic that if they make enough calls, some will be successful, so they should simply focus on making calls. This strategy also helps to distract attention from the numerous hang-ups and abrupt "I'm not interested" responses. Another technique that senior managers suggest to newcomers is to focus their time and energy on setting up lunch meetings in local companies. Here the goal is to provide a certain number of free lunch meetings in which you introduce yourself and explain your services in the hope that some clients will emerge from those events. A novice advisor described the work techniques that he employed to keep working in the face of difficulties. Notice how clear he is about manipulating his own emotions as he has learned to encourage himself:

> I have been more up and down in moods [than in my prior job]. . . . I believe that eventually when you are out of your comfort zone, you are going to start to get a little bit stronger as a person. So I like to think that when I first came here, I was bewildered and dumbfounded and didn't know what to expect. But now, yeah, I am having a bad week, but I can't control that, [so] let's keep going, let's move forward, do what we gotta do to get through the week and make sure we are taking care of all the work that we are gonna get done. . . . Keeping myself busy is probably the most important thing. . . . The reality is that you can't make someone want to be your client. You can't control that. There are certain things you can control and things you can't control. It took me a while to learn that.

Here we see a newcomer learning to do the cognitive and emotional work he needs to do to focus his attention on what can be controlled. He also employs cognitive ideas and linguistic techniques to create a sense of forward movement and tempo in keeping himself busy. When he began the sentence, "Yeah, I am having a bad week, but I can't control that, [so] let's keep going, let's move forward," he actually began speaking more quickly, almost as if picking up the pace in his own speaking voice would help him will his way through a rough patch. I think many of the people whose pay is based on commission sales can relate to this feeling of needing movement (physically, linguistically, and cognitively) to keep going in the face of refusals.

Another newcomer described a seminar he attended as part of his formal training; it was focused on understanding and managing one's emotions and was followed up by discussions he had with informal mentors at his firm:

> We have what is called emotional competence: how things affect you, how they affect your mood. A couple of bad weeks can ruin your mood and put

you down in the dumps. You are literally riding a roller coaster. Some people handle it very well and are very focused. Some people let it get to them a little more, have hard times, and get frustrated. . . . Yeah, it is a roller coaster. . . . I've had very open discussions with people in my firm about what is going on in my head and what I am thinking right now. . . . And I share with someone, saying, "I am having a really hard time. I'm down in the dumps. What am I going to do?" And people that have been here a while understand the way these types of industries go, and they have been through it.

Drawing Lessons

Because the quotidian practices of this job involve seeing people who made wise financial choices as well as those who have not saved enough money for retirement, financial advisors often draw out lessons on a regular basis about money, saving, and investing. Obviously, this experience encourages investment advisors to think carefully about their own investments and to start saving early. However, they also are confronted with examples that suggest that becoming wealthy is not *only* about good investing, as they meet clients who have inherited great wealth. Most of the advisors I talked with reported that they had on occasion become embroiled within complex family dynamics that played out around wealth and inheritance. This was often described as a challenging or even distasteful aspect of their job:

> Here's a classic situation: Someone passes away, and there is an estate that will get divided up among three siblings. I've handled the estate to this point, but there is usually one sibling who dominates, for good or bad. The others say, "Bill, you take care of it." So Bill is sitting there, obsessing over the estate. It is down a little in stocks because the market is weak. He would like it to go up a little bit. And his brother, this money is all the money in the world to him, and the sister is in the middle. And Bill, the dominant one, doesn't need the money [right now]. What they need to do is just . . . get the whole thing in cash, then each sibling can do what they want to do. . . . But what Bill wants is for the market to go up so he can make an extra $50,000 for his brother and sister.

I've seen money do really dreadful things to people where it splits children. When I tell you, I mean, I've seen estates where—the smaller the estate, sometimes the more trouble it is—because, you know, the $25,000 that one child is getting is the most meaningful amount of money that they've ever had. I'm dealing with sibling disputes more often than I'd like.

Not all of these complicated family dynamics, of course, are created by people inheriting significant wealth. Sometimes it can be about struggling over a declining or lost family legacy:

I'll give you a true example. . . . My heart went out to these people. They basically had a net worth of $200,000 and a failing business that the son was handling, and it was basically worth nothing. They had some Social Security but basically no retirement money of any substantial amount. And they wanted to keep their lifestyle, but I told them something has to go: one of their homes. I think [instead] they were trying to find the next stock that would go from $1 to $50. . . . They were accepting reality, but they weren't really dealing with it. . . . And the kids weren't helping them deal with it. They were very nice people, but they could have done something to make Mom and Dad's life better, but that is really not my business [*sighs*]. I do a lot of family dynamics.

What I find very interesting is that advisors tended not to draw out any lessons from clients they met who were born into wealth or inherited wealth, other than that this can cause problems. Instead they mainly told me that they learned through their job the importance of saving money early and regularly to ensure they build a nest egg for their own retirement. Many advisors said that they turned their experiences at work into lessons for their children—namely, lessons of hard work and saving: "I don't teach them right now that you have to work to get money. But if they do something nice for their brother or sister, they get a reward. We have a little jar. They are dying to go to Disney World, and so I'm telling them it's expensive to go. So I told them if they save some money and we put our money together, we can see if we have enough to go to Disney World one day." I assume that advisors only drew lessons for their children from those clients who worked hard to obtain their riches because this fits well with the nation's ideology of individual hard work (whereas the ones who are born into wealth do not fit that ideology very well) and also because they fear that their children will not work hard if the lesson of success coming from hard work is not transmitted and instead they came to believe that wealth is simply a matter of luck, birth, or fate.

Money and Happiness

I also found that many advisors drew lessons for themselves about the connection between money and happiness. Many advisors volunteered without prompting that their work taught them that money doesn't necessarily buy happiness. Although several used this phrase, borrowed from the common lexicon about money, it seemed that they were more precisely saying that they had come to notice that people can feel as if they don't have enough money or security at almost any level of wealth, which is a slightly different lesson from the aphorism that "money cannot buy happiness":

> You know, I actually know a few people who are billionaires. And one of my best friends from where I grew up, his dad fixed furniture for a living, and he is one of the loveliest gentlemen you will ever meet and one of the loveliest families you will ever meet. And more money, or less money, has nothing to do with it. And intellect: there are a lot of bright people who don't have much money, and there are a lot of real wealthy people who are pretty stupid. And it has nothing to do with happiness. . . . There is always someone who has more. Always. Regardless of what level.

> Everybody's goal is to be a little bit ahead of where they are now. If you really have a lot of money, you are worried about the legacy of who you are leaving it to and how it is going to get to them. If you have less money, you want to make sure you have enough to get through your lifetime. If you have enough money, you want to know how you are going to accumulate it, to get to where you can do that.

Interestingly, one financial advisor bounced back and forth about the need for money and the connection between money and happiness, even though he had spoken to me about money not buying happiness. In the end, he seemed to conclude that while money can't buy happiness, it could certainly help:

> I hope to raise my kids right to show them that, you know, money can help, but it's not going to bring you happiness. So for the particular one [of his children] who wants to be a social worker, who may not make a lot of money, but they get happiness out of other things, I want them to bring their children skiing, you know, to do things that cost a few dollars. Therefore I will set up my money properly to reward them.

Investment advisors, of course, sometimes meet individuals and couples who have worked hard all their lives and only have meager retirement savings. In these instances, it seemed that advisors did not draw out lessons about the difficulties of saving on a lifetime of low wage work but instead focused on the lesson that these individuals could be happy despite not having a lot of money.[3]

Swinging for the Fences

Most advisors strongly believe in the idea of disciplined investing and diversification. In this way, they often counseled the generally accepted, prudent advice of most investment advisors: steady, regular investing over long periods of time with diversified investments aligned with someone's tolerance for financial risk will likely lead to a good result. However, I also found that investment advisors don't always take their own advice. I met several who at some point in their lives decided to "play with some money," as one put it, and make some risky bets. Often, they lost a significant sum of money (e.g., in the tens of thousands of dollars) as a result and admitted they had made a mistake dabbling in something they should have known was risky. Probably because they are around money so much and sometimes talk to very aggressive investors who seek much higher returns than safer investments will pay, financial advisors can be tempted to take more financial risk with their own money even while they preach safety and patience to clients. One of my interviewees who prided himself on counseling clients to "hit singles and not home runs" actually swung for the fences a couple of times in his career, occasionally whiffing at the ball. He seemed to imply that having spent so much time in financial markets and around people with significant fortunes, he simply wanted to try his hand at hitting the big home run, rather than only consistently hitting singles.

> Actually, probably the greatest learning experience I ever had—which in hindsight I was fortunate to have—[was] about fifteen years ago, and it was miserable. I was a single guy making a good income, . . . and there was a situation with a local company that I thought would get an FDA approval for something. And I stuck my neck out, and I got it chopped off. . . . To make a long story short, I lost $50,000. . . . God, I will never forget that; it was an awful weekend.

It is interesting that in talking about these moments of "making a big bet" by "swinging for the fences," the advisor linked this to the boredom of the job ("doing the same thing over and over again") and used the psychological language sometimes associated with addiction—having a "moment of weakness." He went on to use this experience as his own cautionary tale by drawing out a lesson for himself about discipline:

> The best learn[ing] is not from our triumphs but from our mistakes. And I really believe that. "[Admonishes himself by using his own name], that was stupid! You had no business doing that trade, based on a whim." If that had worked out, I probably would have had a gambler's mentality. When people go to Atlantic City with $100, and they take it up to $500, they don't walk away; they wait until it goes down to $0. . . . I think it is a combination of human emotions: greed and hope. I am subject to those too. I see things I should have done in my account that are rational. But, you know, the doctor doesn't operate on himself, right?!

He went on to *remind himself* of the need for emotional discipline to curb temptation, both for himself and for his clients. It is interesting to see how this advisor mixes talking about the discipline he preaches to his clients with the discipline he wants to see in himself:

If you stick to your basic principles—and that is the hardest thing, which I am very good at—if you keep your discipline, you are going to hurt a little here or there, but you aren't ever gonna blow up. People can't keep their discipline. . . . The most challenging thing in this job—or anything—to be successful is combating the boredom that comes with the necessary repetition of what you have to do to become successful. You have to keep doing the same thing over and over again. . . . How many times has Tiger Woods used his putter or practiced that drive? How many times has Mick Jagger sung "Start Me Up"?

Midcareer financial advisors, particularly the successful ones, reach significant incomes and become more buffered from the financial roller coaster that the early-career advisors experience. However, as their careers progress, they are also more likely to have more clients of significant wealth. So, interestingly, the actual *gap* between their income and some of their clients can get larger over the course of their career, even while their income is increasing. So the challenge in midcareer is to remain satisfied in one's work by focusing on one's own financial success, while coming to grips with the fact that you may never reach the financial heights of some of your multimillion-dollar clients. One way that financial advisors seem to make peace with this fact is by repeatedly telling others—and I think telling themselves—that money does not buy happiness. They come to this view because they meet clients who seem very wealthy but not very happy and some clients who are very happy absent great wealth. While these experiences are anecdotal and not based on systematic research, they draw the conclusion that you can be happy or unhappy with various amounts of money. Whether it is true or not that money and happiness are unrelated is not the issue here. Rather, I think this assertion is a coping mechanism in the face of becoming intimately familiar with people at differing levels of wealth. How does a financial advisor remain on an even keel after meeting with someone with savings of $200,000, then $10 million, then $150 million? Partly, by repeating the cultural refrain "money cannot buy happiness." I initially thought it was ironic that it was financial advisors, among all the occupations I studied, who most often verbalized the notion that money cannot buy happiness (the other occupation to do this was clergy; see chapter 6). But after understanding it in terms of the cognitive and emotional work that financial advisors perform to remain on an even keel, it made more sense to me. Since they routinely meet people with more than they have—and they know that because they have access to these people's financial documents—they curb their sense of jealousy or envy as well as their temptation to "swing for the fences" by reminding themselves that they can be happy with what they have. I don't believe this cognitive move is ever fully completed, nor is it ever fully satisfactory; so it gets repeated with some regularity in this line of work.

Debt and Credit Counselors

We come now to a group of social class boundary crossers who tend to cross mainly in one direction: downward. Debt and credit counselors spend much of their time counseling individuals who are in dire financial circumstances. Recent bankruptcy legislation requires many filers to seek debt counseling, and as a result, there has been a recent proliferation in debt counselors and some intensification of their work. However, I limited my own interviewing to counselors who worked for established, not-for-profit agencies, deliberately avoiding some of the for-profit firms that have recently sprung up, promising amazing results while charging larger fees that can put their clients into even worse trouble.

Interestingly, several of the counselors I spoke with began their careers in banking. They found themselves attracted to debt and credit counseling because they enjoyed helping people and did not particularly like the increasing pressure to sell financial products that they encountered working for a bank. Several counselors I interviewed had also gone through one or more stressful mergers/reorganizations, common in the industry, and were weary of changes in policies and procedures and demoralized by watching layoffs of colleagues. As banks became deregulated, they were allowed to offer more types of investment products, and they often felt pressed to market and sell these products. As one credit counselor told me,

> When you are in the retail banking world, you are sitting there with clients and trying, for example, to sell them a home equity loan, and you are [also]

trying to up-sell the home equity loan by incorporating all of their credit card debt. Well, here, we don't teach clients to substitute unsecured credit for secured credit just for the sake of getting a better rate or something like that, because they could put their home at risk. And when you are talking to a low- to middle-income person who might not have the most wise use of their credit cards, that is not what you want to do, to give them a clean slate [on the credit cards] and allow them to start over again.

Those who are attracted into the profession of debt and credit counseling are a somewhat self-selected group of people who have a keen interest in financial matters and have a tendency toward wanting to help others. This trait ends up coinciding quite well with the structure and practices in this job, which blends elements of social work and psychological counseling with financial acumen. Even the title "counselor" or "counseling" (rather than, say, "advisor," as used by financial advisors) sends a clear signal of both the individualized and psychological nature of the work. Many of those whom I interviewed take great satisfaction in being able to pass on lessons they had learned about managing money to their clients. Several told me that they were "always interested in money" or that as children "they were good with money" (by which they seemed to mean that they were thrifty or good at saving money).[4] In spending time with debt and credit counselors, you quickly notice that their language blends the financial and psychological lexicons and that their work has a strong element of psychological talk therapy in it:

> You have to really listen to what the client says. You really do have to listen to them, because they will tell you what they need or what they don't need. The other thing that I have learned is that you cannot judge someone at all. . . . I have had people when they come in, . . . and they are in an emotionally difficult time, obviously also a difficult financial time. . . . Sometimes there is crying, so when someone knows that you are there to support them, and they can walk out with their head up: "Thank you for not judging me."

Debt counselors are trained in financial literacy through a rigorous set of online courses and printed materials. However, they also spend a lot of time sitting in on counseling sessions run by more experienced counselors as part of their socialization to their jobs, "You spend a lot of time observing. There is a lot of one-on-one mirroring. And then when you get a certain comfort level, then I would be sitting here [in the main counselor's chair], and another counselor would be kind of walking me through it until I am at the point where I feel comfortable." Some of these elements of debt counseling have long historical antecedents. Viviana Zelizer describes a 1916 campaign launched by the city of New York called "Teaching How to Spend," operated by the New York Charity Organization Society. The goal of this program was "to teach poor families how to use their monies properly." Social workers would sometimes inquire into how money was divvied up among family members and would intervene to improve familial relations. This program included asking poor families to keep detailed records of their spending so that they could see ways to improve their spending habits. Zelizer writes of the larger implications of this program: "By itemizing expenses in extraordinary details, household budgets allow private charities as well as public pension supervisors to step into the domestic economy of poor families more deeply than the charity worker who distributed in-kind relief or grocery orders."[5]

Blending the Old with the New

The contemporary job of credit counseling blends elements transported from the history of poor relief with the profession of psychological counseling, combined with significant elements of financial education. As mentioned, the job title of "counselor" rather than "advisor" reflects the culture of psychological counseling more than financial advising, and I did not find the same stress on psychological concepts and "counseling" among investment advisors, even when they talked about becoming embroiled in difficult family conflicts. When financial advisors described advising someone who had not saved enough money for retirement or when they encountered someone who wanted to hit a home run with a thinly traded stock, they did not rely on any psychological explanations for these behaviors or scenarios. Financial advisors would certainly "counsel" someone away from trying to "hit the home run" and preach patient, diversified investing, but they did this using financial and economic reasoning rather than probing for the psychological trigger points that might lead to any of these behaviors. If anything, investment advisors seemed to push away psychological elements of discussions that occurred in their office, trying to return to the core financial issues at hand.

The financial tools that are at the disposal of credit and debt counselors and the consequent money culture in which they work pushes them toward a very individualized and highly psychologized view of the causes of indebtedness and, in turn, the remedies they suggest for debt problems. There may also be elements of stereotyping the poor as unable to responsibly handle money, which has been around for centuries. All the counselors I interviewed or observed used some form of a budgeting diary (not unlike the one described in the 1916 program in New York) as a key tool to structure their counseling sessions.[6] In the diary, the client is asked to record every penny that is spent each day for a specified period of time (usually either one week or one full month). This diary is supposed to show both the client and the counselor ways in which the person can cut back on spending or, as many counselors put it, to help "locate where the client gets into trouble."

> We go through the budget [diary] with the client. We have a thirty-two-line budget [that we fill in]. In each area of spending, we may be able to offer them tips on how they might be able to cut back in that certain area. We also have a directory we have built up over the years: how they can get breaks on their insurance, with [the electric utility], food banks they can go to, different things like that. We may talk to people about their telephone usage, . . . things like that. . . . People come to us with addictions, all kinds of things.

> You know about 70 percent of the people we counsel do not go under a debt repayment program. They need counseling, a written plan of action; they need—God, I hate to use this word—but they need a budget. People don't want to hear that, so we call it a spending plan, but that is what they need. And when you put them in the right direction, that is where you can be of help to them.

What was once described as "poor spending habits" in the language of the public health campaigns of the early twentieth century (akin, perhaps, to the "poor hygiene habits" attributed to the poor and seen as a cause of their ill health) has now transformed into the psychologically based language of the late twentieth and early twenty-first century. "Poor spending habits" has been replaced by "psychological trigger points," "places that get you into trouble," and "spending addictions."[7] I noticed that some of the pamphlets given to clients even used medical terminology or terminology from the fitness industry, such as "restoring your financial health" or suggestions on "how to get financially fit." Again, these terms suggest an individualistic approach to debt problems: an individual is ill or out of shape but can regain health and fitness with the right treatment regimen.

It Can Happen to Anyone

Not only is indebtedness or the simple lack of money perceived as an individual trait; it is also portrayed in this particular money culture as a more universal problem. Notably, several of the debt counselors told me a story about how they had counseled either a doctor or a lawyer who had gotten into indebtedness. They seemed to be telling this story to underscore the point that anyone can get into debt trouble and that debt was as much a problem of psychological maladjustment as it was a lack of money. Here are typical examples from two different debt counselors of the universalizing of debt:

> I mean, I get doctors, I get attorneys. I can think of a doctor that I can think of offhand. I think his take-home income per month was $10,000, and his expenditures were $14,000 per month. So it is not how much they are making but how they handle what they are making, and are they living above their means. That is probably what it comes down to.

> It seems we all like to live right up to what we are making, and most of us like to live beyond that. I have seen folks who have very high debt and very good income, but very high debt. If you can't keep your payments up and you have creditors calling you, it affects a couple things in your life. It

affects your marriage, it affects your kids; the pressure on you may cause you to get into drugs and alcohol and other things.

It is fascinating that debt counselors don't say, "On rare occasion, I get the unusual case of a doctor or a lawyer who has an overwhelming problem and gets into debt despite having a high income." Rather, they interpret the phenomenon as proving that *anyone* can get into financial trouble. It seems to me that the experience of having counseled one or two high-income individuals is put into this particular interpretative frame precisely because of the individualized and psychologized approach taken to debt in the counseling setting and the tools counselors have at their disposal to understand and mitigate the problem, as well as because of the individualistic tendencies in American society more generally.[8] Since the focus is on individuals (not groups, social classes, and structural pressures that lead to debt, such as lack of medical insurance) and on psychological problems or "issues" (overspending, addictions, gambling, drinking, illegal drugs, "shopaholics," and the like), the doctor or lawyer in debt is used to reinforce the psychologized view rather than a structural view of debt (e.g., that it might be due to a declining minimum wage, high unemployment rates, rising inequality, housing costs, transportation costs). If there is a psychological interpretive framing of the debt problem, then anyone can have this psychological problem, and the doctor/lawyer proves that belief. "Maybe with the higher-income [people], the shopaholics—we have people who buy things and never take the tags off; they are just in their trunks. So we tell them to take them back!" If, on the other hand, debt is caused by poverty, the erosion of the minimum wage, the lack of well-paying jobs, or high medical bills, then the doctor or lawyer might be seen as a rare anomaly to the larger trend that poorer people tend to have debt problems and that once in a while someone with a higher income gets into debt due to overspending or addiction.[9] The leading cause of personal bankruptcy filings in the United States is uninsured or uncovered medical expenses, and these expenses are unlikely to be captured very well in weekly spending diaries designed to locate spending "triggers." Perhaps an analogy to this situation is found in homelessness. While it is certainly true that someone from privilege can end up homeless (for example, resulting from a mental illness such as schizophrenia), it is also less likely that a wealthy person will end up homeless, due to significant differences in access to care, affordability of medication, support from family members, access to legal interventions, and the like. Moreover, if homelessness is viewed as a more structural problem of lack of affordable housing, unemployment, or marital disruption, the incidence of a person of privilege falling into homelessness is viewed more as an exception rather than as an example that proves that anyone can become homeless.[10]

One the other side of the ledger—income—counselors tend to offer their clients suggestions for increasing income that are very immediate and short term, since there is often little time and few tools at their disposal to remedy a person's lack of income. So counselors suggest that clients think about ways they can generate immediate income:

> We have some standard lines, particularly for people who have a home: "Do you have an extra room in your house? Could you rent it out? Maybe you could go get a second job?" We do look at those things. Unfortunately, it is just something that just sometimes doesn't fit into the game plan.

> I try a little bit, by maybe throwing out some things like, "What could you do for a second job? What skills do you have that you could earn money under the table? What can you do out of your house? "Do you"—like, silly things like, "at my house I rent out my garage. I don't have to be there; it doesn't take my time, but it is a way for extra income. Can you rent out a room? Can you rent out a garage? Do you have a large piece of property that someone can put their boat on?" If they are a teacher, "Can you help prepare people for tests, get their test scores up?"

One counselor went on to say that many of her clients are single mothers, so it is quite difficult for them to take on a second job and leave their children at home. Other counselors suggest that clients think about selling their possessions, having a yard sale or tag sale of some sort to try to raise immediate cash. These are clearly short-term solutions and likely to be fairly limited in their impact. While counselors do sometimes talk to clients about going back to school or getting a GED diploma, they express the frustration that clients do not really have the time to do this since they are often facing an immediate crisis of bill collectors or the impending foreclose on a home. Several counselors expressed their frustration at not being able to implement longer-term solutions to their clients' problems.

Every debt counselor I spoke with told me that they had become more sympathetic to the plights of their clients over the course of their career. This suggests that they feel strong emotions and connections to many of their clients. But since they have limited remedies for many of their situations (particularly those due to chronic medical conditions, illiteracy, lack of formal educational credentials, and lack of reliable transportation to get to jobs), they are often left to focus on the unpaid bill notices, the canceled credit lines, or foreclosure notices. Many counselors also told me that a very high percentage of people come to their office just one time and never return (some estimated this to be as high as 80 percent) or never show up for a scheduled appointment (one estimated a 40 percent no-show rate). Whether these statistics indicate the instability of the clients' lives, that they get what they want in a single visit, or that they sense that what is offered in credit counseling cannot effectively address their problems is not entirely clear.

Debt counselors feel a great deal of sympathy for those who are in financial trouble. The tools of their trade push them toward an individualized and psychologized view of financial debt that helps to obscure some of the structural elements of their clients' predicament. As counselors, they are called on to provide individual counseling, which turns them away from commonalities among their clients (for example, the lack of health-insurance benefits for many in the contingent workforce).[11]

In addition to counseling sessions with individual clients, many debt counselors also give presentations to groups of people. Here, they get to talk about such things as repairing credit scores, applying for a first mortgage, paying down debt, or avoiding identity theft. I attended a number of these talks at various locations and found that they were often attended by people who were either poor or of meager means (simply judging by their questions and comments), and many of the attendees seemed to be fairly skeptical or even hostile to the "financial industry." Some seemed to base this skepticism on perceived poor treatment they had received in the past or simply on unfamiliarity with banks, credit unions, and credit cards.

Actually, a lot of the groups I work with I am trying to teach people to actually get into banking. The groups themselves are intimidated by banks, or they don't trust banks or whatever. So for a lot of the groups I talk with, I am trying to get them to use checking accounts and stop using the fringe check-cashing places and tell them the benefits of these particular types of accounts and how they can build wealth through an investment ladder, if you would, that they might have never heard before. A lot of them are just amazed at some of the things we take for granted.

In these settings, I watched credit counselors walk a line between validating the skepticism of audience members (which can align with their own skepticism of the banking industry in which they once worked) and encouraging participants to gain more knowledge and to participate in the system as what they called "an informed consumer." For example, counselors would talk about things that people could quickly do to improve their credit score or to remove bad credit items from their credit report. These discussions would sometimes carry the flavor of "working the system," encouraging the view that people are in a game that can be rigged (to some extent) in one direction or the other. Of course, they could be right about this. However, my main point is that counselors often had to legitimate a system to a skeptical audience while at the same time acknowledge that the credit system may not always be "objective" or that elements of that system might be stacked against them. For example, one attendee asked how she was supposed to build good credit if she could not obtain any credit owing to her past credit history. Another said she preferred to use only cash as that helps her avoid getting into any debt (something that indeed would be recommended in most individual counseling sessions), yet she was being told in a seminar that she should get a credit card and "use it a little bit" in order to build a good credit history that would allow her to get a home mortgage.

The Economic Nested within the Social

While Zelizer showed that even our most intimate relationships have important economic and instrumental elements, here we see that the converse is also true. The occupations of investment advisor and debt counselor, like those of fund raiser and grant giver, are instrumental in nature and on the surface appear centered on economic performance. Yet they are also deeply infused and intermingled with social relationships. In jobs in which people work with other people's money, they become involved in a myriad of entanglements connected to money: brokering a bitter family dispute, helping an aging parent transfer money to a child, talking about old times on a college campus with a prospective donor, visiting a hospital with a donor to talk with the heart surgeon who saved his or her life, or counseling a client who is shaking at the prospect of losing her house to foreclosure. While these are among the deepest forms of social relations, they are harnessed within instrumental, organizational, and economic structures—another example of the difficulty of separating the economic from the social.

The nesting and interconnection of the social and the economic—which seems inevitable when one works with other people's money—presents a range of dilemmas for those who do this sort of work. Individuals in these jobs try to resolve these dilemmas through a variety of cognitive moves and emotional management strategies that emerge from the structural features of their jobs and are embedded in the particular money cultures surrounding their work. For the investment advisor, the money culture is quite different from the money culture of debt counseling, and this difference encourages a very different approach to clients and their money. The distinctive money culture in all the jobs in which one works with other people's money derives from the fact that one is sometimes expected to separate the economic and the social while at other times must deftly combine the two. Succeeding at this balancing act requires the nimble moves of a tightrope walker.

6

Sacred and Profane

Religious Clergy

> In a market-driven culture like ours, things no longer have *inherent value*, but only *exchange value*. "Will it sell?" ... These are first concerns, and sometimes the only concerns, of the *market mind*. ... Once we lose a sense of inherent value, we have lost all hope of encountering true value, much less the Holy.
>
> —Richard Rohr, *Hope against Darkness*
> (written with John Feister)

Richard Rohr captures one of the major dilemmas confronted by clergy members of all faith traditions in their daily work. In the United States, there is a highly developed market economy and a national money culture in which nearly everything has been reduced to its exchange value: "What is this worth on the market?" For example, we have already seen that both time and talent have become calculable in a market that sets a price for it.[1] This market mentality has engulfed the realm of religion, and clergy are often left to deal with the tsunami of the market mentality, or what Rohr refers to as the "exchange value" reading of religion.[2] At the same time, many clergy try to live within a belief system that runs directly counter to a market mentality that reduces human worth to what it can sell for on the market. Robert Wuthnow describes this challenge quite bluntly in his book *God and Mammon in America* when he writes, "As a nation of believers, we would expect our religious commitments to have a decisive impact on our economic behavior. But we are also passionately committed to the almighty dollar."[3]

Certainly, not all clergy take the same view on poverty and wealth. However, when you talk to a wide array of clergy about money, you find that they do talk about many of the same core issues, even though they may say different things about them. All the clergy I interviewed reacted to the trends that Rohr and Wuthnow describe, but in ways ranging from direct and conscious resistance to the market mentality to a somewhat more enthusiastic embrace of aspects of this mentality.[4] For example, some of the clergy I spoke with sounded like the seminarians described in Jonathan Englert's book *The Collar: A Year of Striving and Faith inside a Catholic Seminary*, which follows a group of men preparing to become Catholic priests. These priests-in-training are what one seminarian quoted by Englert calls "thousand-dollar-a-month men," living on very little money but a great deal of the kindness of strangers (and friends), who give them various gifts (e.g., phone cards, clothing, and retail-store gift certificates) to supplement their meager incomes.[5] I interviewed one Catholic priest running a church in a very poor neighborhood who similarly survived mainly on the generosity of others and gave away a significant portion of the $1,000-per-month stipend that he received as a salary. This priest seemed almost to live outside the world of money, as actual currency played a small role in his life.[6] Other clergy I talked with were running larger, prosperous, thriving churches with thousands of members, providing their congregants with an array of services ranging from Bible study to financial education to parenting classes. These clergy, owing to the size and scope of their significant operations, dealt with many business and financial issues on a daily basis and were making peace (to some extent) with the market mentality by drawing activities into their churches. I wondered what unites such a varied group of working clergy, and what is different among them when it comes to their view of money.[7]

Writing Meaning onto Money

Émile Durkheim, in his classic sociological treatise *The Elementary Forms of Religious Life*, argued that all religions deal with the dichotomy between the sacred (things set apart from mundane concerns and reflecting the interests of the group) and the profane (reflecting individual and day-to-day concerns). Durkheim wrote, "The division of the world into two domains, the one containing all that is sacred, the other all that is profane, is the distinctive trait of all religious thought."[8] All religions must deal with both the sacred and the secular world, as religion can be viewed (as it was by anthropologist Clifford Geertz) as a "cultural system."[9] More recently, there has been something of a backlash against taking this dichotomy between the sacred and the profane too far. I title this chapter, in part, after Mircea Eliade's book *The Sacred and the Profane* (1987), with my emphasis on the word "and" to highlight the view that the sacred and profane are not always separable but rather are often intertwined.

Listening to clergy talk about money, one gets the sense that they view money as containing and reflecting elements of both the sacred and the profane. Money, because of its malleability and fungibility, is particularly amenable to having elements of both the sacred and the profane written onto it. To give one small example: many Christian clergy I talked with repeated two well-known biblical quotations: "It is easier for a camel to go through the eye of a needle than for a rich man to enter the kingdom of God"[10] and "For where your treasure is, there your heart will also be."[11] Several Christian clergy argued that the well-known quotation about the "eye of the needle" did not mean that God disfavors the rich but instead that wealth can lead to the love of money over other more important virtues, and what is more important is what the wealthy person does with his or her money—something religious clergy refer to as "stewardship" of God's money. The second quotation was often used by clergy in talking about their own fund-raising campaigns in their churches and in making the point that this stewardship can, and should, be reflected in the immediacy of their own place of worship. They are also stressing stewardship—that the way a person uses money can reflect goodness or good intentions. Here we see a potential dilemma for clergy: they need to raise money to keep their churches in existence, so they cannot simply deride money or wealth. Money, therefore, is talked about as a necessity but also as having the potential to do good, within a cautionary framework ("Do not worship money over God"). These ideals are not necessarily mutually exclusive, but it does seem to make talking about money to me and to congregants a bit of a tightrope walk for clergy. Money, often earned in profane pursuits, can also be assigned the task of representing individuals' intentions, their "goodness," or perhaps even the state of their soul. Thus, clergy must continually juggle issues of the sacred and the profane in their work, particularly when it comes to money.

Foundational Assumptions

Clergy across many faiths have a distinct starting point for conceiving of money: that money belongs to God. As such, money represents qualitative meaning even more than it represents a quantitative measure of universal exchange value. Clergy, therefore, operate within larger belief systems that challenge commonly held assumptions, conceptions, understandings, and practices in modern finance and consumer culture. Those belief systems, of course, differ somewhat from one religious system to the next and also sometimes differ within religious systems.[12] Of course, clergy must also stand with one foot in each world.

It is not surprising that clergy derive their conceptions of money, at least in part, from sacred texts (such as the biblical quotations noted earlier) and their own interpretation of those texts, as well as from a long line of tradition and practice in their own religious order. The particular doctrinal belief system within which clergy operate has an impact on how they think about money and finance. However, it is also true that even within a belief system or faith tradition, clergy have some room for interpreting beliefs about finance in differing ways. I found that the clergy I interviewed took quite a variety of approaches to financial issues, emanating from their understanding of their belief systems, sacred texts, and traditions. I do not mean to imply that clergy can simply think anything they wish to about money. I did find crucially important commonalities in the issues that most clergy were wrestling with in one form or another, and I found that clergy were quite distinctive in the way they thought about money when compared to others I studied. For example, all the clergy I interviewed talked at length about one overriding theme in relation to money and finance: How do clergy manage the role of faithfully representing their understanding of sacred texts and beliefs while also operating in a world that has moved quite a distance from those beliefs?

As a result of clergy's distinct foundational assumption that money belongs to God, they share some unique cognitive dilemmas that are quite different from the dilemmas faced by other people portrayed in this book. For example, one of the first things you notice when you talk with clergy about money is that the topic of mortality frequently arises in conversation. Clergy of all faiths brought up the issue of death by pointing out that every person will die one day and that money is an earthly item that will not be of any value in the eyes of a deity or in an afterlife. This leads many clergy to emphasize the point that "money alone" is meaningless; it is the uses to which money is put that fundamentally matters. Clergy, like some financial advisors but in sharp contrast to most hedge fund traders and day traders, adopt a very long time frame when talking about money.[13] Clergy talk about money and its role in a person's entire lifetime and about how the way people used God's money during their lifetime might affect their afterlife. While mortality often arose in clergy conversations and in conversations with financial advisors, it entered the conversation in different ways. Whereas financial advisors focused on a client's having saved enough money for a good retirement or having enough wealth to pass on to progeny, clergy spoke of putting money to good use during your lifetime because you cannot take money with you. Clergy also stressed that since money really belongs to God or Allah, human beings are simply the "custodians" of it. This means that clergy do not completely accept the idea that individuals possess money or have full dominion over it. In the following quotations, first an imam describes his view of money and then a Christian pastor does. Note the commonality between the two in talking about money as coming from God and holding qualitative meaning and in explaining that a person's "attitude" toward money is a reflection of the person's relationship with God. Neither of the two speakers venerates or denigrates wealth but instead turns the focus toward "meaning":

You are allowed to enjoy it [*speaks in Arabic quoting the Quran*], as who can forget the evidence of beauty that God has introduced to you. You can enjoy. But enjoyment from the Islamic perspective does not mean you devote your life to them. These are tools to help you in life. Money itself is not going to raise you in God's eyes. You will be raised in God's eyes if you try to recognize his commands and that you should gain wealth from lawful aspects. If it is unlawful, then Islam will have concern with it—for example, if you gain wealth from gambling, liquor, drugs. You have to be away from them. You have to start to purify yourself from feelings of stinginess, even what you have; you should have others to share it with you. This is the aspect of purification of the human soul.

The difference comes when we talk about values. What is your relationship with God? Why do you need to have all the most fashionable clothing? What are the real issues behind the way you are spending? And I say that there is a spiritual problem behind the issues. So what is going on spiritually? So those are the questions I am going to raise. Money is not a good in and of itself.

While it might seem an obvious point, this distinctive starting point in how clergy see money (i.e., that money is given by God, carries different qualitative meanings, and in its usage reflects moral values) influences many other views of money that flow from it. In comparing clergy to financial advisors, you find that while both talk about mortality and both can even talk about doing good things with money, financial advisors assume that money "belongs to" the client and that having money brings some sense of security, freedom, or independence; all the clergy I spoke with expressed some version of the idea that human beings are simply custodians of money and that what one does with money is more important than whether or not one has money.[14]

While all clergy that I spoke with shared some similar core assumptions, each religious tradition also has its own particular precepts and concepts that influence the specific ways these clergy talk about money. For example, the idea that money actually belongs to a higher being is a particularly strongly held belief of Muslims and is partly the basis for the prohibition against *riba* (charging or collecting interest or, more accurately, "making money on money") and underlies the rationale for the payment of *zakat*. *Zakat* is the annual contribution or paying of alms made by a Muslim, and it is based not on income but on wealth. *Zakat*, one of the five pillars of Islam, is derived from a verb that means "to purify" and "to grow." It can be thought of as similar, in a way, to pruning a plant to cause it to flourish. This means that imams tend to talk about the way that money can be "purified" through paying *zakat*. Here is one imam speaking of the role of *zakat*:

> The word itself, *zakee*, mean[s] "purity." *Zakat* is an indication that with everything you have to deal with in the world, not everything you can do is absolutely pure. So in giving *zakat*, by giving between 2.5 percent and 10 percent, based on the class of property[15] you have accumulated, . . . you help poor people or help build a mosque. Then that purifies your wealth, and you can enjoy it.

Bridging the Sacred and the Profane

Religious leaders describe money in ways that allow it to take on meanings that blend elements of the sacred and the profane. If money is thought of only in the secular accounting sense, when a person makes a donation of money, he or she now has less money as a simple mathematical formulation. But if money can carry *different qualities*, clergy can assert that by making a donation, you actually increase the value of the money that remains with you. It is the very different starting point in the conception of money (being a representation of the wealth created by God and carrying qualitative meanings) that allows clergy to assert that less money can actually be more money. If money can have different meanings, then having less money quantitatively can logically coexist with having more money qualitatively. In addition to being a fundamentally different way of thinking about money, this view of money also serves to focus the attention of believers away from the fungible, quantitative aspect of money and toward the meaning systems attached to currency.[16] This distinct view of money fits well within the larger worldview of many clergy that the market mentality has become too dominant in society and that their job is to offer a completely different way to think about money. As one imam reflected,

> Giving to God is the best investment, because you are always guaranteed a return and usually the return is in the sense of reward, nontangible reward, that you are accumulating blessings with God and those blessings are multiplied. So basically, the one dollar can equal the reward of giving ten, because the reward that you get from God, he would multiply it for you. That is the basic belief.

It might be tempting to see in this belief system elements similar to what has sometimes been called "prosperity theology." Critics who have been derisive of this movement argue that it is a form of theology that implies that getting wealthy is proof of God's blessings on a person.[17] However, I think this would be a mistaken understanding, as Islam also carries a very strong emphasis on moderation and not living a life aimed at accruing wealth for its own sake. So the idea that *zakat* is a pruning process that increases the value of what remains is not a call for simply gaining more wealth but rather an emphasis on the belief that the qualitative meaning of money can change. Again, the value that increases here is not quantitative but qualitative; it is less about the amount and more about the meaning and uses of money.

In addition, Islam tends to discourage a high degree of savings, as saving money may be viewed as hoarding something given by God and denying its benefit to the community.[18] So, many of the beliefs and practices of Islam stress the circulation of money, rather than the saving of money (and in this way Islam is actually quite compatible with certain aspects of capitalism).[19] For example, notice that *zakat* is charged on retained wealth and not on income. Someone could have a high income but absolutely no savings and thereby owe little or no *zakat*. The prohibition against *riba* also encourages people with assets to invest in projects and to take a financial interest or stake in them (rather than making a loan and charging interest). So, through this religious meaning system, we arrive at a very different place from that of "a penny saved is a penny earned." For imams, there is a stress, then, on money in circulation and money invested in projects. Here we see how a specific religious meaning system shapes the view of money, the understanding of savings and investment, and the value of the "circulation" of money.[20]

The Islamic prohibition against *riba* also can illustrate how differing interpretations of this prohibition have evolved to allow Muslims to stay true to the intention behind the prohibition while charting a course through current-day financial transactions.[21] Christianity and Judaism, of course, have similar dilemmas of living according to sacred strictures in the context of the modern world.

In another Christian church that I visited, a very interesting text was used for what is called "The Prayers of the People," recited during a religious service. Notice the framing of what might be seen as financial issues to imply that it might be as appropriate to pray for those who have a great amount of financial wealth as it is for those who have little. This excerpt of the prayer shows how issues of wealth and poverty are reframed along a spiritual and qualitative dimension and away from a quantitative accounting framework:

> Pray for the hungry. And for the overfed. [*pause*]
> Pray that we all might have enough.
> [*long pause*]
> Pray for the unemployed. And for the overworked. [*pause*]
> Pray that all our lives might be productive and balanced.
> [*long pause*]
> Pray for the homeless and for the house-proud. [*pause*]
> Pray that all our homes might be simple, warm, and welcoming.[22]

Another example of how particular belief systems (and traditional practices) affect the way clergy think about money can be found in the Jewish concept of *tzedakah*. The word is sometimes translated as "charity," but the root of the word is more akin to the word "justice" or even "righteous justice." So giving *tzedakah* is more about "doing justice" than it is about "giving charity." For this reason, even poor Jews are expected to give *tzedakah*, because it is both a spiritual practice and a religious obligation to do justice.[23] The concept of *tzedakah* is deeply ingrained in the childhood socialization of young Jews, as one rabbi describes it:

Tzedakah definitely plays a role in all of our education [with the youth]. It is part of what we do; there are [teaching] units on it. There is a *tzedakah* box that the kids decorate and they pass around and put coins in it. Their parents are usually there, and they feel guilty and put in a dollar. That money—the bar and bat mitzvah class are the oldest in our school, and at the end of the year they go through a decision-making process, and they split the money up three ways: one to a Jewish cause, one to a local community cause, and one to a global cause. And they learn what to do.

Collections

While reinforcing the view from the pulpit that the meaning of money is paramount, clergy also have the mundane daily tasks involved in running churches, mosques, synagogues, and (sometimes) schools, paying for heat and electricity, providing services for congregations, engaging in counseling, helping to plan weddings and funerals, hiring office staff, and many other tasks that require financial resources. While they operate within a distinct belief system that stresses important aspects of the sacred in money, clergy also operate within a world of the profane when it comes to many money matters. Thus, clergy constantly juggle the sacred and the profane. In addition to deeply rooted religious concepts such as *tzedakah* and *zakat*, the ways in which religious organizations support themselves financially in order simply to pay the bills also influences clergy's conception of money. In other words, approached from a cognitive perspective, the structural arrangements of how a religious tradition actually collects money has some impact on how clergy conceptualize money and talk about money with followers.[24] For example, Jewish synagogues are funded typically through membership fees and not through a weekly collection-plate offering, as is common in many Christian churches. Because of the prohibition against collecting money on the Sabbath, rabbis face an interesting economic dilemma. They are unable to raise money on the one day in which they are likely to have the most members in attendance at the synagogue. A yearly membership fee, then, is a way to raise the needed funds to support the work of the synagogue, including the rabbi's salary.

Using a membership fee set by a board of directors and collected by a treasurer allows for a greater separation (though not a complete one, of course) between worship and money, or between the more sacred and the more profane. I found it interesting that several rabbis commented that they also intentionally tried to limit their knowledge of finances of the synagogue and in particular knowledge of individual members' financial contributions in order to keep these issues from influencing their views and actions. This seemed to be made easier to do within the structure of some synagogues, where there is a temporal and physical separation between worship and monetary collection that allows for rabbis to create a separation between their "more sacred" interactions with followers and the "more profane" interactions handled by a membership committee.

> When someone comes up to me and says, "Um, So-and-So has died. How much is a cemetery plot?" I can actually say, "Well, I don't know. I am happy to work with you on the funeral, and someone in the synagogue will be able to assist you with the finances, and it won't be prohibitive. . . . We have a treasurer, a board of governors, and usually someone will speak to the president of the board [about the financial issues].[25]

In many Muslim countries, there is an entirely different way of funding mosques, and this funding mechanism has also had a great impact on the conception of money. As two imams explained,

> Generally, the religious institutions in the Muslim world will be taken care of by a special department of the state. And they take care of the maintenance and the salaries. Maybe in some countries you will find private mosques, . . . but there is no aspect [notion] of "membership" in the Muslim world. . . . Once I was walking by an Islamic center in Philadelphia, and I saw a sign that said, "Only members are allowed to attend." I was astonished.

> We don't mandate that people give the *zakat* to the *masjid* [mosque]. They have that option, and we would prefer that they did, because it would help the *masjid* function. However, people have the freedom to give their *zakat* to whoever they choose. . . . What happens on Friday is that there is not

mandatory giving, but there is encouraged giving. . . . There is a box built into the wall called a "*zakat* box."

The practice of governmental funding of mosques and the fact that Muslims perform the five daily prayers throughout the day means that in Islam there is not a well-formed concept or tradition of a parish or a congregation, nor is there a well-developed notion of membership in any particular mosque. Muslims will pray the daily prayers in whatever mosque is close to them (and it could be different ones throughout the day, as people go to work or to market). This tradition, when transported to countries such as the United States, presents particular challenges for Muslim imams. The U.S. government, of course, does not provide funding for mosques (or for other places of worship). Imams have thus had to struggle with developing ways to generate the revenues to support their mosques in a way quite different from traditions developed in Islamic states. Some have used schools or language lessons and the revenues those create to support the mosque. Some receive gifts and donations, and some have tried to establish fees in either the mosque or a "society" attached to the mosque. Fund raising remains difficult, however, as it is not embedded in the tradition of many of the faithful.[26]

This situation provides a perfect example of how the structural location of a job or profession and the structural conditions of work influence views toward money. Since mosques are state funded in the Muslim world, it is less important that *zakat* be given through the mosque, and it is often given to a number of different organizations. In the United States, and in much of the Western Hemisphere, however, since the state does not directly fund religious organizations (other than granting tax-exempt status), each church, synagogue, or mosque must raise the funds needed to operate. This large-scale structural change (from state-supported mosques to individually supported mosques) leads to developing some sense of membership in a particular mosque and a new structural requirement to financially support a particular mosque. This pushes religious organizations to act more like market participants, as they must compete for members and solicit funds to remain in existence. Thus, the idea of paying *zakat* seems to be slowly evolving into some form of providing *zakat* to your own particular mosque, which may be responsible for providing charitable or social services to "members." Imams in the United States, then, have to absorb an entirely different set of financial concerns than do imams in the Muslim world, as they have to learn new ways to think about money and talk about money to followers in this changed context. Since their structural location has changed, they have to work to change the particular money culture and its views on funding religious organizations.

One imam explained the evolving notion of *zakat* in the new context:

IMAM: There are roughly eight different areas that it can be used for. It can be used for needy people, it can be used for religious institutions, and it can be used to help the poor in general. The Quran mentions the wayfarer, those in need. And so it depends. So the custodian of the *masjid* or the custodian of the *zakat* itself, who deals with that type of situation, would be in fact the treasurer, who would have the responsibility and duty to disperse the *zakat* accordingly.

KD: If I was a member of this *masjid*, would I give the money to this *masjid*, or would I donate my *zakat* directly to a charitable organization?

IMAM: We don't mandate that people give their *zakat* to the *masjid*. They have that option, and we would prefer that they did, because it would help the *masjid* function. However, people have the freedom to give their *zakat* to whoever they choose to.

Passing the Plate and Capital Campaigns

In many Christian churches, there is an offering plate passed around once or twice during each service. As compared to the membership fee common in Jewish synagogues, though, the passing of a collection plate provides significant uncertainty in funding and makes long-range planning difficult. In weeks when attendance is down, so too are collections. To combat this uncertainty, many Christian churches use a "pledge and envelope" system. Here, followers make an annual (or sometimes monthly or weekly) pledge in advance and then place that amount in an envelope on the collection plate. It is usually made clear—through the pulpit and through monthly or yearly "accounting statements"—that the pledge should be paid even for weeks when attendance is missed. If this system works, it provides the church with more reliable funding. Of course, some Christian churches practice tithing, which suggests that members pay 10 percent of their income to the church. Significant debates have ensued over the practice as well as over specific issues such as whether the 10 percent should be calculated before or after the deduction of taxes.

Many religious organizations across different faiths have adapted the idea of "capital campaigns" from nonprofit organizations to raise money for larger projects such as constructing new buildings or infrastructure repair. Many make use of religious or secular consulting firms that help to manage these capital campaigns. Even when religious clergy attempt to keep themselves somewhat separate from the day-to-day financial workings of their congregation, it becomes difficult to do that when they embark on major fund-raising campaigns, particularly if they use the expertise of outsiders. Here again, issues from the world of the profane stream across into the sacred:

> One of the things you do with the consultant is you go through family by family, and you say, "How much do you think they make? And how much do they make?" And when you get to the point when you say, this is somebody who you potentially think can give a whole lot of money, then the consultant has access to data that I don't. I can say, "So-and-So lives here on this street," and the consultant takes that, types in some little code, and what comes back is a profile. And they can say, "This person [has this job]. That guy is pulling down $350,000 per year."

Once religious organizations begin to get engaged in more significant fund-raising campaigns, clergy cannot help but get more personally involved in some of the fund-raising activities and strategies suggested by consulting organizations:

> If you know you have to get a big piece of money up, sometimes you have to ask. We got two or three really large gifts in our campaign. In each of those instances, we knew the people had the capacity to give that gift. . . . You go to those people and say, "We are doing this really important thing,

and we really need five gifts in the range of $75,000 to $100,000, and we are hoping that you would be one of those. If you could give us $100,000, we could do this." . . . There is a principle, you know, if you need big money, you ask people that have big money.

Some of the larger religious organizations have subsidiaries that provide things such as counseling services, television or radio programming, books and recordings, and educational programming. All of these are complex and entail significant business acumen. In managing these initiatives, religious clergy may come to run organizations that are increasingly complex but operate under a different paradigm than more secular types of organizations. Religious clergy underscore this difference by returning often to the theme of the "meaning of money" and stressing its use in the service of God. Some reinforce this message from the pulpit, particularly when trying to orient the congregation to focus on the meaning of money and the good that can be done with it. Some clergy think about how this principle is built into their organizations:

> The thing that is dissimilar to a medium-sized corporation is the spiritual
> side. . . . Love the people, care for the people; they have to espouse the same
> values because if not, you will have a hodgepodge and it will kill the very
> mission of the church. . . . There is not only the organizational side; there
> is the pastoral side, which is equally important. So I have a senior associate
> pastor who oversees a lot of the pastoral aspects. The pastoral side has to be
> driving things, not the organizational side. So my job is to keep a tension
> between the two elements.

While clergy of all types confront rising operational costs and demands for a wider array of services (sometimes as a result of the decline in governmental services), clergy also have to be cognizant of the fact that some followers may resent anything that might resemble a hard sell when it comes to requests for money. Some attendees—probably a very small percentage—may go so far as to believe that any requests for money are inappropriate in a religious setting and that any offering is purely voluntary, in that it should emerge solely from their desire to give. This presents clergy with the difficult task of simultaneously needing to satisfy parishioners who desire (and even may expect) a certain level of service (religious, social, and educational) while also satisfying others who may not desire those services or appreciate the expenses associated with providing them.[27] Some clergy have not been trained in the complexities of fund raising, and not all are comfortable engaging in sophisticated, large-scale fund-raising efforts, as reflected in this exchange about approaching parishioners for large donations: "If you want to know what makes my little rear end pucker up, that's it [asking for large donations]. Somebody told me once, 'It puckers up so much it can grind diamonds from dust!' [*laughs*]. I don't particularly like doing this. It is one of my least favorite things. But it is one of those things that has to happen. And for some people, I am the only one who can do it." Robert Wuthnow, in *The Crisis in the Churches*, wrote of similar dilemmas he found among the Christian pastors he interviewed, who often spoke of juggling two roles: a *prophetic* role and a *priestly* role. In their prophetic role, many pastors could speak critically about prevailing cultural notions of consumerism and self-interest and positively about the need for stewardship of all of God's blessings. However, in their priestly role, ministers must manage the church financially and keep the pews full, limiting the idea of stewardship to donating to keep the church running. As Wuthnow writes,

> The inevitable tension between these two roles arises whenever stewardship is at issue. Prophets want to speak against self-interest, against working too hard, in favor of using one's talents wisely at the office, and on behalf of the environment. Priests know they must focus parishioners' attention on supporting the church. One of the reasons that stewardship in its prophetic sense is not very well understood or applied is simply that clergy emphasize its other meaning.[28]

Because of clergy's religious paradigm (which takes as its starting point the notion that money belongs to God), combined with the structural economic position in which they operate while working, clergy exist both inside and outside the market mentality that Richard Rohr describes in the epigraph at the outset of this chapter. In their prophetic role, clergy can warn against self-interest and working too hard in pursuit of money. In their priestly role, they may need to solicit donations from those who are in the best financial position to give, as well as being called on to counsel parishioners struggling with the stresses induced by a striving lifestyle.

In the book *Passing the Plate: Why American Christians Don't Give Away More Money*, Christian Smith, Michael Emerson, and Patricia Snell estimate that in most Christian denominations, parishioners give 1.5–2 percent of their income to the church, with approximately 20 percent of people giving nothing.[29] Religious clergy and those who study religion have tried to figure out why some followers do not give as much as they might. In part, it may be due to some of these ambivalent feelings about making contributions. Smith, Emerson, and Snell argue that many congregants have not come to grips with the moral teachings of their churches regarding helping those who have less and that congregants experience unclear expectations from their churches about giving. The authors also stress the fact that many give only episodically or irregularly. One Protestant minister I interviewed believed that trends in our culture contribute to the reluctance to give more fully and openly, and in the following statement it is clear that he looks at the issue of giving from both a spiritual and a psychological standpoint:

> I have some hunches. I think that one of the sidebar things that are happening in this culture is that it has created a free-floating anxiety. You cannot see it, but it is there. It is a kind of palpable fear that is there, and it is the fear that somebody is going to take something away from me and I will be hurt. So my suspicion is that this is what is there—it is fear. It is living in fear. These are the people living in great huge houses, with alarm systems on them and attack dogs in the backyard or whatever; that have huge, huge savings accounts to prepare themselves for whatever the future is going to be. . . . That is the place where I stop being angry and my heart sort of melts a little bit. These are people who have something going on. How can you be a whole person and still live in fear?

Issues of church, synagogue, or mosque finances can be particularly sensitive for clergy, as one or two mentioned to me that they have to be very careful about the handling of finances because of media reports (real or imagined) of clergy misusing funds.[30] While all organizations have to be concerned with the proper handling of funds, religious organizations carry an additional burden because they operate under a different paradigm when it comes to handling money. As I have pointed out, religious organizations rely on contributions, and the contributed money is continuously inscribed and reinscribed with spiritual meaning. Funds contributed to a church, mosque, or synagogue are seen as qualitatively different (sacred) than are funds used in a business or corporation (profane), so treating those funds properly means treating them as carrying sacred qualities. Thus, any improper use of these funds would be seen as something qualitatively different (i.e., more heinous) than improper use of corporate funds would be by contributors. So the sacredness bestowed on money in the religious realm adds an additional responsibility for clergy not only to ensure that funds are handled properly but also to make sure that parishioners understand and believe that the funds are handled properly. Similar to other nonprofit organizations, in religious institutions, the perceived legitimacy of the handling of funds is almost as important as actually handling the funds properly, because if those who give voluntary donations do not believe in the legitimacy of their handling and use, they can immediately withhold donations and the organization might quickly collapse. So this extra concern and care in handling funds and in communicating to followers that the funds are handled correctly is necessary because of the sacred quality inscribed on the money. As one minister told me,

> There is a little wooden box with a funnel in it in the sacristy. I never touch it. If money is lying around, I will say, "Kevin, help me. Pick up that, and put it in that, and I will watch, and you will watch, and we both knew it was there, and I won't touch it." It's just—there is so much ambiguity about ministers and money. One of the things that ministers live with, and I suppose every helping profession does, transference.[31] Transference is deadly. Sometimes you don't even know what is happening with transference.... And sometimes you don't know it is happening, and you'll be looking at somebody, and you just see a gleam in their eye, or their eyebrow goes up. Something happens, and you go, "Uh-oh." Money, for me—anything to avoid anything like that, I just do it.

A Higher Calling

Owing to clergy's sometimes unique perspective on money and their understanding of their call to help the least fortunate, they struggle in complex ways when confronted with issues that others may simply take for granted. For example, many clergy are approached by people asking for money, because clergy are often right on the front lines confronting the poor or people suffering with mental illness. These folks come to places of worship looking for help or for a handout, and the dilemma for clergy is this: How do you follow religious ideas about helping others and putting the needs of others before your own if those needs become overwhelming (financially or emotionally) or if your are not even sure whether giving someone money will actually be helpful or harmful to that person? One Catholic priest provided a perfect example of this cognitive struggle:

> We have "regulars" that come for their needs. It is usually canned food, soups, vegetables. There is a neighborhood to the east of here that is pretty derelict, so I wonder if some of them sell the can of food. We have AA [Alcoholics Anonymous] meetings here, and if one of the AA people see me in the foyer giving someone money, he gives me a lecture, saying that I need to practice "tough love" and that I am not allowing them to feel the consequence of their lifestyle.

In this conversation, I could sense the priest's dilemma with wanting to assist someone who was clearly in dire need but (in common psychological parlance) not wanting to "enable" the person's lifestyle by giving money that might be used to buy alcohol or illegal drugs. This priest's strong sense of his religious calling is to give what money he has to others,[32] yet elements in our culture tell him he might be wrong to do so. His own practice, or habitus, is that he himself will be blessed and purified by giving away what little he has, yet others warn him that he may in some way be harming rather than helping another person by doing so. A Protestant minister described a similar internal conflict and how he dealt with it:

MINISTER: [People knocking on the church door asking for money] kind of goes in spurts. It happens occasionally. But right now I don't have a whole lot of money to give.

KD: Do you worry that the money might be used for alcohol or drugs?

MINISTER: I don't worry about it too much anymore. I used to. If it gets to be repetitious, I get less willing to give money. There is a guy, and he was kind of like in your face, like he's entitled: "Isn't this a church? Aren't you supposed to help me?" So I helped him out a little bit, then I found out he was dealing drugs—not *using* drugs; *dealing* drugs. So the next time he came around, I said, "Are you dealing drugs?" "No." I said, "Don't lie to a priest." Two days later, he was in jail, and later he came to see me, and [I said], "You lied to me." We had a long conversation. He was trying to get clean. So I really helped him a lot, really bent over backwards.

KD: Does this make it more difficult to be open to the next person who asks for help?

MINISTER: No. It used to. But part of where I am is that it is a terrible time to be a poor person. And I can't imagine what it would be like to have to come and beg money from somebody you absolutely don't know. So anything I can do to make that process more human and easier. The thing about poor people is that they understand joy in a whole different way. It's that place . . . that place of—I really think it is true that the only universal experience of all human beings is the experience of suffering. Not everybody dances, not everybody is joyful, but everybody suffers sooner or later.

A third clergyperson, a Catholic priest in a very poor neighborhood, responded this way when I asked him about a sign I had seen on my way into the rectory for our conversation. This exchange gives just a small taste of life on the front lines of poverty:

KD: I noted that you have a sign on the door that reads, "No Food."

PRIEST: Yes, the women in the office put that up there. It is relentless with the ringing of the doorbell [*weariness in his voice*]. We have food about half the time. The ladies are eager to put that up when we don't have food. So that is when we put the sign up there.

Some of our current cultural understandings of poverty and addiction present a significant challenge to the way that some of these clergy think about money as a means to help the poor, the needy, and the lost. Clergy, however, seem to have a more difficult time than most people in shutting out the poor, as they believe strongly that they are specifically called to help the most needy, even when these needs seem overwhelming and they are not always sure about how best to help.

Being a clergyperson also means having many blurred boundaries around your work life. Many people in the congregation think that the clergyperson is, or should be, available twenty-four hours a day, seven days per week. Yet clergy (at least in some faiths) have their own families to tend to. Clergy of all faiths talked to me about the high potential for "burnout" if they did not actively work to create some sort of boundary between work and leisure (or at the very least between work and "rest").

I have been in these sorts of [poor] neighborhoods almost my entire forty-five years as a priest. I guess what I do is not so much traditional church or ministry work but hand-to-hand charity, going to court with people who are in trouble with the law, serving poor people at the church door, listening to them, talking about their needs. I also have a history as an activist. . . . I try to incorporate the idea that one of the tasks of a spiritual life as I understand it is letting go of one's own needs. . . . The old Latin word for virtue is *habitus*, a way of life, a way of being, a habit, like driving a car. So if someone is at my door with a story, you hope that story is true; they have a need, and that need is as immediate as your own.

Some religious clergy also struggle with issues around the payment of their own salaries. This is something that is shared to a certain extent by leaders of secular nonprofit organizations—the notion that to attract people to a job they need to be paid at least relatively well, pitted against the idea that someone should be doing this work out of a moral calling and that high financial recompense is wrong. Again, we see that because clergy operate with at least one foot in an alternative paradigm for financial issues, they confront issues such as salary, benefits, and even retirement differently than many others do. Some use their theology to think about these issues from a somewhat unique angle, but that doesn't mean the issues don't present certain continuing frustrations.

KD: Do you have any savings?

PRIEST: I do. I don't know how much it is. There is some family money left by my parents and split among the four children, . . . but I don't know if there is enough to keep me during my older years. I think there is a pension that the diocese provides. There is a nursing home, but it is not very attractive unless you are ill.

KD: Would you like to retire?

PRIEST: It is attractive, yeah, but sometimes my ideology does get in the way. Dorothy Day and all that.[33] Retirement is actually a pretty middle-class concept after all. People around here [a very poor neighborhood] are just here. They are just here. They don't "retire." My image of a priest is not that of having a "job"; it is shaped by the biblical passage from St. Paul read at Easter time: "You are dead now, and your life is hidden in Christ and with God." So I believe in inserting yourself into a community like this and being here and hanging out here.

The Role of Gifts

Many clergy survive on relatively low salaries (given the work they do, their educational credentials, and the long hours they put in). One of the things that helps them survive is that they are often given gifts—sometimes basic necessities such as clothing or a gift card to a grocery store, other times gifts that give a taste of some of the luxuries in life. But when given these gifts, clergy can have mixed feelings about them. They are grateful for the gift but realize that it can sometimes come with a sense of reciprocity. As Lewis Hyde put it (describing Marcel Mauss's 1900 essay on the gift), a traditional gift economy is based on "the obligation to give, the obligation to accept, and the obligation to reciprocate."[34] While gifts are typically seen as being given "voluntarily," they can also create a relationship of dependence of the recipient on the gift giver, even if that relationship is a subtle one. There is a cognitive difference in the experience of earning the salary one deserves and being given a gift of a car or the use of a beach or lake house for a week. The first is experienced as deserved, earned, and due; the second, as something to be grateful for and to feel fortunate to have, that can be withheld and may carry reciprocal obligation. As Hyde writes, "It is the cardinal difference between gift and commodity exchange that a gift establishes a feeling-bond between two people, while the sale of a commodity leaves no necessary connection."[35] This "feeling-bond" can include gratitude but also a sense of owing the person or being somewhat dependent on the gift giver.[36]

Gifts can raise other tricky issues for clergy. A minister I interviewed had been given an automobile by a parishioner. He mentioned his concern about driving this car around the Boston suburbs (where his church is located) and being seen by parishioners. He worried this might alter the way parishioners would receive his appeals for money for the needy. On the other hand, it was a reliable car, and he needed the transportation. This story represents the additional cognitive struggle that clergy experience when confronted by a gift that others might be able to accept more cheerfully and fully. Clergy are particularly visible members of the community and must consider how symbols, such as an automobile, will be interpreted by the community. I sensed that it was hard for this minister to fully enjoy the car because of these concerns.

There are many ways, though, that gifts are essential to the very existence of the religious organization. One priest I spoke with talked of the ways in which friends of his church pitched in with everything from accounting expertise to plumbing expertise to keep his church going. These sorts of exchanges allow many religious organizations to operate partially outside the world of money and in a world of gifts and kindnesses. Several of the clergy I talked with were paid partly with "book allowances" and "housing allowances" rather than only straight salary. Again, this is compensation not directly in fungible dollars and cents but in targeted goods (shelter, books).

Some of the phenomena that clergy experience in their money cultures can militate against the value of independence that is deeply ingrained in American culture. Relying on gifts, donations, and the kindness of others may not contribute to the notion of being independent. Depending on others, however, can fit within the religious paradigm in a very positive way, in that many clergy preach the notion that people are interdependent, that we all must rely on others and that community is built on mutual involvement with one another. Some clergy even challenge the notion of independence as an illusion. Thus, clergy are in a sense practicing what they preach when they model the dual notions of dependence and interdependence as valid ways of living a full life. This is another example of how a larger system of belief that challenges more hegemonic cultural notions is intertwined with the financial features of a clergyperson's life. Put another way, it shows that cognition (how one views and values the meaning of "dependence," for example) is enwrapped with elements of a structural financial position that almost necessitates certain dependencies. Within this local money culture, then, there are some important and recursive alignments between practices and cognitions. How a clergyperson comes to a cognitive understanding of the experience of "depending on others" is related both to his or her structural location (in that he or she must depend on gifts for survival) and to his or her spiritual and religious understanding of the meaning and spiritual value of concepts such as independence, interdependence, and dependence.

Trust and Money

Both clergy and hedge fund managers raise money in their jobs—clergy from congregants in the form of donations and hedge fund managers from clients in the form of invested capital. Thus, both rely on a significant amount of trust. In the case of clergy, followers must trust that there is a supreme being, that the clergyperson faithfully represents that deity, and that the clergyperson is personally trustworthy and will act as a good steward of the donated money. So a person making the donation to a religious organization must have a certain amount of doctrinal trust (or faith, if you prefer that term) as well as a form of personal trust in the clergyperson and the religious organization as a whole. The customer or client of a hedge fund also demonstrates a large measure of trust. Because hedge funds have significant minimum investments (i.e., rules governing who can be a "qualified investor"), and they are loosely regulated in a way that often grants very wide trading discretion, a client turns over large amounts of money and nearly complete discretion over how that money can be invested. Some hedge fund prospectuses come close to allowing managers to do most anything with the money (within legal bounds, of course), and there are even "lockup provisions" that the investors agree to in advance that make it difficult to remove money from the fund quickly. The client, then, is trusting that the fund is not a Ponzi scheme and that the returns that get reported are real returns. I don't think it is a stretch to make the argument that in some ways the person investing $50 million in a hedge fund is showing more trust and faith than is the person giving a $1,000 donation to a church, synagogue, or mosque. This may be why both hedge fund traders and clergy I interviewed showed a sensitivity toward any media stories of fraud in their professions: they run a great risk if they are tarred by the same brush that paints stories of fraud in media coverage. Any threat to trust and legitimacy is a threat to the entire operation.

But what is the nature of this trust? For the religious adherent, one trusts first in God and accepts (to some extent) the notion that one's own money comes from the goodness of God. So there is a belief, promulgated by religious texts and clergy, that the potential donation does not fully belong to the person anyway. Second, there is a belief among many people that donating the money to a religious organization is not only a right and good thing to do but also may help one gain the afterlife. Finally, there is a belief that the money will help other human beings here on earth and that if money is not misused, then making a donation is a noble thing to do, in and of itself. With a religious donation, of course, one will never know (on earth anyway) whether some of these beliefs are in fact true, so trust must be earned and maintained as part of faith.

For the client giving money to the hedge fund trader, the motivation is entirely different than it is for someone donating money to a religious organization—it is mainly the desire to gain a significant monetary return rather than a significant heavenly return. One could even argue that the motivation for the investor in the hedge fund is partly greed—if only in the sense that the investor is trying to get a higher return than might be possible with a safer investment or one with greater oversight and regulatory control; if you prefer, investors are willing to take on greater risk in the hope of higher return. Unlike in the case of clergy, however, there is no required or expected belief in a higher being, and people making an investment in a hedge fund are likely to believe that their money belongs entirely to them and that they have full dominion over it. So what is interesting in this comparison is that each party—be it the hedge fund investor or the donor to a religious institution—shows significant trust and even a form of faith in whom they are investing: one is motivated by a faith in God, Allah, or other deity, while the other is motivated by a faith in the hedge fund management and perhaps a faith in the economic system that has created hedge fund investing. Interestingly, I found that people who make religious donations are more likely to try to attach strings to their donations than are hedge fund investors (e.g., by attaching their donation to specific projects rather than giving the clergyperson complete discretion over it). People investing in hedge funds not only accept but often advocate for the idea that the fewer restrictions put on hedge fund traders, the better. One could argue that their faith (particularly in the face of recurring stories of Ponzi schemes and the publicity of the Madoff investment scandal) may be stronger (or "blinder" perhaps) than the faith of a religious contributor is. This level of faith may tell us as much about the power of mammon as it tells us about the power of God.

It is also interesting to compare clergy with fund raisers for secular institutions (such as public universities or hospitals). Fund raisers ask individuals for donations just as clergy do, yet they do not invoke the assumption that money belongs to God. Instead, they rely on the idea of putting money to good use during one's lifetime (or as a bequest to be used after death). Despite this foundational difference regarding who owns money, I found it interesting that both clergy and fund raisers use the same vocabulary in talking about the "stewardship" of gifts. Clergy talk of acting as a "steward for God" when they ask for donations and when they put money to work, directing it to uses that are in keeping with their view of God's intent. The secular fund raiser acts as a "steward" for both the person making the donation and the institution receiving the donation. This use of "stewardship" implies that the secular fund raiser should communicate regularly with the person who made the donation and demonstrate that the money was used for the purpose designated by the donor. "Stewardship" for God is a somewhat different matter, however, and can lead to conflict when the person who has made the donation believes a clergyperson (or religious organization) is not representing the donor's own individual wishes, and clergy may very well believe that they are not bound to do so if they are God's steward over the money, rather than being the representative of the donor. This is an interesting example of the translation of a concept such as "stewardship" from one fund-raising context to another.

Clergy have a unique standpoint from which to view and understand the market economy. They are able to see and engage in market exchanges based on money as a universal currency, but they also are more aware than most people that market exchange is just one form of exchange, rather than the only form. Because clergy regularly receive gifts and donations (either personally or organizationally), witness numerous acts of generosity, and espouse and explore a message that emphasizes time, talent, and treasure rather than just treasure, clergy seem much more conscious of the market mentality as just one possibility for thinking about one's place in the world. Put another way, many people who are fully immersed in an increasingly market-based culture have come to believe that the only answer to the question "What is this worth?" (or even the question "What am I worth?") is the price that can be fetched in the market. The answers to these questions are likely to be very different if you ask them of clergy because they operate in a world in which money is only one arbiter of value. It is clear from my conversations with clergy that they spend an incredible amount of time writing meaning onto money by reminding their followers that the money represents God's bounty and that its use should be thought of in those terms. So, while money has a universal exchange value in the society, clergy point out that each exchange can represent something about one's faith, beliefs, or purpose in life.

Philip Goodchild, in his book *Theology of Money*, writes, "A distinctive feature of religious life is that [human] flourishing is normally attained by means of a renunciation: time spent on productive activity or enjoyment is interrupted by ritual or sacred activity."[37] While Eliade argued that modern men and women have become increasingly closed off to "the sacred" as they confront the market economy, Goodchild (among others) counter that this position is overstated. Clergy continue to encounter people seeking the sacred on a daily basis, and a large part of their job is helping people chart a course through the modern world while keeping an eye (or as they might put it, an "open heart") toward the sacred. Put another way, clergy are simultaneously encountering the sacred and the profane as they are called on to provide comfort, guidance, advice, and leadership to their congregation in many matters, not the least of which are money matters. And these money matters reside within a culture of commodification, the market mentality that tempts people to ask even about their religion, "What's in it for me?" Clergy do not have an easy task.[38]

7

Testing Limits

Experimenting with Currency, Prices, and Salaries

There are many things that we would throw away if we were
not afraid that others might pick them up.
— Oscar Wilde, *The Picture of Dorian Gray*

There are some people who intentionally—and quite self-consciously—
use money in their work in highly innovative and unexpected ways. What
these people are doing is conducting experiments with money that are
designed to directly challenge our unspoken assumptions about money.
In making this challenge, they also hope to change—or at least to make
commentary on—major social issues of our time, such as globalization,
values, inequality, or community. I wanted to understand some of these
experiments with money and to ask what impact they have on the people
involved, as well as inquiring into what these experiments teach us about
the malleability of money. These experiments also allow us to see the
limits to malleability, as we can pose the question, Can money be *anything* we want it to be? While clergy use religious texts, traditions, and the
power of the pulpit to remind followers that money has a spiritual dimen-

sion, these individuals who are experimenting also make strong statements about the qualitative meaning of money, but this time in a more secular context. These experiments include creating alternative currencies or setting prices and wages in new and innovative ways. These experiments all demonstrate that money is a practice as much as it is an object.

Designing Money

One of the most interesting and complex experiments with money is the alternative currency system developed in Ithaca, New York, and later copied in dozens of other places.[1] In these alternative currency systems, local communities literally print money that can then be used to pay for local goods or services. The system in Ithaca, New York, known as "Ithaca HOURS" is one of the longest running alternative currency systems in the world. The system began in 1991 in the midst of a national recession. A community activist and writer named Paul Glover knew that the economic problem in his community was not a lack of skills or a lack of useful things needing to be done but (literally) a lack of money. As he told me,

> I had gotten a grant and had done a comprehensive survey of the Ithaca fuel system, with cartoons and diagrams. And [then] I got a grant from the Fund for Investigative Journalism to do a study of Ithaca's financial system. So I studied formal economics, independently, and I studied community economics, such as it was known, and it became evident to me that wonderful things could be done in our community to meet our needs, to transfer control of the economy to people in general, and in such a way to benefit the environment at the same time; notwithstanding that there were always wonderful ideas of good things that could be done, they didn't happen significantly because money was moving in a different direction.

From this initial idea, Glover went on to make sketches of a local currency that he called Ithaca HOURS, which could be used to buy and sell local products and local skills. He went door to door in Ithaca, getting local businesses and individuals on board with the new currency, which was priced in hours of labor. "I started out with people affiliated with the Food Coop, and then I just walked around town asking people to sign on, and about half a dozen businesses. I got a list of about ninety pioneers, issued the first edition of the newspaper, *Ithaca Money*, with a coupon inviting everyone to join in. So within a very short time we had two hundred people trading the money." At the program's height, Ithaca HOURS were accepted for full or partial payments at about five hundred businesses and service providers and by thousands of individuals. The alternative currency was also accepted by the local hospital, the public library, and the transit system. One of the major coups, which occurred early on, was the decision by an alternative credit union in town to accept HOURS for partial and sometimes full payment of bank fees and later as partial payment for home mortgages. One supporter of the HOURS program stressed just how important the credit union was to providing legitimacy for the alternative currency: "They are a good partner of ours. Just the fact that they are a bank, and they will take the local money; that's a big symbolic thing for people. It is like, 'The bank takes them? They must be OK!'"

Ithaca HOURS was never intended, however, as merely an adjunct to traditional national currency, and it was never intended to be fully fungible nationally or globally. Instead, Ithaca HOURS was intended to keep money in the local community. At the same time, Ithaca HOURS was also intended to cause cognitive disequilibrium to those who take currency for granted, to suggest that we think about money in a new and different way. For example, the program asks us to think about the qualitative meaning of money and to move away from seeing it simply as a neutral medium of exchange. Several distinctive features of the local currency highlight the qualitative meanings associated with the currency. Each bill carries a local design that reinforces the image and importance of local community. The words "In Ithaca We Trust" are on the front of each bill, as is the statement, "This note is useful tender for many local needs." These images and text underscore the goal of using this money to support the local community and to maintain wealth locally. The drawing on each bill highlights a particular feature of the Ithaca community (e.g., "Ithaca's children" on the quarter-hour note, a local spotted salamander on the one-eighth-hour note, a "Cayuga Lake Steamboat" on the half-hour note). The back of the bill stresses the idea that the currency is priced in labor hours and encourages its acceptance and circulation: "Time is Money. This note entitles the bearer to receive one hour [or one half hour] labor or its negotiated value. Please accept it and then spend it." There is also a statement that explains and defends the very idea of an alternative currency: "Ithaca HOURS stimulate local businesses by recycling our wealth locally, and they help fund new job creation. Ithaca HOURS are backed by real capital: our skills, our time, our tools, forest, fields, and rivers." Intended as a local currency, Ithaca HOURS travels in a much narrower circuit of exchange than does a national or global currency.[2] If the currency is to achieve the goal of keeping money local, then by definition it must travel this narrower circuit (or else it would simply become a direct substitute for a national currency with nearly complete fungibility and thereby lose its distinctive use in keeping dollars local). Partly owing to this more local circuit, transactors in exchanges using Ithaca HOURS come to know one another better. Reinforcing the social connection between transacting parties is the fact that they tend to talk about the shared experiences of accepting Ithaca HOURS, reinscribing the alternative currency with its intended meaning as a currency that builds a sense of community. Contrast this local circuit with the global circuit that U.S. currency typically travels, as described by Barbara Garson in her book *Money Makes the World Go Round*. Garson deposited half her author's advance in a small local bank and then tracked the movement of those dollars through New York commercial banks to places as far away as Malaysia and Thailand. She found it very difficult to track the movement of her own money in a bank account or a mutual fund, as it moved rapidly into, and out of, emerging markets or new investment opportunities.[3] Glover points out that Ithaca HOURS are backed by something just as tangible, and probably more comprehensible, than a national currency in the era of globalization: "We regard Ithaca's HOURS as real money, backed by real people, real time, real skills and tools. Dollars, by contrast, are funny money, backed no longer by gold or silver but by less than nothing—$4.3 trillion of national debt."[4]

The idea that there is a tension between money having complete fungibility and easy global movement and the idea that money carries important social values is an interesting reflection of the same ideas that Georg Simmel wrestled with in *The Philosophy of Money*:

The greater the role of money becomes in concentrating values—and this occurs not simply through the increase in its quantity, but through an extension of its function to more and more objects and the consolidation of even more diverse values in this [money] form—the less it will need to be tied to a material substance; for the mechanical sameness and rigidity of a substance will become increasingly inadequate compared with the abundance, mutability, and variety of values which are projected upon, and consolidate in, the concept of money.[5]

In other words, if a currency becomes national, or even global, and serves to concentrate all values as everything in a society (including love, interpersonal relationships, and religious beliefs) becomes monetized, then money has a mechanical sameness and cannot become a carrier of any particular value as it may become itself the universal value. Or as Simmel put it, "Since money is not related at all to a specific purpose, it acquires a relation to the totality of purposes," and "money tends toward a point at which, as a pure symbol, it is completely absorbed by its exchange and measuring functions."[6]

The significant efforts that the creators and proponents of a local currency expend to resist this process appears in a new light, not as something inconsequential or trivial but as something essential and perhaps even threatening to global capital. If proponents did not consistently work to inscribe Ithaca HOURS with particular values (whether that be in its aesthetic design, its actual usage in practice, or the way it is represented in conversations), then it could become simply an adjunct to a regular national currency, losing its very purpose. So the design of the currency carries many crucial messages about the money: that it is real, that it is useful, that it pursues local goals, that it reinforces and strengthens community, and that it is backed by the significant assets of the community. There is also a hint of environmentalism in the illustrations chosen for the currency and in statements about "forest, fields and rivers," as well as a bow to the history of the town and region. It is not an overstatement, then, to say that this currency carries a great deal on its shoulders.

One additional meaning that Ithaca HOURS take on is the message that labor is the important commodity being exchanged and that one hour of someone's labor should be equal to an hour of someone else's labor. As Glover puts it in his book *Hometown Money: How to Enrich Your Community with Local Currency,*

> We have been taught to think that teachers should be paid less than bankers, that psychiatrists should be paid more than shoe store clerks, that muscle work is valued less than mental work, that male work is valued more than female work, that black labor is valued less than white labor, that office labor is valued more than home labor. But we all need each other to make Ithaca function. Everyone's honest labor has the same dignity.[7]

Holding to this ideal that all labor is equal, however, has proven difficult, and the program coordinators recognized that in order for HOURS to be accepted, they would have to make the practical choice of allowing people to value some skills more highly than other skills. They treated the ideal of all labor being equal as a goal to strive toward, rather than a hard-and-fast rule that might lead to problems with getting physicians, lawyers, and accountants to trade their labor in a one-to-one hourly fashion with a house painter or a massage therapist. As Glover put it, "More hours of labor are worth one hour but some people may have rare skills and might want 1/5, 2, 3, 4 or 5 hours for their hour of work. Eventually, the Ithaca HOUR list could bring so many skills into the local market that rare skills become less rare, and more affordable."[8] This sentiment reflects one of the reasons, in my judgment, that the HOURS program has lasted as long as it has: the founder, program supporters, and participants were willing to continually assert principles while allowing for practical solutions to the problems that could be created by sticking to principles too rigidly. Rather than giving up on the principle, however, the coordinators continue to assert the principle as a goal. In this way, the currency continues to carry meaning, even if the meaning might be a processual and dialogic one as opposed to a fully actualized one in practice at any moment in time. In many ways, then, the reason that a program such as this generates a great deal of discussion is that it challenges the trend toward a global capitalism that removes all meaning from money, and it makes consumption more thoughtful by slowing down transactions and capital accumulation as it acts as a barrier to the rapid global movement of money.

Supporters of the program whom I spoke with continued to strongly believe in the founding ideal of keeping local dollars in the local community. They practice the use of Ithaca HOURS because doing so both reflects and promotes their values. Three different people who became very involved with the program described it in these ways:

I was familiar with it when I lived [elsewhere] because I had friends here that I kept in touch with, and I started reading about it in alternative journalism, like *Mother Earth News* and places like that. So I'd be talking with my friends like, "Hey, you're starting your own money. What's happening with that?" Even from far away, I was very proud of that. I thought, "OK. That's my home town. If there is not enough money to go around, we'll make our own!"

I knew about it because it was like this legend: Ithaca has its own money! I had an awareness coming in, and then I would see people use it. I worked at the farmers' market, and there were a lot of HOURS transactions that happen at the farmer's market.

Ithaca is one of those places, . . . and I think a lot of places are like this, . . . there are not a lot of jobs, so if you are unable to carve out a [work situation], then you got to change your class or change your city. I think Ithaca HOURS is one of those things where they are into Ithaca enough that at some point it is just a term that you are aware of on some level. . . . You know, "It's fake money used by hippies," something like that. Then I became involved in it. I did accounting work for the [Ithaca HOURS] organization, and then I became really involved in it.

In addition to how labor is valued, the alternative currency program has encountered several other challenges that are also instructive about local money. First, the program had to ensure that the alternative currency kept circulating, so that people would see the usefulness of accepting it. There was the ever-present possibility that people would simply treat it as a novelty or as a business write-off rather than keep it circulating. Another danger for the alternative currency is that it could "clog" at one or two major locations that accepted the money. Glover spent a good deal of his time making sure the currency circulated by suggesting, for example, that some businesses begin by accepting only a portion of payment in Ithaca HOURS. According to Glover, one of the major lessons he learned in the HOURS experience was the need for a full-time community networker who got new people and businesses involved in the program and who worked to ensure the smooth circulation of the money. As he put it,

> Then for the next several years, my prime effort was both to promote the money and then to facilitate the trading, so that it doesn't clog in few hands.... It needs constant attention. The food co-op had been taking it for a significant part of the price of groceries, and I was very concerned about that because it is a very easy way to move the money. If all the money clogs in one place, I was very concerned to keep it moving there.

If money began to clog in one place, Glover would study the problem and then make a recommendation to the particular business that was acting as a "choke point" for the money. He might suggest that a business limit the percentage or amount of Ithaca HOURS it accepted on a single transaction or that the business begin making grants or donations of the money to community groups once its accumulation of HOURS reached a certain threshold (e.g., two hundred HOURS). It might be tempting for critics of alternative currencies to see in the need for a full-time person to unclog the system or to solicit new participants as proof of the limits of an alternative currency. However, one only has to think of the number of people, organizations, and agency involved in keeping a national currency working properly to see that this isn't so different. One could reasonably argue that since the financial meltdown caused by the housing bubble and ensuing credit crisis, a substantial portion of the federal government has been involved in trying to unclog the credit system and to ensure that the national currency moves more smoothly through the economy. Even in more sedate economic times, huge amounts of labor and money are expended monitoring and keeping national currencies operating properly.

Glover and others in the Ithaca HOURS program have found additional key players to participate in the currency, such as Alternatives

Credit Union, the Food Co-op, the local farmers' market, Ben and Jerry's ice cream store, and a grocery store. A plan was even discussed to get local government to accept a portion of taxes (or other government fees) in Ithaca HOURS, although that has not materialized.[9] Another supporter of the program described ways in which he wanted to work for greater acceptance of HOURS among a wider array of vendors, and he also stressed the importance of keeping HOURS circulating within the local economy:

PROPONENT: I saw [one retail vendor] with a drawer of five thousand dollars' worth of HOURS. . . . I see his relationship with Ithaca HOURS as one of charity, which—and I think I said this to the board directly; I know I feel this—that's very risky, to have a major player in the circuit be there for charitable purposes. You have a currency that has its own little economy; people have to be there because of a need, at least on some level.

KD: Yeah, [do you mean] it's not right to resort to hoarding because then you just keep printing more because it's not enough in circulation?

PROPONENT: Right. When I saw that drawer of HOURS, I know I thought it, and I believe that I communicated that to them, that I saw that as something that could potentially ruin the organization, even as thoughtful as it may have been [to accept Ithaca HOURS].

Even alternative currencies must be in circulation to be of use. This is particularly heightened in the case of an alternative currency because it is the very practice of exchanging it that creates the conversations necessary to forge the social relationships and the discussions about community and social good that the proponents desire. Most proponents wish to challenge the complete fungibility and "meaninglessness" of money:

When you use it, you begin to establish relationships with people, for instance, the people that painted this house. They take HOURS. Then I know them, and they know me. And if I need a carpenter or this or that. And you begin to get this circle of people, and it started with Ithaca HOURS. And it continues to use Ithaca HOURS, but it becomes an established face-to-face relationship, which is possible in a smaller community anyway. But I think the use of a specific piece of paper, though a symbolic thing, sort of nails it down, gives it a kind of shape, something tangible.

Problems of Translation

The Ithaca HOURS program continues to operate almost two decades after its founding and has spawned as many as one hundred other alternative currency programs in places around the world. As I have suggested, one of the more interesting feature of alternative currency programs such as Ithaca HOURS is the way in which money is intentionally used to carry various meanings. However, it is also true that these multiple meanings can sometimes come into conflict. Unlike regular currency, which touts its complete fungibility and interchangeability (or, one might say, its attempt to ignore meaning), alternative currency is intended to do something quite different—to carry meaning, to initiate political and social discussions, and to challenge the status quo and taken-for-granted assumptions about the economy and about the role of money in the economy.[10] Not all supporters of the currency, however, stress precisely the same meaning for the money; some might favor localism, others environmentalism, and still others community building.[11] While I was in Ithaca participating in the program, there was a supporter who wanted to approach a local retailer about accepting Ithaca HOURS. This person knew that to convince this particular business owner to begin accepting Ithaca HOURS, the best approach would be to highlight the competitive advantage that accepting the currency might provide to him against some of the "big box" chain stores that had recently moved onto the edge of town. Another supporter, however, argued against approaching this store to participate because it sold chemical pesticides for gardening and farming. Here we see the clash of meaning that can occur when a currency is not portrayed as fungible and soulless. Supporters of the HOURS program have goals and passions attached to them. Most are not supporting the program simply to create a substitute for money. In this case, one board member was stressing the goal of supporting a local retailer over a chain store and expanding the number of retailers that accept Ithaca HOURS, while the other board member was stressing the goal of supporting ecologically friendly uses of the currency.

While it is tempting to conclude, then, that this sort of a conflict is proof of the inherent problem with an alternative currency, it is probably more accurate to say this is evidence of exactly the point of having an alternative currency: to stimulate conversations about competing social goals. The presence of conflict over goals, then, is not necessarily evidence of a problem with Ithaca HOURS, though it may be evidence of a particular problem created by a currency laden with meaning. The presence of conflict over goals actually illustrates the difference between a soulless currency and one that is used to pursue particular meanings. Put another way, the *absence* of conflict over the uses of money could equally be seen as evidence of a problem with an alternative currency.

Similarly, critics of alternative currencies often complain that the money is not as fungible and interchangeable as a national currency is and cite this as a major problem with alternative currencies. However, I think critics miss the point here. An alternative currency is not meant to be a fully interchangeable currency. Rather, it is *supposed* to slow money down, as the motivating idea behind many alternative currencies is to generate conversations about meaning and values. As Garson demonstrated in *Money Makes the World Go Round*, financial traders around the world seek to benefit from the increasingly rapid movement of money around the global system, as these powerful players are often taking a piece of the action each time a transaction occurs. Global electronic currency can move rapidly into emerging markets as well as into various speculative bubbles being created in the global economy. Then, money rushes back out if a new market is found or a bubble is about to burst. Global traders usually resist anything that will slow the movement of currency—in part because they argue that any effort at slowing currency's movement is a barrier to the working of markets but, more pointedly, because they are likely profiting from each and every exchange.

A few years ago, the Ithaca HOURS program issued a one-tenth-hour note, and the discussion and controversy over this seemingly small decision are also instructive. Recall that Ithaca's currency is priced in hours of labor. So it made sense to have a one-hour note, a half-hour note, and a quarter-hour note (i.e., notes denominated in typical units of time). As a result of being conceived in terms of labor time, Ithaca HOURS are not a denary system like most national currencies.[12] However, Ithaca HOURS might be used as an adjunct currency rather than a replacement currency. By that, I mean that Ithaca HOURS typically operate alongside, and sometimes in conjunction with, U.S. dollars and not as a complete substitute for them. Therefore, in actual practice at the point of exchange, merchants are often accepting partial payment in HOURS and partial payment in U.S. dollars, and they may also give change in either Ithaca HOURS (if they have some) or U.S. currency.

Supporters of Ithaca HOURS have always discussed these sort of issues at length (because again most believe that the point of the HOURS program is to stimulate discussion about currency), debating their principles versus the practical aspects of the system. They are often willing to bend principle just enough to make the system work better in practice—as long as the thoughtful conversation continues and the system stays alive.[13]

What Does It Cost? Or What Is It Worth?

In addition to interesting experiments with creating alternative currencies such as the Ithaca HOURS program, there are also people who have experimented with alternative pricing schemes. Take, for example, the system of "pay your own price." In these systems, rather than setting a price for, say, a meal, restaurants ask customers to pay whatever they think the meal is worth. I interviewed a proprietor of one of these restaurants located in the western United States.[14] She explained to me how she had come upon the idea of not charging a set price for a meal:

About two months had gone by [since I opened]—and I am really working like 24/7, and it is really difficult. But some big energy comes over me. Like the front door had opened, and this breeze of energy gets my attention, and I have this phenomenon. . . . Except it is like, "Go to donations. Let people price their own food." It was this sort of communication. I don't know how to explain it to you. I didn't hear it, but I got it. Like something pitched me a ball of communication. And I am like, "Oh, God, I am screwed. I am screwed. This is crazy. I am out there, but this is *too* out there. But I remember my promise [to listen to such communication]. To my own credit, the next person who walked in the door, I did it. No more pricing.

Note that the explanation of an alternative pricing system ("name your own price") is not described, or defended, in terms of being "good business" (which it could, in fact, be) but rather is described as something more akin to a mystical revelation. It often seems that when a financial practice is outside the accepted status quo, it is nested within a wider set of alternative practices, ideologies, or paradigms. In the case of this particular restaurant, the larger ideological apparatus revolves around a call to feed the hungry and to end world hunger, a call for establishing a greater sense of community and a set of more egalitarian labor practices, as we can see in this description from the founder:

KD: When someone comes into your restaurant, how do you explain your policy to them?

OWNER: We say, "Hi, welcome to [restaurant name]. We are a regular business, but we are different. We serve all organic food, and we dedicate ourselves to eliminating waste in the food industry and also world hunger. So the soups are self-serve, in whatever portion you like, and the drinks are also self-serve. After you are done eating, we just ask you—we just ask that you put a fair price on the amount of food that you ate.... So make yourself at home." And most people get it. And what is really interesting is that we get a lot of regulars.

Similar to the Ithaca HOURS program, this unusual pricing mechanism is seen as a way to start conversations and build community, in a way that might not be of particular importance at other restaurants. "This has been a real community builder. You wouldn't believe it. A lot of people take ownership of this place because they want to see it succeed, so a lot of people, if they know someone is new here, will say, 'Oh, let me show you around, and I will show you how it is done.' So we don't even have to do that." This doesn't mean, however, that the restaurant is completely freed from the economic realities that other businesses face. For example, the restaurant provides suggestions for how much to pay for a meal, and it also combats the possibility that someone could take advantage of the system of payment by simply paying nothing and always eating there for free, as the following exchange indicates:

OWNER: We just ask that you put a fair price on the amount you ate. . . . And there is a little gauge there, [if] you are interested in a range. And if you don't have enough money, we offer a voucher for every hour you volunteer, and then you can use that or pass it on. . . . This is called our "hand up" policy. If someone has no money to eat the amount of food they want, for every hour they volunteer, they get a voucher for a full meal.

KD: Do you get a lot of homeless or poor people, and is that a problem?

OWNER: It is not. You know, a lot of people ask me that, and originally that was a concern of mine. What I call the chronically homeless are not really interested in my "hand up" program; whether it is just a habit or not, they'd rather go a few steps up from here and get a free bologna sandwich from the Good Samaritan program.

The owner makes clear, then, that it is not a "free food" policy but a policy of "paying a fair price." She nests this belief within her own goal of paying decent wages to her employees as well as giving people who have little or no money the opportunity to perform labor in exchange for the food voucher. She used the phrase "hand up, not hand out" in describing this policy to me.

OWNER: This is all an honor system. But most people, given the chance, are very honorable.

KD: Do you think some people put more in the box than what might be the suggested or typical price?

OWNER: I think so. Somebody who is inspired by this. And I think the two spectrums then kind of average themselves out. I get a head count, and the average pay per meal is between eight and ten dollars.

Interestingly, a few years after my initial interview, this restaurant adjusted its pricing policy, asking people first to name their price to servers, and then their portion would be prepared to align with the price. This was done to avoid people taking very large portions and paying little or nothing for them. Here we see that alternatives to traditional pricing can present significant economic issues with which a business must grapple. Apparently, underpayment or nonpayment was enough of a concern to merit this change in policy. The new policy will bring some social pressure to bear on the individual to name a price publicly as opposed to slipping money into a payment box, which allowed some to drastically underpay for the portions they took, without any public disclosure of the fact. The restaurant owner, however, is still a major proponent of flexible pricing schemes and has helped many other entrepreneurs in other cities set up similar types of restaurants.

The national chain of cafes and bakeries Panera Bread has begun opening a few of its locations using a similar "name your price" system. One of the first locations to open using this system is in the St. Louis suburbs, and managers report that the system has worked well. The company also prints a "suggested price" on its menu and reports that about 70 percent of the customers pay that price, about 15 percent pay less than that (or nothing at all), and 15 percent pay more than the suggested price. Occasionally, people leave significantly more as a donation, which suggests that they are inspired by the model of sharing.[15]

I encountered another interesting experiment with money that one could also call an alternative pricing scheme but would probably be more accurately termed a "no pricing" scheme. An artist opened a facility called The Free Store in Williamsburg, Brooklyn, which has no prices, as everything in the store is free. People are encouraged to bring things to the shop and leave them for others to take. Customers (if that is even the right word to use) are welcome simply to take what they wish. When I visited the store, I could find no one working there, as it appeared empty. I spent several hours at The Free Store, and interestingly, when people came in, they would often ask me questions, assuming that I worked there. So, for example, one man came in and walked right up to me and said, "Do you have any *National Geographic* magazines?" Without really thinking, I replied, "Well, there are a lot of magazines over here" (by then I knew where the magazines were stacked), and I proceeded to help the man search through boxes and stacks of magazines. We did not find any *National Geographic* magazines, but he did leave with some other magazines that he found of interest. I believe he continued to think that I worked there during this entire experience, which lasted maybe fifteen

minutes. My overall feeling while at The Free Store was one of disorienta-
tion, which I think may have been the artist's point. The Free Store raises
some fundamental questions: Can something be a "store" if nothing is
being sold? Am I a customer or a clerk, or am I a part of an art installation? The very absence of clerks seems to encourage people (like me)
to help one another in a way they might not in a typical store. I seemed
unable to say, "I don't work here" (which I would have typically done in a
retail store if the same situation had occurred), because that implies that
someone else who is being paid to help customers does work there and
that it is that person's job to assist the customer. So it seemed that I *should*
help the person find the magazines for which he was looking.

It was also obvious that the space occupied by The Free Store had
come to serve as a place to communicate activities among neighborhood
groups. There was a bulletin board with lots of flyers for local community
groups, mostly of the political or musical variety. Most of the goods in
The Free Store were similar to those you might find in a thrift shop—lots
of used clothing, old children's toys, plenty of used books and magazines,
records and CDs, and some things for the kitchen (used utensils, for
example). The place was in more disarray than most thrift shops I have
visited, presumably because there was no one there to tidy up the place.

I think The Free Store is intended to make us think about commodities, consumerism, value, and price as well as the meaning of art and
its relationship to the economy. For example, the very existence of The
Free Store makes the point that many people have excess items they do
not need and are willing simply to give them to others at no cost and
that commodities can change hands without an intermediary currency
of any sort (not even bartering is necessary there). Just outside The
Free Store, I saw several plastic garbage pails that seemed to belong to
the store. Interestingly, these were chained to parking meters and poles.
Could it be that the most valuable thing at The Free Store—or at least
the thing that no one wanted stolen—was the garbage pails? One or
two were overflowing with old clothes that seemed similar in quality
to the clothes in the store. I wondered, then, what the distinction was
between the clothes in the garbage pails and the clothes in the store.
The Free Store makes us think about value in a different way because
you have to judge value completely divorced from price, as there simply

are no prices. Even in a Salvation Army thrift store or at a tag sale, one is judging whether a shirt is worth, say, one dollar or not. But at The Free Store, you are judging whether a shirt is useful to you or not, since it is free. The calculus seems to become this: "Is this worth something to me or nothing to me?" But then, one finds oneself also thinking, "This might be worth more to someone else than to me, so maybe I should not take it." Unlike when I shop at a typical retail store, I found myself considering the needs of others against my own. Later, when I visited a coffee shop just down the block, I wondered why nothing there was free. The Free Store certainly served its purpose if its goal was to make one ask questions about taken-for-granted assumptions.[16]

Experimenting with Salaries

In addition to experiments with currency and with prices, some organizations have tried new ways to set wages and salaries. I encountered one very interesting organization that was attempting to mitigate the effects of internal wage inequalities, as well as trying to send a larger message about the "soulfulness" of their corporation.[17] This fairly large nonprofit human-services organization had about $125 million in revenues and three thousand full- and part-time employees, and it engaged in a number of innovative workplace practices that reflected the philosophy of the organization's founder. He described it to me this way: "What we are doing is combining monetized thinking with social theory, and we are very much involved in the study, if you will, of human behavior, when you shift the way that a number of things are handled, not unimportantly money."

One of these shifts in thinking is the 1% Club that the organization started. All employees are invited to join the club, which amounts to a salary-sharing club. It is completely voluntary, but if you sign up, you contribute 1 percent of your own salary into a pool of money, which is then equally distributed back to all club members. It is a relatively simple device for shifting money from the higher-paid employees to the lower-paid employees. At the time of my visit, the club had been running for about four years and had forty members. At that time, anyone earning $40,000 and below in salary was a "net receiver" of proceeds from the club, while anyone earning over $40,000 was a "net giver." One executive I interviewed, for example, earning approximately $190,000, would contribute $1,900 to the club each year and, indeed, receive something on the order of $500 back as payout. Therefore, approximately $1,400 of his annual salary was being redistributed to employees making under $40,000. For some of the very lowest paid workers in the organization, the redistribution in a given year could represent as much as a 3 percent increase in their own salary. This obviously is not a tremendous change in economic conditions, but it is certainly enough to make a noticeable difference to a lower-paid employee trying to pay bills or shop for holiday gifts. The club could suffer from the problem of having many lower-paid workers signing up, as they would get payouts, and few higher-paid workers signing up, as they would suffer a net economic loss. However, the opposite had occurred, as the trend was for an increasing number of higher-paid workers to sign up, and thus the redistributed amount was gradually increasing. Thus, the culture of the organization and the value obtained by those who were sharing with others seemed to be trumping the pure economic calculation of monetary gain or loss. Like other people I interviewed who were testing the limits of money, the chief executive of this nonprofit said he believes that it is just as important to shift the way people think as it is to redistribute dollars:

> Let me emphasize that I am very interested in small community building as part of a larger corporation. In this case, it is the creation of a community. . . . Whether we are talking about space, bonuses, vacation time, we have a group of people, and when we meet and pull together, we talk about the separation of the haves and the have-nots. . . . Whether it is this 1% Club, or talking about health-care issues, it is an attitude of a community toward saying, "If there is inequality"—and there is gross inequality in our society—"what can we at least do within this community?"

This same organization also limits the compensation of the highest paid employee to no more than fourteen times the pay of the lowest paid employee. This ensures a flattening of the pay hierarchy compared to other organizations of the same size and revenues, even in the nonprofit sector. I asked the chief executive if it was difficult to find executive talent with this limit, and he replied,

> It is difficult, but it has convinced me. It is not true that everyone is focused on money. Most of the good people we get in this business are in it for more than the money; otherwise we would never find the caliber of people we find at the salaries we are willing to pay. It is a challenge, . . . but the thing we are probably giving up is the individual stardom . . . , that culture; that is what they are really giving up.

Another person I interviewed had a very interesting view of his own salary—considering how low a salary he was willing to accept for his work. He had previously worked as a commission salesperson and was a top performer with a good salary, much like those I described in chapter 3. However, he experienced a significant change in his outlook toward money due to his own deepening religious faith. As he began to explore his own religious beliefs and the relationship to money, he found himself less and less interested in commission sales. It seemed that his consciousness around the role of money was undergoing a substantial shift. As he put it, "What was happening over time was that I was transitioning in my own money story and its relationship to my faith story. So the ability for them to motivate me by dangling money as the primary motivating tool, which is the primary motivating tool of commission sales, was losing its impact on me." He eventually left his sales job and began working for an organization that would lead retreats to help others look at the relationship between money and faith in their own lives. As part of this work, he would lead what the organization called "reverse mission trips" mainly to South and Central America and Africa. He described the thinking behind the term "reverse mission":

> That is the way we describe our trips: . . . a typical mission trip is to go somewhere for a short period of time and usually engage in a project—to build an orphanage, to paint schools, whatever—we flip the model around, and that is why we also call them "trips of perspective." We don't go to engage in a project. . . . If you go and work on a mission trip, you can get lost in the mission and never really experience what's going on where you are

and not really be transformed personally. You can come back feeling good because you did the project, but are you transformed?

Throughout my conversation with this person, he used the word "flipping" or the phrase "flipping on its head" several times to describe the "rules" and "framework" he was now following in his life. So, for example, he said he was "flipping the culture on its head" to indicate that he was moving directly opposite from the consumerist trends in the current culture. The use of this phrase indicates just how different he feels he is from some of the cultural currents swirling around him. He also used the word "journey" to describe his own changing consciousness. This word seemed to have a connotation of a spiritual or religious journey. He described the impact of reverse mission trips on his own thinking, sharing a story about when he was involved in some prison work in Uganda:

> One of my most memorable conversations there was when . . . I was talking with one of the prisoners through a translator—and you never know what is real and what is not—but he told me some of his story. And his story was that his children were hungry, and he stole a radio and got caught. So he got sentenced to six months because he couldn't pay the fine. The fine was the equivalent of seventeen U.S. dollars, and I had way more than that in my pocket. But what am I going to do, start bailing out everyone in the prison? You know, I could go to court and pay his fine and get him out instead of having to serve six months for the theft of a radio to feed your hungry children. So, really, it created a huge internal struggle for me to be told that story. There were all kinds of struggles coming out of that first trip there, but that was a particular one that sticks with me to this day.

The significant change that was happening here, however, was also the change in the way he was thinking about money and how his own life in the United States compares to others' lives in the places he has visited. As he put it, "Each time I come back [from a reverse mission trip], they are life changing, and it gets harder and harder to just settle in to the comfort that has been built around me. Because while I am on this journey, I still live, you know, a middle, comfortable lifestyle with a lot of security. And I really struggle with that. I am in the middle of struggles with that."

Each time this person took a new job accompanying what he describes as his "faith journey," he would experience a significant drop in income. But rather than talk about this decline in income as a problem, he instead described it as an opportunity—a good example of flipping an economic paradigm on its head.

Money Lessons

What is interesting about the experiments with money described in this chapter is that they have a number of things in common that provide interesting insights into the malleability of money and the reasons why people desire to experiment with money. These experiments often attempt to use money as part of a larger desire to change people's thinking or to alter their basic perceptions about currency. They do this by making clear that money is a carrier of values beyond being a mechanism for exchange. So, for example, in the case of alternative currencies, the alternative currency is different from dollars in that it is consciously designed and used to represent the collective interests of the community. Moreover, it is said to help keep the currency in the community, limiting the flight of global capital, which can move anywhere. Because it is priced in hours of labor, Ithaca HOURS also assert the notion that labor and units of labor are really what are being exchanged. With the 1% Club and similar salary experiments, organizations are sending a message that they wish to fight rising inequality in salary and are indirectly implying that tremendous inequality in wages within an organization is wrong and should be mitigated.

Notice that the systems and practices that these alternatives are upsetting, however, also have impacts or carry their own implicit values, even if they are unacknowledged or are treated as inevitable. For example, giving all workers within an organization a 3 percent raise serves to increase wage inequality because those at the high end of the pay scale get significantly more money than do those at the lower end through an across-the-board raise. Across-the-board raises compound inequality over time, as the next 3 percent raise only makes the disparity grow ever larger. So the system currently in place at many organizations already has an impact, in that it increases internal wage inequality. Treating dollars as simple placeholders or mechanisms of exchange serves to avoid conversations about whether treating dollars as neutral actually favors some people at the expense of others. The Free Store, for example, points to the fact that consumer purchasing is not the only way that people can obtain goods and that money may not be needed for some forms of exchange.

Each of these alternative practices is meant to disequilibrate, to lead to more questioning and new insights, or to flip things on their head. It is also true, however, that each experiment illustrates the limitations and barriers confronted by these experiments and underscores the enduring power of money as a fungible means of universal exchange. Alternative currency systems run into problems of keeping their money in circulation, as people are tempted to treat an alternative currency as a novelty item or simply an adjunct to "regular" money. Alternative currency has to continually gain legitimacy, as some people mistrust it or fail to accept it. But perhaps most importantly, proponents of alternative currencies can have differing beliefs about the main goal of the currency, and this can inhibit its spread and limit use to a smaller set of activists and believers. While you can trust most people to pay a fair price for a meal at a restaurant without fixed prices, and you can even count on some people to pay in excess of a fair price because they believe strongly in the alternative model, you continue to run the risk that some people will take advantage of the model and underpay. This presents a potential crisis, as the business has to make ends meet financially.

I think it also must be said that there are some people who simply prefer not to have conversations about the meaning of money. They wish to enter an establishment, make a purchase, and leave without creating any kind of connection with the people from whom they are buying something. This sort of person might find a discussion of price at a "name your price" establishment unwelcome or unsettling and not return again. One of the major characteristics of a national currency is its universal acceptability (except perhaps in times of financial crises) and the way it tends to generate anonymity for those who prefer it.

An additional hurdle for many of these experiments with money is extending them beyond the small handful of people who find them immediately appealing. In Ithaca, for example, a constant tension exists over trying to extend the use of HOURS beyond a group of well-educated professionals and free thinkers. Poorer residents are sometimes reluctant to participate, or are simply financially shut out from participating, because the lower-priced grocery chains and Wal-Mart–style box stores do not accept Ithaca HOURS. So, for a family struggling to make ends meet, they may choose to buy the one-dollar loaf of white bread with U.S. currency in a chain store that does not accept alternative currency rather than the artisanal seven-grain bread for four dollars at a food co-op that accepts Ithaca HOURS. For the "pay what you want" restaurant, healthy meals may still seem more expensive than the dollar-menu items at the fast-food restaurant. This problem reflects in microcosm the larger dilemmas in a global economy. The very largest players can often realize economies of scale that allow them to sell goods at the absolute cheapest prices. People in society with the lowest incomes are often able to afford only such goods (and often express gratitude for these stores because of their low prices). It is much harder to attract these people to a program like Ithaca HOURS, which stresses paying employees a living wage, caring for the environment, keeping money local, buying local goods, and presenting higher-quality craft items (rather than very cheap imports). Put another way, when money carries important meanings of value and community, it adds a cost that in the long run could be better for individuals and communities but in the short run may feel out of reach for those who are most vulnerable in the economy.

None of these obstacles means that these alternatives are not useful or that they do not achieve some of their goals. Rather, they mean that those who believe in the importance of alternatives have to continually work to explain and advocate for the advantages of their alternative, as they do not have the force of law or the support of powerful national or global institutions. It may be that the most important contribution of these alternatives is to point out that there are other ways of doing business and to ask people to confront taken-for-granted assumptions about the way things supposedly have to be.

Enacting Money

Many of the people in this chapter stressed the idea of trying to create a sense of community through their experiments with money. Like clergy, they seem dissatisfied with the model of amorphous transactors meeting in the marketplace to exchange goods. Some also challenge the "scarcity model" that seems to accompany transactions and stress that there is enough for everyone on earth. These people desire something more from money. Rather than pursuing religious goals, they want money to reflect and even to facilitate shared communal bonds. In some ways, I have come to see these experiments as a reaction to the loss of connection that many people feel as a result of individualism, consumerism, the growth of anonymous chain stores, and the feelings of disconnection they are left with after market transactions. As one board member of Ithaca HOURS put it,

> It's like our entire political economy, entire money economy, all of it is built on this idea that we are separate, we are against each other, we are fighting against each other, . . . squabbling for a limited amount of resources, 'cause we gotta get and have as much as we can. But it doesn't work. We are all still very insecure and very scared, and all it would take to change that is to acknowledge that we are part of something larger than ourselves and that we are all in this together.

While I found that every group in this book talks about money in distinctive ways, for this particular group of people—those who challenge unspoken assumptions about money—the actual *talking* seemed particularly crucial. In order to achieve their goal of altering the taken-for-granted view of money, they need to speak with others. In one sense, this talking is simply a necessity, as they must, for example, explain to someone who walks into a "pay what you want" restaurant exactly how the process works, or to take another example, they need to explain to people how and where they can use an alternative currency. But in a larger sense, these individuals also need to talk because they are engaged in a form of performance politics. They are performing alternative ways of conceiving of money and using money, so the performance is as important as anything else. They wish to communicate to new adherents a new way of thinking about money as they seek to change perceptions. Publicity is also important, as they desire to spread their message so that others might try their way, and they wish to attract kindred spirits to come to their places of business because they see those businesses as places of community. So for a restaurant owner adopting a "pay your own price" model, an economic calculation can only be made wrapped within a social calculation: Will enough people pay a bit more for a meal to make up for those who pay little or nothing, *and* will the publicity of something new and different attract additional customers who find this appealing to outweigh any potential customers who might be turned off by such a system? An owner hopes that people who find this system more egalitarian and like it for that reason will come to the restaurant and be generous in how they decide to pay for a meal. It seems, however, that people do have some discomfort in not knowing the price, as they often ask for a "suggested price," and many of the "pay what you want" places end up suggesting a fair price. So these experiments teach us about both the ways in which money can be stretched to carry new meaning and the obstacles faced when challenging the hegemonic view of money as fungible and interchangeable and prices as set and nonnegotiable. Through these experiments, then, we learn about both the malleability and the resiliency of currency. We can also see that engaging in these experiments affects the participants in significant ways. Almost like a social movement, experiments in currency need new adherents as well as consciousness-raising efforts that occur through *conversations* about money and the *performance* of new ways of conceiving of and using money.

8

Money Cultures at Work and Beyond

While conducting research for this book, I watched people working to dissociate the value of money from very large trades on Wall Street or from a pile of poker chips on a table in Las Vegas. I witnessed people struggling to figure out whether they were spending their time wisely or whether they could stay on an even keel with their sense of self on the line in the sale of a product. I saw others using mental gymnastics to turn their raw emotions in the face of poverty into an appreciation for what they had in their own lives. I marveled at clergy who straddled the worlds of the sacred and the profane as they handled money at work. I came to understand how the tools available to do one's job could shape the cognition of debt as rooted in psychological dysfunction. I saw the significant investment of time spent by people who wished to inscribe specific meanings onto money, whether that meaning was religious, spiritual, communal, or secular in nature. In all these instances, I came to see how these varied conceptions of money were rooted in the quotidian practices of someone's work and how distinct money cultures developed out of the type of work that people do. But I also found myself wondering how these money cultures affected a person outside of work. When people develop a certain way of thinking about money in their work, this is bound to influence their identity outside of work as well. Although my research was not designed to study life outside of work, some very intriguing pieces of evidence suggest that there is a significant impact on people in their home lives.

Developing a Certain Quality of Mind

How money is used at work shapes how an individual conceives of money. We have seen that pokers players and hedge fund traders, in order to do their jobs well, learn to balance fear and greed, risk and reward, courage and caution. Poker players and hedge fund traders try to establish the right balance between being excessively risky and excessively timid, and they must do this within an environment of significant and constantly changing uncertainty. One common cognitive dilemma that arose for poker players and hedge fund traders was trying to understand and recognize when one was becoming excessively risky or excessively cautious. This core dilemma got handled in a variety of ways, and those practices became embedded and reflected in the money culture of this type of work.

The telling of stories—both the tales of bravado and the cautionary tales—provides the essential socialization for newcomers into the characteristics needed to do their work well, as well as providing relief valves for the pressure felt by those trying to work out the balance between risk and caution in daily experiences of high-stakes contests with much to be won or lost. In other words, the gasconade common among people in these occupations is rooted in the money culture of poker playing and hedge fund trading that flourishes because of the structural location and cognitive and emotional requirements of the job.[1] In this sense, seeing greed as individual characteristic and psychological attribute misses the fact that the behaviors and attitudes that outsiders perceive as greed are structured responses to a specific location in the money economy, as they are rooted in a particular stylized money culture.[2] Also, owing to the structural features of the work done by poker players and hedge fund traders, large amounts of money pass through their hands on a routine basis. This structural feature of both these jobs presents another cognitive dilemma that calls for cognitive work and emotion work: "How do I manage my emotions when dealing with huge amounts of money and the potential of large gains or large losses while still being prepared to make a large bet when the odds are in my favor?" By dissociating the money you use in your work from the purchasing power of money in the larger world outside of work, money becomes a way of keeping score.

However, this cognitive and emotional practice of dissociation bleeds across from work life to home life. In other words, when people spend many hours per week at work developing a certain quality of mind around money, they do not simply turn off that conception of money once they leave work. Even one of the small-stakes poker players I interviewed had already begun to change his views on money after having played for only about a year:

KD: We have talked about how you think about money differently now. When someone talks to you about a $15-an-hour job, it doesn't seem so great now?

ONLINE POKER PLAYER: Yeah, it seems like nothing. That is kind of the one thing; you become kind of disillusioned with it. I remember seeing some on line pros talking about it. One of them paid a $2,000 water bill that was supposed to be $50. He didn't know. He had no clue. The money was in his pocket, the money meant nothing. You win and lose so much on different days that the money becomes like nothing. Like some of the biggest players in the world that play in the biggest games, some of them win a million dollars one day and lose it back the next day.

Another midlevel player I interviewed talked about money in this way: "Well, you, . . . you become kind of detached from the whole thing. Yeah, . . . you stop thinking about money in terms of, 'Well, this was a car payment, or that was a house payment.' It's more like, you know, 'I won a rack here; I lost a rack there.' You know?"[3]

For poker players and hedge fund traders, the cognitive stance that facilitates the emotion work necessary to do their jobs well leads them to ignore money as the universal value that can be used to purchase anything, by saying repeatedly (to themselves and to others) that money is "just our way of keeping score." As one poker player put it to me, "You can't think of what that money can buy you, because it could buy you a lot. So you can't think of it in those terms, [or] you would not be able to take risks and do what you need to be a winning player." This helps us better understand the braggadocio that happens among traders and poker players: talking cavalierly about large sums of money serves a very different function for poker players and hedge fund traders than it might for other people, in that it normalizes the large sums of money at risk, thereby reducing fear. So what sounds crass to the average person's ear sounds quite different to the poker player or hedge fund trader.

Hedge fund traders also discipline their emotions by building checks into organizational rules and risk models, and poker players perform a similar trick when they separate their money into a bankroll and will only risk the bankroll. Segregating a bankroll is, in essence, a way of capping risk, as it installs what market regulators might call a "circuit breaker" allowing poker players who have exhausted a bankroll to pause and reassess their situation. This gives them time to take stock of whether they might be having an emotional meltdown causing them to play poorly or whether they are simply having a bad run of odds that will statistically occur every once in a while.

All these techniques help to conceive of money in distinct ways, but as we have seen, none of these fully resolves the dilemmas at hand. Rather, they momentarily manage the pressure. There are still plenty of opportunities to hesitate, flinch, back off, make foolhardy trades or bets, or unknowingly give off a "tell" that tips off your opponent to your trading position or poker hand. This keeps hedge fund traders and poker players highly engaged in their work. As information constantly changes, finding the right balance between risk and caution is never a completed process. This process can be exhausting because cognitive and emotional work is constantly required to find the balance, and this may be a reason why poker players and hedge fund traders so often talk about how long they can keep going. The money culture found among hedge fund traders and poker players can appear quite alien to the outsider, but after understanding the role of money in their jobs, along with the cognitive and emotional work that is done on money and on the self, the characteristics of the culture become more comprehensible.

The recent trend in research on how identity is formed is to recognize that there is multidimensionality in any individual's social identity, "challenging notions of identity singularity and coherence."[4] In a complex postindustrial economy, it has become less clear how—and to what extent—consciousness is formed at the point of production.[5] We have seen that there are some particular types of consciousness that are formed around the relationships of money and finance inherent in various types of work. For example, the hedge fund trader who speculated that $10 million "wasn't enough" had clearly developed a certain consciousness in relation to money from his immersion in the culture of hedge fund trading. Professional poker players who learn to dissociate poker chips from their monetary value develop a particular quality of mind necessary to do the job well. But, at the same time, poker players develop a particular consciousness toward money more generally. When you experience $100,000 in losses one evening and $100,000 in wins the next, you are neither ahead nor behind, but you are certainly changed. You have had $200,000 pass through your hands in just forty-eight hours, and when this experience comes to feel routine for a professional poker player, it makes giving the pizza delivery person a $100 tip seem quite unremarkable. That is because for a professional poker player, money becomes simultaneously crucial and largely beside the point.

When I began scheduling interviews with poker players, I quickly noticed that they kept very different hours from most people. One player wrote in an email response to my request for an interview that 3 a.m. was the best time to schedule an interview with him, as he was always up at that hour; another player asked me to interview her at 6 p.m., "before I start work." Poker players are often around a great deal of cash, and this seems to have a significant effect on their attitude toward money. Several told me about generously tipping service workers, and they linked this practice to the amount of cash they often have on hand and to the amount of money that flows through their hands on a nightly or weekly basis. They also work in a tipping culture, where it is routine to tip dealers, waiters, and waitresses. Being around so much cash makes giving a $100 bill as a tip seem normal. A few of the poker players I talked with said they kept significant amounts of cash and chips in safety deposit boxes at their favorite casino but also carried around a lot of cash. One showed me a safe he kept in his home to store cash. When I asked another poker player how much money he carried around on a typical day, he replied nonchalantly, "Maybe about $500 in cash." Another player pulled out his money clip and said, "I think I have $1,700 here. In case I want to get into a game, I have it." Poker players also talked about weighing odds all the time in their lives outside of work—it seemed almost like practicing ways to figure out odds on things but also a habit of the mind to think of things in terms of odds. In a similar way, several of the debt counselors told me that they had replaced their credit cards with debit cards because this is something they had recommended to clients to prevent the amassing of credit card debts. In all these instances, money lessons from work translate into money habits in life.

A more subtle example of the way a money culture at work shapes an individual outside of work was provided by a hedge fund trader. In talking about his work, he spoke at length about balancing risk and reward and about the need to try to make rational decisions in the face of uncertainty and incomplete information (he was not a strict quant). When I asked him later about buying his lunch, we had the following exchange:

KD: When you are outside of work, are you the type to worry about something being overpriced, like a sandwich is $7, and you think it should be $5?

HEDGE FUND TRADER: I am conscious of price. As a trader, I know how much I pay—from a sandwich to a car, I know the price. Pricing makes a difference to me. But the convenience premium, I will usually pay it. So that is the way I think about it. Usually I am standing there and thinking, "You are charging me too much, but I don't care, because it is convenient." So I am willing to pay the price, so I am saying, "Are they really charging too much if I am willing to pay it? I could just walk away."

His use of the term "convenience premium" here is an interesting one. He appears to be using the same system of logic and rational decision-making in picking up his lunch as he might use in making a trade. He thinks about price and is very aware of price. Yet he also weighs that up against the convenience premium of getting the sandwich quickly and nearby as opposed to walking further for a cheaper sandwich (or making one at home). Presumably, he considers the opportunity cost of doing so as greater for him, so he is willing to pay the higher price, as he even asks himself, "Are they really charging me too much if I am willing to pay for it?" apparently putting his full trust in the power of market forces. While many people would complain that they are being charged too much for a mediocre sandwich, the hedge fund trader has learned to think, "Well, I purchased it, didn't I? Then it must be fairly priced once you account for the convenience premium."

Hedge fund traders learn to believe in the market because they must do so to do their work. They talk frequently about "mispricings" in the market because they believe that there must be an accurate price, and if they have an informational edge, they can make money from that mispricing. Notice that the hedge fund trader, while contemplating the purchase of a sandwich, also used the phrase "walk away," which is also something I heard traders use when describing a decision on a large trade, as in, "Do I pull the trigger, or do I just walk away?" It is this quality of mind applied here to a sandwich purchase that appears completely natural and unremarkable for someone who spends his work hours in trading and has learned to think about price, trade-offs, and markets. Buying your lunch is perceived in terms similar to making a trade: "Do I pull the trigger, or do I just walk away?"

Of course, it gets more complicated than this. Poker players and hedge fund traders must also be cautious about using the money they may make from a successful trade or a winning bet as the sole or prime motivation for their work, lest it get in the way of rational decision-making. They must constantly think that if they have the slightest edge (for the poker player that might mean being a better player, and for the hedge fund trader it might mean having more information), they will win over the long run, even if they lose sometimes along the way. Someone who makes a living flipping hamburgers at a fast-food restaurant or driving a taxicab can get through another grueling hour of work by focusing on the value that the extra hour of work will give to his or her family. But if poker player or hedge fund traders focus too much on what a win or a trade can buy for their family, they are likely to lose, as it will distract them from the discipline of weighing the odds correctly without emotion or of accepting a big loss as just part of what the laws of statistics will produce in their profession in any individual trade or hand of poker. So the poker player and hedge fund trader also dissociate from outside forces (such as the family) for motivation, while the cab driver associates with outside forces for work motivation. This difference demonstrates how the social and economic structures of work help shape the boundaries between working life and personal life. The differing structures of work lead to completely different types of emotion work and different strategies of integration or segregation between work life and personal life. For the cab driver, focusing on the family keeps him or her going for another grueling hour of work, but for the poker player or hedge fund trader, *dissociating* from the family may be the emotion work needed to succeed at work. The structures of work lend themselves to deeply embedded ways of thinking that cannot help but bleed over into personal life.[6]

Salespeople provide another good example of how the way one learns to conceive of money at work shapes the individual into a *type of person* at work and outside of work. Since many of the salespeople I interviewed were from the food and beverage industry, they showed a high degree of interest in new consumer products. While their interest was obviously centered on products similar to what they sold, I noticed that they also were intensely interested in new products more generally, including new electronic gadgets and cell phones, which most of them relied on heavily in their work. Most salespeople also had a great interest in how *any* new product is developed, marketed, and sold. One food salesman, for example, told me how much he loves to try all sorts of new products. A salesman through and through, he got a charge out of seeing new products enter the market, understanding how they are packaged and sold and how they might be differentiated from existing products. Another food salesman I interviewed showed me, with palpable excitement, his garage, in which he had an additional refrigerator stocked with many of the latest beverages, including a few that he described as "still in testing" or "not yet on the market." This salesman appeared to be the ultimate consumer in some ways, embracing consumerism not only as essential to his own livelihood but also as integrated into his own lifestyle. He had a deep belief, developed through his daily work, that buying and selling products helped the national economy thrive. Salespeople, then, do not just learn to be good at selling; they also learn to be avid consumers as they develop a larger consciousness about the role of money in the economy. Among all the people I interviewed, for example, salespeople were the most interested in talking about the state of the overall national economy and the most likely to view consumption as essential for keeping that economy growing. They saw their own role as essential to making the world go round.[7] Salespeople not only learn how to sell at work; they learn how to be consumers, and they gain a quality of mind that says that selling and buying are *good*—perhaps even morally good—as they believe that buying more products keeps people employed and keeps the economic engine revving.

In a much more subtle way, salespeople are so often bouncing from one client to another and troubleshooting one problem or another that their jobs seem to induce a set of feelings akin to attention-deficit hyperactivity disorder (ADHD). After riding in a car with one salesman who was using a mobile telephone headset and switching from a call with a customer to one with a supplier to one with his home headquarters and then to one with another customer with a different problem, all the while still managing to answer my questions remarkably coherently in between calls, I found my own head spinning. When he joked that he felt like he had ADHD (and was the third salesperson I talked with who had invoked ADHD in one way or another), I understood why salespeople say this. Because the medical, psychological, and pharmaceutical models are so dominant in our national culture, invoking ADHD is a handy, logical, and easily understandable analogy to draw to the feelings they experience. Yet what he could have equally said (but didn't) was that the structure of his job was causing this feeling, rather than a biological or psychological disorder. The job of commission sales is structured to induce a set of responses to the unrelenting pressure of feeling that your time is scarce, that demands on your time are multiple, varied, and unrelenting. With your salary always riding on the volume of sales, you have to constantly bounce from one issue to another while simultaneously questioning (along with your sales manager) whether you are spending your time in the absolute best way to maximize your earnings.

This doesn't just happen because one works in sales. Rather, it is structured into the job of commission sales, with its ever-higher quotas, sales contests, and commission payment systems. This can begin to affect a person's core identity. As a salesman told me, "[My manager] would shake hands with you at the end of the day if you had a good day but wouldn't if you had a bad day. I really hated that." In David Dorsey's book *The Force*, he describes the life of a leading salesperson of office equipment. Dorsey observes from the point of view of the salesman's spouse that "the company had tinkered with his soul. It has turned him into something other than the man she married. She feels the company, over the years, has tried to adopt him into its own household, its own family, like a cult. It has taught him to motivate himself with a discontent that never seems to die."[8] That last phrase illustrates how learning to motivate oneself with a never-ending discontent (or a quest for more) reaches well beyond the workplace. Over a long career, the discontent that is used to drive sales ever higher may come to reside within a person, working on him or her from the inside rather than from the outside.

For hedge fund traders, poker players, and salespeople, it is crucial that money keeps moving. Traders learn through their work that money cannot simply accumulate; it needs to move. Each year, you must try to get a significant return, and you are trying to beat the average return on investment for funds in the same class as your own. Allowing money to sit in one place is difficult to do, as you always feel that you are missing out on potentially larger returns. Add to this the fact that your firm likely profits from each trade that is made, and it is imperative to keep money moving. Poker players must also keep putting money at risk in order to realize their income. You must keep pushing chips into the pot if you are going to win; of course, knowing when to push them all in is the difficult part. Salespeople must keep their product moving and keep selling, as they get paid based on each sale and they succeed by beating the ever-higher sales goal each successive year.

The constant pressure in these professions to keep money moving affects people's cognitive and emotional relationships to money, in that money must always be doing something, or else you are leaving returns on the table or allowing the competition to beat you. This adds to the feeling that there is never enough, whether we are talking about increased sales goals, growing the hedge fund, increasing your own earnings, or satisfying your own yearnings. If in your job it is your responsibility to create ever-higher returns or ever-higher sales each and every year, then it becomes difficult to feel that there is ever enough in your own income.

In fact, you are taught and trained through workplace stories that if you begin to sense the attitude that you are satisfied with enough, then that is the surest sign that you are losing your competitive edge. If you don't battle that attitude and drive it out of your consciousness, then managers will surely try to do it for you. From the standpoint of the clergyperson, this produces the "restless soul" of the modern world that finds it difficult to settle and find solace, having faith simply in the bounty provided by God. From the point of view of the poker player, hedge fund trader, and salesperson, this unrelenting restlessness is what is needed to succeed, and it is deeply ingrained in you by the central and overriding features of your work.

A grant giver, described in chapter 4, illustrates yet another way in which the money cultures at work extend into private life. She spoke at length about how her job had changed her family, making them more grateful for what they have. Her children and spouse have been significantly affected by their visits to poorer communities, meeting children with many fewer opportunities than her own children have. She mentioned that this experience has altered even how she sees her own upper-middle-class community, in that it allows her to recognize privileges more readily and has changed how she hears grumbling from her children, such as about not having a built-in swimming pool. The job of grant giver, because it entails crossing an important economic divide, provides for an interesting experience for the entire family related to issues of financial (and other) inequality in the United States. The work of grant givers provides readily available opportunities to address the issue of inequality in very direct ways with their own family, which they probably do more regularly than many other middle- and upper-class families. While they articulate to their own children that all children are the same, they simultaneously reference poor children in order to impress on their own children an appreciation for their more fortunate circumstances. This is an unexpected use of the poor to provide a context of appreciation that becomes part of the daily practices of grant givers but not part of the daily practices of many other types of work that never entail crossing social class boundaries. It is the specific social and economic location in the economy and the money culture in which grant givers are embedded that affords them this experience of moving across social class boundaries, presenting them directly with crucially important and compelling dilemmas of inequality that people in other types of work do not experience.

Several of the debt counselors I interviewed told me that their work spilled over into their home lives, in that they have become much more aware of their own spending habits since they took their job. All the debt counselors felt they had become more sympathetic to people in financial need, and a few mentioned that they thought they could live more frugally now that they have worked with clients and seen how people live without many of the extras. This feeling was not universal, of course, as one debt counselor mentioned, almost sheepishly to me, that she loved to shop for clothes and charges too much on credit cards herself. But, even here, this person thought about her shopping as a guilty pleasure because of the mental mindscape she developed at work, which described shopping sometimes as a psychological addiction.

Fund raisers often mentioned that because of their jobs, they had developed their own "giving plans." Before entering a fund-raising career, they might have given here and there to various solicitations that came to them. But after several years in fund raising, they learned a new vocabulary and a new process: "having a giving plan." This means being very mindful about how much money you will decide to donate each year (often expressed as a percentage of income) and to which charities you want to give this money (usually splitting it up carefully among charities and organizations). Several mentioned they were thinking about giving gifts as part of their estate planning. In addition to these plans, fund raisers had a keen interest in the pitches made to them by charitable organizations. They wanted to hear how others in the business do their jobs. For example, they were curious about how another fund raiser would "make the ask" to them and how much they might ask for. Recall the university fund raiser who, when asked for money by someone from his own alma mater, joked, "Is that all you got? I'm insulted!" Investment advisors, of course, talked about their own investment decisions, sometimes being fairly conservative ("hitting singles") but also every once in a while being tempted to take bigger risks ("hitting home runs").

The individuals who were experimenting with money used money to make their points, rather than eschewing money altogether. For example, those who experiment with salaries raise the question of fairness in an internal labor market. In the organization experimenting with wage sharing, managers openly raised the issue of how much more is one person worth than another and then allowed individuals to voluntarily participate in a mechanism to reduce wage disparity. While on the face of it, systems like the 1% Club for wage sharing seem unique, it isn't as if mechanisms that *increase* wage disparity are not already in place in most companies. Any organization that uses a form of an across-the-board salary increase gives larger actual wage increases (in dollar terms, not percentage terms) each year to those at the higher end of the pay scale than to those at the lower end. If across-the-board increases were the only type of salary increase used, workers at the top of the scale would continue to move further and further away from those at the bottom of the wage scale. Seen in this light, the wage-sharing club merely mitigates an already entrenched system that structures increasing internal wage inequality into its salary mechanism.

Even the man who was intentionally taking an ever-lowering salary would reference the amount of the drop in salary as a way to measure what he was giving up. It almost seems as if we need to use money as a quantitative measure of the rejection of money. As Simmel wrote, "Much more difficult and dangerous is the lot of those who don't make any money with their activities, but can only evaluate them objectively and in accordance with inner demands."[9] The money form has become so dominant that it becomes tempting to use it as a measure of what is being given up or rejected—particularly if we are unable to discern any other measuring rod of value. This may be the greatest change in a completely monetized society—the inability to recognize any other metric of value, other than the money form. Are we in danger of losing the ability to measure and evaluate people, ideas, and values without money as the measuring stick?[10]

David Harvey has written that "[t]he advent of a money economy . . . dissolves the bonds and relations that make up the 'traditional' communities so that money becomes the real community."[11] Those who experiment with money challenge this trend, and in one way or another, each of them asks us to revisit our unspoken assumptions about money and the way money works. Experiments with pricing, for example, suggest that we start first with the value that something has to us and only then put a price on it, rather than the other way around. For consumers in the United States and other countries where haggling over price has largely disappeared, most shoppers look at a price tag, note the price, and then ask, "Is this worth it?" or "Do I want to buy this at this price?" They rarely consider first arriving at the value it holds for them and then asking the shop clerk if he or she will accept that amount.[12] In restaurants and other establishments that have a policy of paying what you consider a fair price, customers must think about value and fairness first. Just as interesting to me, however, is the fact that customers find this so disequilibrating that many of them ask for a suggested price, as if they are simply unable to arrive at an accurate answer to the question "What is this worth to me?" and perhaps fear underpaying or overpaying by too much (which assumes there is an accurate price to begin with!). This may also suggest why "pay your own price" systems are fundamentally threatening to a consumer economy. If individuals are asked to do the independent work of thinking and deciding what something is actually worth to them, they may slow down in their decision-making or decide to buy fewer things. In a world of set prices, every item has an exchange value that is immediately comparable to every other item, which seems to induce purchasing because there is always something that appears to be a good deal in comparison to everything else.[13] Our attention becomes fixed not on something's value in use but on its value in comparison to all other values. Combining this with a heavy dose of messaging that money needs to be put to work provides the ingredients for a potent consumer culture.

Economists typically take the position that money emerged to make transactions easier since it was an efficient alternative to bartering.[14] In a barter system, people who wish to trade have to find another person who has complementary needs to their own: "I have extra bread and need shoes, while you have extra shoes and need bread." Simple enough, but this makes barter a stickier form of exchange because you must find someone with needs that complement your own, or else you need three-party swaps, which can get ever more complicated. While bartering is less efficient in the sense of the ease of transaction, notice, however, that it also has the potential to lead to deeper social relations, in the sense that each person must come to know the other's needs and excesses. It is undoubtedly true that money, *once legitimated and accepted as a universal currency*, eases and perhaps even encourages transacting.[15] Yet it also encourages anonymity in transaction, which could bring its own host of problems, including distrust, atomization, or alienation.

With a legitimate money system, I can purchase shoes from you, whether or not you need bread, because I can pay you in currency that you can in turn reliably use most anywhere you want or even store for future use. Note, however, that if a particular currency is not accepted as a legitimate holder of value (e.g., consider the case of hyperinflation), bartering can then be seen as a wiser form of transaction than trading a commodity for a currency that is possibly worthless or rapidly losing value with each passing minute. Thus, unmistakably, money rests on the social belief that it will hold value, and this is a necessary condition for money to be a more efficient form than barter for transacting.[16]

From an anthropological view, the origin-of-money story works a little differently than it does for the economists and puts communal relations at the center. For anthropologists, money did not appear on the scene in order to ease transacting. Rather, anthropologists begin with the observation that for centuries prior to currency, people transacted, traded, shared, and gave gifts to one another. As William Bloom writes in his book *Money, Heart, and Mind*, "In all of the different [anthropological] theories of the origin of money what we have is tribal people in relationship. They are giving or exchanging something in order to help that relationship." Bloom continues, "Objects that were habitually gifted or exchanged became what we call money."[17] Notice the slight, yet crucially important, switch in emphasis from the economists' view (exchange occurs; money arrives as a more efficient way to exchange) to the anthropologists' view (humans desire and need relationships in their communities; they exchange in order to nurture the communal bonds necessary for survival; the things that societies use to cement bonds—shells, beads, ornaments—become universal money). For the economist, money is an efficient solution to an economic problem, and exchange is viewed as the central driving force of life; for the anthropologist, social relationships and communal bonds are the driving force for survival in life, and money is one form of exchange that evolves to allow for the further cementing of important social relationships.

These two origin-of-money stories neatly foreshadow the ongoing debates over the meaning of money that I found at work. Money does both these things: it eases and facilitates exchange, *and* it carries important social and symbolic meanings, fostering and tracing social relationships. Ignoring one to focus exclusively on the other ensures only a truncated, and ultimately unsatisfying, view of money. The more we move toward complete fungibility, the less we need to be aware of the needs of those with whom we are transacting. If the goal of an economic system is speed of movement and ease of transaction, then the more one can do to reduce transaction costs, the better (and in this sense, hard currency even gets in the way, as electronic exchange is much quicker). However, this ease of transaction comes at the cost of a reduction in social ties. So while a program like Ithaca HOURS might get attacked for reducing fungibility, it is doing so in order to reinsert social ties into the transacting relationship as it enhances conversations and negotiated meanings between transactors.[18]

People experimenting with alternative currencies raise fundamental questions about the meaning of money itself. They work to generate conversations about how currency *should* work by asking questions about how to keep money in a community rather than letting money drain away from a community. By pricing alternative currency in labor hours, they draw a direct connection between work and money, so that when you use a one-half-hour note to purchase something, you confront a direct reminder of the source of earned income and the precise amount of your own labor required to purchase something. Alternative currencies also tend to slow transactions down, as they seek to create a bond between transactors. As Paul Glover has written, "Many people have said that HOURS personalize their exchanges. That means HOURS help satisfy our need to live in a friendlier world: the more people you have personal exchanges with, the more people you can trust and rely on."[19]

These experiments run up against barriers and challenges that underscore some of the inherent features of a national currency, as each swims upstream against a tide of expected assumptions and behaviors. Promoters of alternative currencies must consistently work to gain acceptance of the money by various merchants. While some people argue that the transition from hard currency to electronic currency makes money devoid of meaning, the Internet has spawned more types of alternative monies that carry all sorts of meaning systems. Online gamers, for example, often amass a type of alternative currency in video games to purchase characters or avatars or to buy weapons or various tools that can then be used in online communities and games. This online phenomenon of a specific form of electronic currency gets people accustomed to thinking about all different sorts of money and makes the concept of an alternative currency more readily comprehensible. If people get used to trading and amassing online currency, they become quite comfortable thinking in terms of different currencies with highly particularized uses that work in a parallel universe with a traditional national currency.[20] The website Facebook has its own virtual currency called "credits"; users play online games to earn and trade credits. The company Zynga creates many of these games, and users pay national currency (it seems odd at this point to call it "real money") to purchase virtual goods in the games.[21] Thus, we see that the more money becomes electronic rather than paper and coin, the easier it may become to imagine virtual monies and alternative currencies. In fact, in the online universe, using actual national currency is seen as a waste of time and a hindrance to moving virtual money around. New systems of exchange begin to blossom. If a web company can earn advertising revenues through increased visits to its website by using credits in a virtual currency to encourage people to visit and play games on the site, those credits can then be used to make microloans to a poor farmer or to purchase consumer goods (and the consumer-goods company can get paid an exchange in either hard currency or virtual currency for the credits from the web company, which has gained more advertising revenue). The need for using a national currency lessens as the alternative currency finds more uses.[22] In a similar vein, more and more poker players start out as online players, getting used to systems of credits in the online system. This makes it even easier to view chips as just a way of keeping score. If the online credits earned playing poker can then be traded for other goods, tangible money becomes less necessary. Since we are all socialized into our understanding of money, it appears that younger people are being socialized into not using money in the traditional way and into trusting in the use of alternative currencies. If people are socialized in childhood to trust and use alternative forms of money, they may come to see hard currency as archaic, anachronistic, and increasingly irrelevant.

Differences within a Money Culture

The money cultures that develop around certain lines of work not only differ from one another; they may also differ within one type of work. One of the best examples of this, I think, is the very different culture I found in hedge fund trading firms that are quantitatively driven as opposed to those that have a more trader-driven ethos.[23] In the strictly quant firms, there appears to be a more subdued culture that feels more akin to a scientific or research organization, with lots of talk of modeling, testing, and refining models. There are many meetings held to review data and improve models. Many of the senior officers of such firms have Ph.D. degrees in physics or mathematics, and some have spent significant amounts of time working in universities or research institutes before joining a quantitative hedge fund firm. There seems to be less talk of meltdowns and emotions, and there is less swashbuckling. In one or two of my interviews with quant traders, there were even overt attempts to distance themselves from the stereotype of a Wall Street trader. As one head of a quantitative hedge fund told me emphatically, "I've never hired a single Wall Street guy in the firm."

Within the diverse group of clergy, not surprisingly, there were some interesting differences in money cultures. Some of the clergy were more likely to delve into more traditionally secular issues of money, offering seminars to congregants on basic money management, handling debt, and basic investing, while other clergy limited their activities to preaching about sharing God's abundance. I also found some differences in how biblical phrases were interpreted, including the classic passage about the difficulty of a rich man entering heaven. Some pastors interpreted this passage simply to mean that the rich person should do good works with his or her wealth, while others leaned toward the idea that God has a special place for the poor. How to interpret this biblical passage is emblematic of a larger dilemma for clergy, who rely on donations from parishioners and don't wish to offend people with significant wealth or make them unwelcome in their church. For Muslim imams, this issue is somewhat less of a problem, since *zakat* is calculated based on retained wealth, and this allows an imam to appeal to the payment of *zakat* as a means for people with wealth to put their wealth to work for the good of the society. If a Christian church has tithing as a well-accepted practice, then it also can appeal to the 10 percent tithe. However, many Christian churches do not practice tithing, and the tithe is typically based on income rather than wealth.[24] In the Jewish faith, some rabbis leave it to their membership committees to wrestle with issues of giving, and this can help create some sense of separation between finances to run the synagogue and the spiritual and religious needs of the membership. I am sure this separation is breached on occasion, but there is a structure in place that encourages the laity on the membership committee to take more charge of financial issues. The structural arrangements, then, of a religious organization combine with doctrinal beliefs and with the interpretation and style of different religious leaders to create somewhat differing money cultures within the widely accepted foundational belief that money belongs to God.

Nested Money Cultures

The distinct money cultures that I found at work seem to be nested within a larger national money culture. Take, for example, those who cross social class boundaries as part of their work. Owing to the structural location of their jobs and the role money plays in their work, boundary crossers have to handle the cognitive dissonance resulting from crossing class lines in a society that is often thought to be largely free of social class differences. Similar to many of the other people I studied, storytelling plays an important role in their response to the central cognitive dilemma of their jobs. These stories are used to manage the cognitive dissonance created by boundary crossing and by the structural limits (found in the job and in society writ large) and to resolve the dilemmas at hand. For debt counselors, the story told about the doctor or lawyer who gets into debt helps prove (to themselves as much as to others) that being in debt can happen to anyone. This story is chosen and emphasized, I believe, because it dovetails with the individualistic approach to debt that is built into the job through the tools that are at the disposal of debt counselors to assist their clients. After all, they cannot remake the social class system, nor can they redistribute income or even remedy a client's weak educational background in the short time frame they have. They can, however, identify problem areas in someone's individual spending diary, and they are able to make quick, small-scale suggestions for people to bring in extra income by looking for a second job or by selling something they possess. Reminding oneself that "this can happen to anyone" frames the problem of debt not as a result of structured inequality in a society but rather as a result of an individual's psychological problems that can be treated within a paradigm borrowed from other counseling professions.

Here we see how a specific money culture at work is nested within the larger national money culture. As Robert Bellah and his colleagues argued in *Habits of the Heart*, the ideal of individualism is at the heart of American society and helps shape responses to all sorts of social phenomena.[25] Economic matters are particularly prone to an individualistic interpretation because of the strong ethos of the self-made man or woman embodied in the American Dream. In a culture that asserts that wealth comes from an individual's hard work, debt and poverty are also likely to be treated as self-made. This individualism combines with a contemporary cultural ethos that stresses the psychological causes of all sorts of social problems. At one time, debt was considered a criminal and moral problem (e.g., the use of debtors' prisons); later it became an issue for civil law (e.g., the development of bankruptcy laws and the restructuring, reduction, or dismissal of debt). Today, as seen in debt "counseling," the tools, vocabulary, and epistemology of psychology are often used to treat debt. Soon, we may see a shift to a more biological view of debt, as we are able to measure the brain chemicals released during shopping. So debt may one day soon have a pharmaceutical treatment. With this historical lens, we see how elements of the larger national culture shape the money culture nested within it that in turn shapes our understanding and approach to an economic phenomenon such as debt.

Similarly, as grant givers come to know the people to whom they give grants, they see the structural obstacles people confront owing to poverty, limited opportunities, poor-quality schooling, or the dangerous neighborhoods in which they live. They also become painfully aware of the lack of needed social services, and they are aware that their grants help in important ways but do not remedy the hidden injuries of social class.[26] Since their own structural position limits how much they can remedy these problems (and they certainly do make some difference, of course), they also teach their children lessons of appreciation (reminding themselves as well) that manage some of the sadness felt in working with children and adults in poverty. Grant givers gain a sense of appreciation for their own lives and the lives of their children as their job creates a disequilibrium that results from moving across social class lines rather than being insulated from class differences. Their cognitive dissonance is transformed into a lesson in appreciation through the renderings they provide to their own children.

Clergy operate within a specific money culture often at odds with the national money culture it is nested within. Because clergy start from the assumption that all money belongs to God, they are faced with the ongoing task of writing spiritual and religious meaning onto money and resisting the idea that money is devoid of meaning as a lubricant of exchange. Owing to this starting point, whatever is done with money will be seen as honoring or dishonoring God. Clergy must also operate in a secular world, running their churches, paying the bills, and talking with followers who face what might seem to be mainly secular money problems. The core cognitive dilemmas for clergy become how to straddle a world in which money has essential spiritual meaning but also is used as a secular facilitator of exchange and how to write religious meaning onto money in a larger culture of hyperconsumerism. How do clergy honor and live up to their unique starting point in a larger culture that may not readily accept this view?

One lesson drawn from studying clergy is that the distinction between what is sacred and what is profane is not so neatly drawn; nor do they necessarily support a binary opposition, with some money having meaning and other money not. After spending time with clergy, I believe that a more accurate way to think about money in this type of work is to say that money can carry meaning when effort is expended to write meaning on money (or, as some clergy might put it, when effort is spent reminding people that money has meaning). Absent that energy, it becomes very easy to lose the meaning in money. Particularly at this moment in our culture, which is ridden with consumerist tendencies, writing a sacred or religious meaning onto money takes greater effort (as advertising writes entirely different meanings onto money: you are only as good as you look; this car will make you happy, choosing this peanut butter will make you a good parent). This is why clergy spend so much of their time discussing their view of the meaning of money in their conversations with parishioners and in their preaching. One might argue that we live in a society replete with messages that money is really useless unless it is turned into a purchasable product that will bring us worldly enjoyment of one sort or another. In Benjamin Barber's book *Consumed*, he argues that we are entering an era of the "consumer republic," built on an "infantile ethos" of insatiable desires that undermines civic culture and democracy.[27]

Within this culture of consumerism, clergy are faced with an increasingly difficult task. They might wish to argue that using your money to help another human being in need is a greater honor to God than is using it to buy a sports car. They wish to write an alternative meaning onto money, then, and it is often (though certainly not always) a meaning that runs against the current of consumerism. Clergy must figure out how they can live faithfully in a world of consumerism and how to preach to parishioners who are living in such a world. How do they insist that money belongs to God and that it should be shared, for example, without sounding anachronistic, shrill, scolding, hopelessly idealistic, or overly ideological? If they avoid the topic entirely and make their place of worship completely compatible with consumerism, they run the risk of losing legitimacy as an institution that is different from, say, a for-profit corporation. If they address it, they must do it gently yet insistently if they hope to counter strong messages about money and consumerism that are accompanied by significant financial backing and that are provided insistently and not so gently.

While managing this dilemma, clergy's own enterprises (churches, mosques, temples, and synagogues) must survive and thrive in the world of money, and bills must be paid. More and more, parishioners seem to be looking for more services from their churches, mosques, temples, and synagogues as religious organizations come to be seen as competitors in a market for members. Clergy (and their organizations) benefit from the money donated by those who may themselves earn money through a consumer-laden economy. Therefore, clergy must show some caution by not condemning this economy too harshly, lest they bite too forcefully the hand that also feeds them. I found that some clergy try to walk this tightrope by constantly returning to the foundational theme that money belongs to God and that as long as we are good stewards of that money, there is nothing necessarily wrong with having a lot of it. They must reiterate this foundational assumption often because if it is not acknowledged or heeded (even if only partially), then the game is lost for them.

Clergy face other structural dilemmas related to the role of money in their work. We saw how the structural arrangements for the funding of mosques differ significantly in the United States from funding mosques in predominantly Muslim countries. This structural difference means that imams in the United States must take on a set of secular financial concerns that they would not have to handle in a society that does not separate church and state. This structural change can alter the way a fundamental practice such as *zakat* is conceived of and carried out, as it pressures Islam in the West to develop the unfamiliar idea of a congregation with financial membership obligations. This is a profound example of the connection between large-scale structure (as reflected in the national-level belief surrounding separation of church and state that leads to an aligned mechanism of funding for religious organizations) and the type of money culture that develops in religious organizations, as it presents imams in the United States with a different set of challenges to interpreting the lines between the sacred and the profane.

In all these examples, the specific money culture that is formed at work is nested within a larger national money culture, replete with its own set of values and preferences. The particular money cultures formed at work can contribute to the national money culture while also drawing from it, or they can challenge elements of the larger culture. Debt counselors have only individualistic and psychological tools at their disposal to conceptualize debt because their job is created within a national money culture that emphasizes individualism and personal responsibility both in the conceiving of problems and in finding solution to those problems. In a different national context that stressed communal and structural understandings, we might see a more social conception of debt and efforts targeted at communal or societal solutions. The profession of debt counseling and the framing of the problem of debt in turn contribute to the national money culture and its insistence on individual approaches to a problem such as debt.

The lessons that people draw from their work experiences with money also show this nesting of a work-based money culture within a larger national culture that shapes the repertoires available to people as they make sense of the role of money. When investment advisors and grant givers draw out lessons from their work experiences to transmit to their own children, they do so within a national context that stresses individual responsibility and hard work as the keys to success. This leads them to ignore certain features of their work that do not fit the national context while transforming the features that do into lessons for their children. In a national money culture that stresses a classless society, the lesson is that anyone can enjoy success if he or she works hard and that poverty can be addressed through helping others. In a different national context that stressed the rigidities of social class, different money lessons might get drawn about the serendipity of being born into wealth or the difficulties of breaking the generational cycle of poverty in a class-based society.

Money at Work Shapes Who We Are

How we earn our money and how we use money at work helps to shape who we are—as individuals, as family members, as consumers and producers, and as citizens. That is why I think the argument that identity is becoming more a matter of consumption than of production is slightly off the mark. My evidence suggests that the ways that we experience consumption are intertwined with our experiences as producers.[28] Salespeople, for example, embrace consumption more than most other people do. They tend not only to enjoy it but to believe in it as a way to help the economy thrive. This belief comes from their work experience of constant selling and extends quite seamlessly into their private consumption lives. Debt counselors often think about their own consumption differently than others do and differently than they did before they became debt counselors. Many debt counselors think carefully about their own spending habits, and one who talked about spending too much money said it was because she was a "clothes shopper" and described her passions as a sort of "guilty pleasure." Her experience of consuming is affected significantly by her daily work practices. As she purchases clothing and pulls out her credit card, she does so with a certain consciousness about consumption that is shaped by what she does at work every day. Unlike the salesperson who sees consuming as helping others have employment and keeping the economy growing, she thinks of spending as a guilty pleasure that ought to be checked, using the psychological and individualistic terms learned through work. The hedge fund trader uses the logic he has learned at work to think about his purchasing decision when he buys lunch, weighing up and trading off quality, price, and the "convenience premium" that he is willing to pay for a sandwich obtained very close to his office. He explicitly trusts both the market and his own behavior as constituting the correct trade-off—or else why would he be doing it? The grant giver, after spending time in poor neighborhoods for her work, has trouble engaging in the hyperconsumption she sees around her in her own neighborhood and begins to see the lifestyle of her surroundings in a slightly different and somewhat critical way. She also uses those experiences at work to frame her children's complaints about not having a built-in pool like their friends have. She talks with her children about "having so much while others have so little." The decision to resist those complaints and the pressure to keep up with the Joneses by buying a built-in pool seem to be held in check by these work experiences.

These are all ways in which work affects cognition of money, consumption attitudes, and even behaviors. My evidence leads me to believe, then, that production and consumption are tightly interwoven in forming identity rather than operating in separable spheres of influence. Our work lives structure our experiences with money in important ways that often spill over into our lives outside of work. This suggests the importance of studying the money cultures that form around particular types of work. For example, economists argue that each individual has a set of preferences. These preferences create demand, and where supply and demand curves meet, price is set. Sociologists play a major role in understanding where preferences come from, as they do not emerge from thin air or even from an individual's desires.[29] Desires and preferences are shaped socially, as consumers are created, not simply born. The activities that people engage in at work, along with their experiences within the money cultures that grow out of those practices, may play a major role in fostering preferences. Working in sales shapes a person's preferences very differently from working as a clergy person or a grant giver. While work is not the only place where preferences are shaped, it is certainly an important place where we learn attitudes and habits surrounding money. How we learn to use money at work shapes the people we become—as consumers and as citizens.

It is interesting that the two groups of people most pointedly asking the larger question of "How much is enough?" were on such different ends of the wealth spectrum: hedge fund traders and clergy and spiritual seekers such as the man who ran reverse mission trips to Africa. It seems paradoxical, at first blush, that the hedge fund traders were likely to think that $10 million might not be enough, while the man who took an ever-lower salary thought he would always have plenty. But it is the work that a hedge fund trader does and the money culture in which he resides that makes life feel always at risk, as one can always lose it all. If, on the other hand, you can count on God and fellow human beings to care and provide for you—and your work experience demonstrates this to be true each day—you feel less afraid of losing it all.

This brings us full circle to classical debates over the nature of money itself. Because money has a certain evanescent quality, it can be difficult to grab hold of; but it is also this very quality that allows money to be inscribed with all sorts of values and meanings. Part of the problem with talking about the meaning of money is that it represents so many different things to different people and, at different times, can even carry contradictory meanings for any individual. This is because, as Thomas Crump put it, "[Money's] nature is not easy to understand, for money gives no information about itself. In revealing itself as money, it is nothing more than a cultural tautology."[30] This idea leads Crump to propose that we view money as a "ritual system" in which money is "enacted" on a daily basis, although it is precisely when money is working well that we fail to notice its enactment.[31] In this sense, money *as it is used at work* comes to take on particular meanings, as it is enacted each and every day. As money is used at work, it also shapes who we are.

As money becomes less tangible, we can imagine even more for money. There must be something in the nature of money that allows for such diverse uses, and I think it is the fact that as a universal measure of exchange, it can simultaneously be both everything and nothing.[32] While poker players try to disentangle money from all the things that it can buy to treat it as a way of keeping score, clergy perform exactly the opposite cognitive work on money—insisting that money be viewed as a representation of core value and meaning. Here we see how money presents the paradox of being both meaningful and meaningless. Because it represents a universal measuring stick against which all value may be measured, it allows for the conception that money itself is without meaning. However, at the same time, because money reflects the sum of all values and social relations, it can be viewed as the final arbiter of all meaning and pursued as an end in itself. In some work contexts, we strive to make money as fungible and meaningless as possible, while in other settings, we work to write meaning onto money, using it to represent our most deeply cherished values.

METHODOLOGICAL

APPENDIX

One of the most challenging parts of this research project was trying to figure out how to get people to talk about money at work. At the outset, I wondered whether I was asking people to describe a process that was simply inenarrable for those experiencing it. Unlike other types of interviewing I had done in prior books, I learned that simple, direct, and straightforward questions did not always work very well for the kinds of processes I was trying to uncover. For example, it did not take me long to find out that you cannot sit down with someone and begin by saying, "So how do you think about money here at your work?" The most likely response to this question is, "Well, what do you mean by that?"[1]

I was faced with the challenge of getting people to talk about issues that I thought would matter to them and that they could indeed talk about once we got going in conversation. The problem was in how to start them talking. So after much experimenting, I found success with a pair of opening questions that I would use to get the ball rolling. The first was this: "If you were talking to a third- or fourth-grade class as part of a career day at their school, how would you describe what you do in your job?" This helped respondents give a very clear, concise, and somewhat simplified explanation of what they did for a living. Since children often want to know what someone does for a living and why someone would get paid for doing that particular activity, answers to this question were often quite revealing. One salesman, for example, replied, "I sell wine to stores for people to buy. If I sell a lot of wine to the store, I get paid for that." In this short description, the commission salesperson has already drawn the tight connection between selling and payment, indicating the centrality of commission payment in this job. The second question I would ask was, "Now, what does that simplified description of your job leave out?" This question would elicit more complicated and detailed aspects of their job.

Often these two questions were enough to begin a very long conversation about money and work.[2] I had to rely on my ability to adjust during the interview to probe for the issues that seemed most interesting in a particular job. I centered on how money played a role in the respondents' job, how they thought about money in the job, and what led them to think about money in these ways. I would try to probe for connections (if they existed) between daily workplace practices and cognitive dilemmas and resolutions that emerged related to money issues at work. I also asked some straightforward questions that worked well, such as "Tell me about a typical day at work?" I tried hard to listen for stories that got told at work, although I never found a good way to ask for this directly. So I ended up just hoping stories would come out (the one that begins the chapter on hedge fund traders is a good example of a story that emerged after the respondent had trouble finding words to answer my direct question about what hedge fund traders are like). I found that the illustrative story often spoke volumes.[3]

As I became more and more comfortable with this particular style of interviewing, I came to think of what I was doing as a "sociology of revealed cognition" and viewed my challenge as figuring out ways to get people to describe the ways they engaged in the cognitive work needed to conceptualize money in the specific ways they did. Sociologists tend to study outcomes, actions, and behaviors, as well as what people say about things (opinions, viewpoints, life narratives). It is quite tricky to get people to reveal and describe cognitive and emotional processes, as these tend to happen inside the head, even though they may become revealed in actions. I found that elements of these money cultures were observable, patterned, and revelatory because different kinds of work led to recurring cognitive dilemmas. By paying attention to how individuals wrestle with these dilemmas—through cognitive work and emotion work—we gain a window on how structure and culture are connected and intertwined. The many ways in which money is embedded in different types of work (what can be called a structural feature of work) are what create the cognitive dilemmas that are reflected in storytelling, tropes, and cautionary tales found in the workplace (what can be called the money culture of work). As incumbents in these positions attempted to resolve these dilemmas, they drew from the existing money culture and from the available cultural repertoires surrounding money in their workplace. It is the money culture at work that made certain forms of resolution to dilemmas seem reasonable and preferred, though not necessarily inevitable or determined, because the money culture is both reflective of, and contributing to, the structured relationship to money in that line of work.

When we see observable patterns in these cognitions, we gain a glimpse into how culture and the economy are intertwined as we witness individual decision-making within the structured context of work. All jobs are structured to function in a specific location within a larger money economy, and as such, they contain daily practices related to money and finance that are built into the job and embedded into their work routines. These daily practices produce a series of challenges, and as incumbents wrestle with these challenges and dilemmas, they engage in both the cognitive work and the emotional work to help make sense of the meaning of money.[4] They reveal those cognitions as they relate the ways in which they come to conceive of money and integrate it into their work and home lives and into their own identities. These behaviors and cognitions in turn contribute to a specific money culture at work that is often rich with symbols, rituals, stories, and scripts that are all in play within organizational and other workplace settings. In my view, it is the structural economic location of different types of work and the specific role of money in that work that creates the distinct cognitive dilemmas common in any line of work. In the various resolutions of these dilemmas, structure and culture shapes the individuals in those jobs as well as producing and reproducing the money culture at work.[5]

Cognitive sociologists have developed interesting ways to get a window into cognitions, such as asking people to sort things into categories and having them talk about the rationale behind their sorting process. I tended to ask people about how they thought about money and what types of dilemmas or issues concerning money arose in their jobs and then to have them talk me through how they confronted or resolved the dilemma. This was a way to have them model their thought processes for me. Of course, this is ex post facto modeling, so you still run the risk that what they describe may not be exactly how the cognitive process worked at the moment it was occurring. I had originally planned to devote a part of the interview to how thinking about money at work might spill over into home life. In the end, I retained a few questions about this subject—and these elicited some interesting findings—but I realized I had bitten off more than I could chew. A future project needs to be designed that specifically addresses the issue of connections between work and home life that I only hint at here.[6]

I found that storytelling and humor could reveal some of this cognition, and I use these throughout the book to show how people think. Metaphors are also an interesting way to understand cognition. James Geary, in his book *I Is an Other*, points out that people use metaphors every ten to fifteen words when they are speaking.[7] Thus, metaphors are essential to how people conceive of things and explain them to others. This is particularly true when it comes to talking about something like money that can represent so many different things—we talk about money being "liquid," stock markets "responding smartly," and savings representing "security" or "freedom."

Often, I would end my interview by asking, "Thinking back now over your career as a [*insert career here*], how do you think you might be different as a person today if you had never become a [*insert career*] but instead had become an accountant or a teacher or any other line of work?" The response from most people was something along the lines of "Wow, now that's a tough question. . . . Hmmmm. . . . Let me think." For a few people, the question completely flummoxed them, and they never were really able to say much more than "I can't even imagine that," perhaps proving the point that careers can be so deeply embedded within us that it is almost impossible to imagine ourselves as something else. It may also support the idea that without actually experiencing another career, we cannot really know how that would have shaped us into a different person. For those who were able to answer this question, they often did so using comparative language such as "I think I would be more this and less that," and this proved helpful in highlighting the ways they understood the impact of their work on themselves and their views on money. An obvious example is the investment advisor who said, "I think I pay a lot more attention to my own investments, as I know so much more now," or "I am a lot more aware of how money can pull families apart since I have seen it so many times in my office." Other examples include the debt counselors, who all said they became more compassionate toward people in debt after working in their jobs.

In addition to the interviews I conducted for this project, I also used fieldwork to help me understand the money cultures described in this book. I looked for any opportunities to be an observer or a participant-observer in activities related to the work I was studying. For example, I attended a weekend retreat and intensive training program for new fund raisers. At this retreat, I attended seminars where I learned how to "make the ask" for money, how to cultivate prospects, and how to make use of the latest research tools for ascertaining someone's capacity to give. Just as importantly, I learned a new vocabulary and a new way of thinking about money, as I was temporarily immersed in a new money culture. During this weekend, I was able to have many informal conversations with both experts and newcomers in the field of fund raising. Similarly, I attended a weekend retreat on money and spirituality at a monastery. There, I and the other attendees slept in sparse quarters, talked and sang hymns, wrote our own "money biographies," and engaged in a dinner in which each person was served according to the distribution of food in the world. This retreat was designed to make attendees aware of the religious and spiritual dimensions of money. I attended a number of seminars run by credit and debt counselors on topics such as "how to get out of credit card trouble" or "how to buy a house if you have poor credit." I observed several talks given by credit card counselors to various groups. I hung out at the Free Store for the better part of a day. I spent several days in Ithaca participating as fully as I could in the Ithaca HOURS program, buying coffee, eating lunch, and going to the farmers' market several times, always using my Ithaca HOURS for purchases. I toured the New York Stock Exchange with a financial regulator, talking about trading floors. I observed hedge fund trading rooms before and after my interviews. I spent as much time as I could listening to sermons and other messages delivered by religious leaders when they spoke about money issues (several of my clergy interviewees invited me to events or to services, and some provided audiotapes they had made on the topic of finance and religion). I spent several days in Las Vegas casinos, interviewing poker players and observing poker rooms. I collected several file drawers full of newspaper and magazine articles on all the jobs I was studying. All of these helped inform my interviews and my analyses.

I should also say a few words about how I chose the professions and the people whom I interviewed. The group of people I interviewed is not meant to be a random sample of some population of people. I was not trying to understand how work affects the average person but rather to explore a set of ideas and a new way of thinking about money and work. Thus, I deliberately chose types of work in which money was likely to play a central role. So my first concern was to select an interesting group of professions or types of work to begin exploring. I did this by first thinking about the ways in which money might be important at work. Once I decided that an occupation might be interesting, I used contacts to find people who work in that profession or simply wrote letters of introduction to people whose names I found in professional directories. Once I had one or two contacts, I simply asked for more referrals.

I was also on the lookout for occupations to pair with each other as interesting comparison cases. I did not originally conceive of poker players and hedge fund traders as a natural pairing, until I found out that several traders liked to play poker, and I began hearing some similar types of stories and language used in the two professions. Other pairings came after data collection was complete, and I was trying to structure the book in the most useful and interesting way. There is nothing sacrosanct about these groupings; they just seemed to be the best way to present my findings and to highlight similarities and differences.

I knew from the outset that I was taking some risks by including so many different types of work in one study. Certainly a very satisfying book could be written about each of these occupations as a single case study, and a book could be written comparing any two of these occupations. A book written in this fashion would allow a deeper and sustained analysis of these issues than I provide here. But by doing it that way, I would have lost the power of the larger set of comparative cases and would have missed many of the similarities and differences across occupations. I chose the strategy I did trusting that by putting each type of work in juxtaposition to all the others, I could see things I might not see if I chose to study just one or two occupations. Because one of my primary goals was exploring a new way of thinking about money and work, I needed a large comparative array of cases to accomplish this. I think it was the very process of interviewing a poker player one day and a minister the next that led to the insights contained in this book.

NOTES

Notes to the Introduction

1. There is an old bartender's joke that plays on the alleged practice of bartenders helping themselves to some of the money from the operation. It goes like this: The owner of a bar confronted his longtime bartender, saying, "I have been watching you over the past several years, and I know that with the money I pay you, it is impossible for you to afford the house that you live in, the in-ground pool you recently installed, and the fancy sports car that you drive. I don't know exactly how you do it, but I know you've been stealing money from me, and so I am going to fire you." The bartender quickly replies, "Well, that's pretty stupid. Now you're going to hire a new bartender who doesn't have any of those things yet!"

2. Some good examples include Jordan Goodman's *Master Your Money Type: Using Your Financial Personality to Create a Life of Wealth and Freedom* (2006), Shelia Klebanow and Eugene Lowenkop's more psychoanalytic approach in *Money and Mind* (1991), and Klontz et al.'s article on "money belief systems" (2011).

Notes to Chapter 1

1. Even the titles of many books give a sense of the bravado that is used to write about Wall Street trading. See, for example, Frank Partnoy's *Fiasco: The Inside Story of a Wall Street Trader* (1999), James B. Stewart's *Den of Thieves* (1992), and Michael Lewis's *Liar's Poker* (1990), all of which provide rich, vivid depictions of the culture of Wall Street. For somewhat broader treatments, see Steve Fraser's *Wall Street: America's Dream Palace* (2008) and Charles R. Morris's *The Two Trillion Dollar Meltdown: Easy Money, High Rollers, and the Great Credit Crash* (2008). Finally, for a more fully academic treatment, see Mitch Abolafia's *Making Markets* (1996). Karen Ho provides a richly textured ethnography of Wall Street in the 1990s in her book *Liquidated*, which has a slightly different take on the bravado common among traders than I do. She tends to stress what

she calls "the culture of smartness," the elite replication achieved through insular recruiting as well as the hypercompetitive atmosphere and transient human relationships common on The Street. Michael Lewis's *The Big Short* (2010) gives a richly textured description of the logic used by traders, while Niall Ferguson's *The Ascent of Money* (2009) situates trading practices within a larger history of finance. Sebastian Mallaby's *More Money than God* (2010) provides an inside look at some of the approaches specifically taken by hedge fund investors and the advantages afforded them by looser regulation.

2. I use the term "Wall Street" to refer to the collection of investment banks and other large financial institutions that are engaged in financial transactions. Many of these firms are located in the area surrounding Wall Street in downtown Manhattan, although more and more have moved to the area bounded by 46th and 56th Streets and Park Avenue to Broadway (Ho 2009).

3. I introduce this person more fully in chapter 7, on individuals who are consciously experimenting with uses of money.

4. If there is such a thing as money culture, one could reasonably argue that there are national money cultures as well as very localized money cultures produced, for example, in particular families. To understand any individual person's view of money *as an individual,* you would have to consider the competing pulls of workplace money cultures, familial money cultures, national money cultures, and others that could be relevant. Since I am studying money culture as it relates primarily to work, the more accurate term for me to use might be a *work money culture,* but I find this phrase awkward and hope the reader will accept the shorter term *money culture,* with the caveat that I am studying mainly one variant of a money culture: that which is produced through distinct types of work. Since I think it is a more commonly accepted belief that family money cultures shape who we are, I emphasize the idea that money cultures are also produced through the work people do. See also Baudrillard 1975 and Ingham 1996, 2001.

5. See Hochschild 1979 and Leidner 1993 for elaboration of the concept of *emotion work.*

6. Fevre 2003, 190.

7. Smith 1985 [1776]; Weber 1930; Throsby 2001, 9. There are a few interesting exceptions, of course. Amy Wharton (1993) detailed the consequences for workers of having to constantly manage their emotions at work. Rebecca Erickson and Amy Wharton (1997) demonstrated that service workers who have to be "inauthentic" in their jobs are prone to depression.

8. The idea that differing cultural capital is held by different social classes is an example of the lineage from classical economic sociology to more modern variants in the field of economic sociology (see Portes 2010; Bourdieu 1977).

9. Edwards and Wajcman 2005, 19.

10. Hughes 1958, 7.
11. Hughes 1958, 8. It is impossible not to note the sexist language in a book entitled *Men and Their Work*. Published in 1958, the book is an important contribution to the sociology of work and was typical of much of the dominant research at the time, which did not seem to take any account of women and their work (the word *women* does not appear in the index to the book). It is interesting to think about the impact on "conceiving" of work and its role in shaping identity in an era in which gender was ignored.
12. Ransome 2005, 91.
13. See Edwards and Wajcman 2005, 22–23. When economists look at the non-economic rewards for work, they sometimes put a monetary value on those noneconomic rewards equal to whatever salary is forgone to do that kind of work. So if I could be a stock broker and earn $200,000 per year but choose to be a social worker who earns $30,000 per year, I must value the noneconomic rewards of social work at $170,000 per year. This is an example of monetizing everything.
14. Many researchers point out that it is less and less likely for an individual to spend an entire career working for a single organization. With all the fluidity of a working life, one wonders how someone develops an identity from work. Edwards and Wajcman (2005), in their book on working lives, devote an entire chapter to this issue, titled "Is the Organizational Career an Outdated Concept?" They consider the possibility that a career should now be thought of as a "project of the self." This project does still often happen in social and organizational settings; the settings just shift more frequently (e.g., working in a small company, working in a large company, working from home while an employee, working as a self-employed consultant providing work for the large company you formerly worked for, and the like). I would argue that due to this fluidity, one's work identity comes as much from the nature of the work you do as it does from the organizational setting in which you do it (see also Du Gay 1996). More generally, Richard Sennett writes in *The Corrosion of Character*, "How can a human being develop a narrative of identity and life history in a society composed of episodes and fragments? The conditions of the new economy feed instead on experience which drifts in time, from place to place, from job to job" (1998, 26–27). This trend not only presents dilemmas of identity for the individual working in what Sennett calls the "new capitalism" but also presents challenges to researchers studying work and identity, as they tend to study these identities within single organizations where they can only capture a snapshot of someone's larger career, which might unfold in and out of particular organizational settings. It is important for sociologists and others to figure out ways to study the "postmodern worker" who works for multiple organizations and in

multiple settings over the course of a career. Having said all this, it is still true, as Edwards and Wajcman write, that "the workplace remains a central location for the realization of employees' personal identity, their sense of autonomy and their will to connect with society" (2005, 43). See also Connor 1997.

15. Abolafia 1996, 16.

16. Abolafia 1996, 20. See also Hardie and MacKenzie 2006; and Lepinay 2011.

17. I highly recommend Beunza and Stark 2004, 2005; Callon and Caliskan 2005; Callon, Millo, and Muniesa 2007; Hardie and MacKenzie 2006; Maurer 2005; Tett 2009.

18. Swedberg 2005, 129; emphasis in original.

19. Weber 1978, 636.

20. Weber 1978, 635–36.

21. Biggart 2002, xiv.

22. Granovetter 1985.

23. Granovetter 2002.

24. Zelizer 1997, 1. She also refers to tips as "not quite a payment, not quite a bribe, not quite charity, but not quite a gift either." Historically, "tips indicated distance and social inequality between donor and recipient," and because a tip was "discretionary and 'dependent upon the whim of the patron,' [it] further established the inferiority of the recipient." It wasn't until 1917 that tips became more fully recognized and established as wages by the courts (Zelizer 1997, 95–96).

25. Zelizer 1997, 10. See also Zelizer 2005, 2010.

26. Zelizer 2007. See also her earlier article on the establishment of markets (Zelizer 1988).

27. Swidler 2001, 25.

28. Swidler 2001, 189–90.

29. It is not my task here to ascertain the larger cultural repertoires surrounding money, as I am studying local repertoires specific to particular types of work, but I think it would be interesting to tease out the larger repertoires of money from which people draw in American culture writ large (see, for example, Wachtel 1983). George Akerlof and Rachel Kranton attempt to incorporate social and cultural norms into existing economic models in their book *Identity Economics* (2010).

30. It is interesting to think of how thinking and talking are related when it comes to major cultural topics like love or money. Most likely the connection is an iterative process in which cognition shapes language while language shapes cognition. One of the most pointed versions of the Jungian idea that there are larger money repertoires rooted in our collective psyches can be found in William Bloom's *Money, Heart, and Mind: Financial Well-Being for People and Planet*, in which he writes, "Millennia of anxiety and greed, as well as millennia of inspiration and fulfillment, have created a money entity—a thought form or

archetype—which exits in humanity's mass psychic experience. This *Zeitgeist* is the collective inner life of our psychological attitudes" (1996, 16–17).

31. See Nippert-Eng 1996.

32. Zerubavel 1997.

33. Zerubavel 1991, 32.

34. Moeran 2006, 115.

35. Christena Nippert-Eng, in her latest book *Islands of Privacy* (2010), shows that we are constantly negotiating what we reveal about ourselves to others. As in all research that relies on narrative interviewing, it is difficult for me to disentangle whether people are reporting "the truth" of their life (assuming there is any single truth in describing a life) or engaging in "telling a story" about their life in which they align means and ends to make logical coherence ex post facto out of what at the time of occurrence might have seemed incoherent or simple coincidence. I tend to side with the approach of Marya Shechtman, who uses the term "narrative self-constitution" in her book *The Constitution of Selves* (1996) to describe the process whereby people develop autobiographical identities that take into account the environment, their understanding of themselves as a person, and their view of other people's conception of who they are. These narratives are stories that rely sometimes on storytelling devices but are also a type of truth in that they are revelatory of how individuals engage in sense making of their own story and identity. I also agree with Pablo Vila, who argues that people "use social categories and interpellations to understand who they are and who 'the others' are" (2000, 21)—or in my research, to understand who they are and who they are not. As Mary Jo Maynes, Jennifer Pierce, and Barbara Laslett (2008) point out, recognizing that the telling of a story is an act of self-construction on the part of the teller is the greatest value of narrative evidence. Susan Chase (1995) makes a good case for thinking in terms of narrative in interviewing, and Jaber Gubrium and James Holstein (1995) show that understanding both biography and ethnography can be revelatory in getting a comprehensive view of social experiences. Ruthellen Josselson and Amia Lieblich's edited collection ties narrative to the interpretation of experience, and Michael Humphreys and Andrew Brown (2002) discuss ways to use narratives to understand the taking on of, or resistance to, organizational identities.

36. See Barley and Kunda 2001.

37. Magali Sarfatti Larson (2006) once described professions as "disciplinary cultures," as she and other sociologists recognize that professions create cultures that transcend individual organizational and workplace settings.

38. Geertz 1973, 89.

39. An obvious next step is to understand how a particular workplace culture might make a difference to the money cultures shared across different organizations.

40. It is interesting to see in chapter 2, for example, how professional poker players develop similar ways of thinking and talking about money, even though they do not necessarily share a particular "workplace" with one another in the strictest sense. If one considers the gaming tables in casinos as their workplace, they do share in a loose, ever-shifting work culture. They engage in similar work with one another and sometimes share gaming tables with a sea of interchangeable faces. Many converse with one another quite a bit while playing or during downtime between games or while waiting for an opening at a table. With the increasing flexibility of many types of work, it is interesting to think about whether a more traditional work life is becoming more like the shifting work culture of poker players and to speculate on how workplace culture develops in these more flexible workplaces. Online poker players play in their homes, but even they report some level of engagement with other players, chatting online during games or in chat rooms and discussion forums for online players.

41. Gianfranco Poggi writes, "For every institution, there is . . . a set of people who are specifically and exclusively identified with and committed to it; and such people often reflect and embody in a particularly intense manner the institution's distinctive traits—whether because the involvement has so shaped them, or because they already possessed those traits and on that account have specifically involved themselves in it" (1993, 142). This summarizes a piece of my dilemma in choosing people to interview. I wished to interview people who embody the characteristics of certain kinds of work, yet I could not always know that in advance; nor did I want people unrepresentative of the others in that line of work. Similarly, it is impossible to disentangle whether individuals have certain traits because they have worked in an occupation for many years or whether they had some version of those traits before starting their career and were attracted to a particular career because they were already that type of person. Without true random assignment—which in this case would mean taking a random group of people and making them poker players for twenty years and taking another randomly chosen group of people and making them commission salespeople or religious clergy for twenty years—this problem is never completely solvable.

42. Swedberg 2003.

43. DiMaggio 1994, 27.

44. DiMaggio 1994, 30–31; 1990. See also Neil Smelser and Richard Swedberg's *The Handbook of Economic Sociology* (1994).

45. Zelizer 2002, 108; 2010. Additional research on culture and the economy can be found in Mark Jacobs and Nancy Weiss Hanrahan's edited collection, *The Blackwell Companion to the Sociology of Culture* (2006), and in Kieran Healy's (2002) article on culture and the new economy.

46. I might have taken this approach had I wanted to understand from what larger national repertoires people drew in talking about money.

47. As Herb Goldberg and Robert Lewis write in *Money Madness*, "Money behavior, like all complex behavior, is learned; and it is because it satisfied certain psychological and emotional needs. Positive and negative experiences during infancy and childhood, cultural impact, and early training all help define attitudes and behaviors toward money. If those attitudes and behaviors prove troublesome or inappropriate, they can be unlearned" (1978, 65). I differ from this approach in pointing to an entirely new set of socialization experiences around money that occur in adulthood through work experiences and through a person's own family formation experiences (e.g., having a partner, having children).

48. See Beunza and Stark 2004; Hardie and MacKenzie 2006; Nippert-Eng 1996; Zerubavel 1991, 1997.

Notes to Chapter 2

1. Notable examples of works that have explored this subject include Mitch Abolafia's *Making Markets* (1996), which shows how trading markets are social constructions as traders develop trust to perform their jobs, and Iain Hardie and Donald MacKenzie's "Assembling an Economic Actor: The *Agencement* of a Hedge Fund" (2006).

2. Laura Hansen and Siamak Movahedi (2010) show that the most common explanation for the 2008 global financial crisis is one that centers on individual greed as a character defect. Rather than examining the systemic roots of the crisis, they argue it has been easier to blame "a few bad apples on Wall Street who created havoc for Main Street" (367). This is a common response to financial crises. See also the Financial Crisis Inquiry Commission's report (2011).

3. Scannell, Solomon, and Zuckerman 2006, 1.

4. Ellis 2010. To the best of my knowledge, none of the hedge fund firms where I interviewed went out of business during the financial meltdown that followed the piercing of the housing bubble and the difficulties experienced by Bear Stearns in its mortgage-backed securities (resulting in its acquisition by JP Morgan Chase) and the bankruptcy filing of Lehman Brothers.

5. "Two-twenty" is the typical fee structure in hedge funds, which means that a management fee of 2 percent is charged as well as a performance fee of 20 percent of earnings. This has allowed the 20 percent performance fee to receive more favorable tax treatment as a type of capital gain rather than as regular income, but this also means that it is dependent on performance. Some of the more successful funds have been able to charge even higher performance fees.

6. McCrary 2002, 2005.

7. Weiss 2006, 110.

8. The reverse can also be a problem for hedge fund traders and poker players: getting "giddy" from a good run of luck, leading to overreaching based on the odds in front of you. Some traders and players use the phrase "playing with house money" to describe the looseness with which some people play or trade when they have been winning.

9. Reuven Brenner, Gabrielle Brenner, and Aaron Brown, in their book *A World of Chance: Betting on Religion, Games, Wall Street* (2008), show how important gambling and risk taking were to the development of modern finance. Susquehanna International Group, a well-known financial trading firm, hosts its own poker tournament and uses poker as one way to teach trading, as it provides a training ground for thinking about risk.

10. These types of wagers are called "proposition bets" and are particularly popular among poker players. I think one reason for this is that poker players like to "practice" calculating odds for all sorts of unusual activities.

11. Zelizer 1997.

12. I interviewed a number of small-stakes online players who try to think of their playing as a way to earn an hourly wage above what they might earn in other fields of work. Most told me they earned somewhere between ten and twenty dollars per hour over the long run. (There are many computer tracking programs that keep statistics on earnings, so players would often know their exact hourly rate.) Poker players enter games based on the stakes of the game, starting in the lowest-stakes games, until they feel they are good enough to move up to the next level. Moving up is a tricky decision because players have the chance to earn more money per hour, but if they move up too quickly, they may find themselves beyond their skill level. It is important to remember that I was interviewing those who tended to be successful enough to still be playing. A huge number of people try playing online, lose fifty or one hundred dollars, and then stop playing. Some of the more seasoned online players reported making between thirty and sixty dollars per hour over the long run, with some of them playing thirty or more hours per week.

13. The most obvious form of this is detecting a "tell" in an opponent. A tell is an unintended tip-off by an opponent that indicates what the player might have in his or her hand. For example, if a player tends to bet more quickly when he has a good hand, this is a very straightforward tell that can be used to clear advantage. A less obvious tell might be that an opponent glances back and forth between her hole cards and the community cards (called the flop, the turn, and the river in Texas Hold 'Em) when she wishes to confirm that she has a straight or a flush. Most good players carefully monitor their own

tells and work to eliminate them. A few players try to create "false tells"—for example, betting more quickly when you have a good hand for several rounds but then bluffing by betting quickly with a weak hand. Beyond these basic tells, good players simply seem to have a very keen ability to read other players' emotions. This can even be an unconscious ability that cannot be easily described in words. Interestingly, some online computer poker players (who don't actually see their opponents) claim there are tells in online games (e.g., betting more quickly with good hands).

14. Siler 2009, 1. For more information on the technical aspects of Texas Hold 'Em and other variants of poker, see Bellin 2002; Brunson 1979; Craig 2005; Hayano 1982; Sallaz 2009.

15. I am not talking here about illegal insider information, which usually involves making a trade based on nonpublic proprietary information about a company that has been revealed by someone who gains access to that information through their duties working in or with a company. Rather, I am talking about knowing something about a market that not everyone recognizes yet or knowing about a world event that might lead to a decline or rise in a major commodities market or even having a better sense of the psychology of a particular market before others.

16. McManus 2009, 15.

17. McManus 2009, 8.

18. I thank one of my outside reviewers for helping me nail down this insight. One difference between poker players and hedge fund traders is that poker players generally think of what they are betting as "their money," whereas hedge fund traders may think of what they are trading as "other people's money." But even this difference can become cloudy. Some poker players are "staked" in tournaments or big games, meaning that investors will put up a piece of the entry fee or the money for chips in exchange for a cut of any winnings. Most hedge fund traders have some of their money invested in the hedge fund to show investors that they have "skin in the game" (to use the term du jour), so they are also trading some of their own money.

19. Derman 2004, 269. In addition to Derman's book on his own life as a quant trader, Lindsey and Schachter's profiles of twenty-five quant traders in their book *How I Became a Quant: Insight from 25 of Wall Street's Elite* (2007) provides interesting insights into the making of quantitative traders and the way they learn to think about markets and trading.

20. Schiller 1990, 58.

21. Black and Scholes 1973.

22. See Edwards and Wajcman 2005.

23. Edwards and Wajcman 2005, 222; see also Lowenstein 2001, 70–72.

24. As Emmanuel Derman puts it, "The success of the theory of options valuation, the best model economics can offer, is the story of a Platonically simple theory, taken more seriously than it deserves and then used extravagantly, with hubris, as a crutch to human thinking" (2004, 269).

25. Lowenstein 2001, 70.

26. Lowenstein 2001, 72.

27. All of this might also be thought of as an example of the point made by Donald MacKenzie in *An Engine, Not a Camera* (2006) that financial modeling can be seen as "shaping markets" just as much as they are "describing markets." In other words, the models themselves (and the logics behind them) drive traders toward certain shared behaviors and modes of acting under particular conditions. MacKenzie, Muniesa, and Siu (2007) examine the way economic thinking and the work of economists help to make markets, and they study the way markets come to perform in concordance with economic thinking. Millo and MacKenzie (2007) have made the argument that the Black-Scholes model and its progeny operate as a set of instructions and practices that serve as a basis of behavior for hedge fund traders. Ironically, as they put it, "as the consensus around risk management systems was established, the accuracy and validity of predictions produced by them became less important" (1). In other words, if everyone is speaking the same language using versions of the same model, they all can be in general agreement as they do their work, even if they are all wrong in the same direction. This offers insight into systemic market breakdowns, as Beunza and Stark found in their ethnography of a trading room: "If enough traders overlook a key issue, their mistake will reverberate to others" (2010, 1).

28. In most hedge fund firms, there are one or more risk managers in charge of following the level of risk for the entire firm. Typically, risk managers use some form of a quantitative formula called "VaR" (Value at Risk). VaR models try to measure the short-term risk of an entire portfolio. Since it is based on a normal curve, it tends to work well 95 percent of the time but often falls apart at the tails of the normal curve. Since major market crashes happen at the tail, VaR is not as good at predicting extraordinary events such as the freezing up of credit markets after the housing bubble burst in 2008.

29. There are several different ways to "mark"—or set a value for—a portfolio. The most straightforward way is to "mark to market," which means the value is set by the price in a real market (so, for example, the closing stock prices for a portfolio of stocks determines the value set for the portfolio). This valuation should then reflect what people are willing to pay in the market for the items in the portfolio at any given moment. But what happens when what is being traded has an unclear value or a value in dispute, or when there is no clear "market" for a something like a derivative or a highly specialized and

esoteric bundle of securities (e.g., timber land, water rights)? In these cases, there may be no clearly set "market price" at any given time, so some firms use what is called "mark to model" pricing. The "model" referred to in this pricing procedure might involve using computer forecasts of such things as cash flow or interest rates or default rates, depending on the securities being priced, to set a price. But if a market starts to completely unravel, these "mark to model" prices can become quite disconnected from what anyone is actually willing to pay for a bundle of securities. The speaker in this case seems to imply that in the particular hedge fund "blowup" he is describing, there was wide discretion in the firm's ability to "mark" the value of a portfolio or a particular tranche of mortgages, for example.

30. A "leak" means that the poker professional loses money at other forms of gambling in which he or she is not particularly skilled or for which the casino or "house" has a significant edge; this player is said to have a "leak."

31. The organization is called 100 Women in Hedge Funds, and more information about the organization can be found at http://www.100womeninhedgefunds.org/.

32. A "fund of funds" is essentially a hedge fund pool that invests in a group of other hedge funds as a way of spreading risk.

33. See Reskin and Roos 1990 for an excellent discussion of the ways to study gender dominance in particular professions. See also Tomaskovic-Devey 1993; Bielby and Baron 1986; and Baron et al. 2007.

34. One of the female professional poker players whom I interviewed believes that poker playing is actually a good profession for women who want to combine work and family, because you can be home with children much of the day and play poker in the late evenings and into the night, presuming your partner or caregiver can be with the children at that time.

35. I have always found it interesting that those who explain male dominance in the hedge fund industry or among poker players often cite the fact that men are more aggressive, which they believe provides men with an advantage over women. Yet they also cite the importance of reading the emotions of others, understanding one's own emotional reactions to stressful events, and having good gut instincts. They rarely note that these traits are usually seen as more common among women. This selective use of stereotypes seems to justify the status quo more than anything else.

36. Lehrer 2009.

37. See also Gladwell 2005 for an examination of the importance of intuition. For an excellent look at the science behind the brain and decision-making, see Pesaran, Nelson, and Anderson 2008.

38. After the meltdown of the two Bear Stearns hedge funds, Steven Begleiter, a former Bear Stearns employee, began to focus more exclusively on poker playing

and reached the final table in the 2009 World Series of Poker. When interviewed about his two careers, he said, "When I'm good I'm processing everything that's going on around me and making good decisions under pressure" (Kadlec 2009, 2).

39. Do not read this as an apology for sexism and misogyny. There is no reason why these insoluble dilemmas necessarily lead to these particular forms of language or belief.

40. Zelizer 1997, 10.

41. De Goede 2005, 48.

Notes to Chapter 3

1. There is terrific sociological research on salespeople and selling, including Robin Leidner's *Fast Food, Fast Talk* (1993), Nicole Biggart's *Charismatic Capitalism* (1990), and David Dorsey's *The Force* (1995). Each of these includes dilemmas of identity and boundaries.

2. In addition to these three areas of sales, I also interviewed a few salespeople in other industries, including a head hunter who straddles the two occupations discussed in this chapter: sales and agents.

3. Agents have been portrayed less often in literature. However, the most iconic image of an agent is found in the film *Jerry Maguire* (1996), in which actor Cuba Gooding, Jr., delivers the famous line, "Show me the money!" In this scene, Gooding (portraying a football player) teaches Jerry (his agent) how to scream, "Show me the money!" For a quick primer on the role of sports agents, see Conrad (2006).

4. This reminds me in some ways of sociologist Michael Burawoy's classic book, *Manufacturing Consent* (1979), in which he found that machinists on a shop floor who were given some discretion over how to use their time to make parts would obsess over the best ways to allocate (and account for) their time working on different jobs. The men (they were all men) played various games to try to maximize their pay, which was based on a modified piece-rate system in which they would get additional money per piece if they exceeded certain goals or quotas for each type of piece. As Burawoy pointed out in the book, it was the uncertainty of the outcome and the discretion afforded to the machinists that got them so engaged in the game of maximizing their pay. See also Evans, Kunda, and Barley (2003) on the way that independent contractors think about different types of time.

5. Being on "stop" means that because a customer has not paid its bills, the accounts receivable department and/or the CFO has placed a hold on the account such that, say, the restaurant cannot order any more food until it cuts

a check and pays at least a portion of its outstanding balance. Most customers have a credit limit, and if they are sixty or ninety days past due on that amount, their account is placed on hold until they pay off. This is a constant source of friction between salespeople and the "bean counters" back at the home office. In this particular quotation, the salesman hints at his irritation that the unpaid balance is at "another restaurant" the customer owns and not the one that is trying to place this order. This is the typical sort of dispute that arises between salespeople and the accounting department. The tension is endemic because of the differing interests at work here: the salesperson wants to sell, and it is excruciatingly painful to salespeople to know that someone is trying to order from them, yet they cannot make the sale (and gain the commission). The accounting department, well aware of the high rate of failure in the restaurant industry, is worried about never getting paid and throwing good money after bad. I noted that of all the professions I studied in my research, salespeople were the most likely to spontaneously talk about conflicts at work, and I think a major reason for this is the way that work is structured, so that, on the one hand, the salesperson is loaded with incentives to sell (from commission salary to sales contests to direct and sometimes intense pressure from a sales manager), yet the company also sets up "brakes" on selling (ranging from stop orders to pressure to hold margins within a given range) that are often out of the control of the salesperson. This conflict is embedded in the structure of many sales organizations, to balance the drive for more sales against the risk of nonpayment.

6. Christena Nippert-Eng analyzes the cognitive dimensions of work and home in her innovative book *Home and Work: Negotiating Boundaries through Everyday Life* (1996). Nippert-Eng shows how people use symbols and transformational practices to try to draw boundaries between home and work. One of the ways people transition from work to home (and vice versa) is through their commute. I found that salespeople have a particularly difficult time drawing these boundaries and often don't really have a traditional commute to and from work. When salespeople stay in their driveway to talk on the telephone, they are deciding not to enter the home and to remain in a place that "feels" more like work to them. When I asked salespeople specifically about their commute, several said they don't think in terms of commuting but rather think of entering their car as the beginning of the workday. However, when I asked if exiting their car ended their workday, several said no and that they carried their work into the home with them (sometimes in their mind and sometimes by being on the phone or checking email messages). Michael G. Flaherty provides an interesting cognitive sociology of time in his book *The Textures of Time* (2010).

7. I did not hear any allusions to ADHD from sports and entertainment agents, who seemed perfectly at ease in the office environment. Agents spend

significant time reviewing contracts, a more typical form of office work, and spend less time on the road.

8. In this chapter, I use the term "agent" to refer to those who represent talented individuals in contract negotiations typically for a percentage of the contract value. The term, as used in common parlance, is a catch-all term that could refer to an entertainment lawyer or a registered agent with the National Football League. The term can have differing meanings depending on the professional context. For example, in the National Football League, there is an actual training and certification process for agents, and only registered agents may represent players in negotiations. In the music business, on the other hand, some bands employ agents, managers, booking agents, and lawyers, and sometimes these roles can overlap. To complicate matters even further, one individual can be an entertainment lawyer by profession and training but also gain certification as an agent in the NFL. The majority of those I interviewed for this chapter trained as entertainment lawyers (or trained as contract lawyers and then moved into the entertainment field). Several became certified as agents by various governing bodies. Many of the entertainment lawyers did take on some standard contract law to help provide steady income while they acted as representatives for musical groups, hoping to strike it rich as agents for those groups. Literary agents, however, rarely have a legal background and instead usually have industry background, working first as an editor. These agents have skills at recognizing promising writers, helping writers to shape or market their work, and finding suitable publishing houses for their work, but usually they do not have formal legal training.

9. Agents can actually be paid in all sorts of ways. Most earn some sort of percentage or commission on the deals of their clients. For example, literary agents tend to earn a standard 10–15 percent fee. Sports agents tend to get a percentage of a contract (and this percentage is sometimes regulated by a professional sports league). Entertainment agents can, and often do, earn commission fees, but those who are trained as lawyers can also do contract work for a flat fee that is not commission based. Many music agents, for example, do some work on a commission basis and some work for an hourly or set fee. Regardless of all these variations, usually the earnings of agents are highly dependent on the success of their clients in obtaining contracts and in some form of commercial success as an artist. More and more, major sports and entertainment stars also sign endorsement deals in addition to their contract with a team or a record company. In these cases, the deal structure is more wide open, and agents can be more creative in how they structure compensation both to their clients and to themselves. The major dilemma for agents, however, is that they can do significant work on behalf of some clients with little or no economic payoff if the client never "makes it."

10. Perhaps the best book on this topic is Derek Bok's *The Cost of Talent* (1993). Bok makes a persuasive argument for the significant salaries of talented people. However, the agent's job is to be able to pick from among many talented people the few who have the best chance to make it big. Knowing what a person might be worth, in advance of his or her making it big, is a very difficult proposition. Boris Groysberg's book *Chasing Stars: The Myth of Talent and the Portability of Performance* (2010) suggests, however, that talent may be misunderstood as a characteristic of individuals. He found in a study of "star" performers in Wall Street banks that when stars left their original place of employment, they often could not replicate their success at a new firm.

11. I don't mean to imply that other commission salespeople do not have strong feelings about their products as well. A musical agent, however, might be a trained classical musician who doesn't like rap music (or vice versa) but has to put aside that predilection and learn to judge and represent talent from a musical genre he or she might even detest. I think it is less likely to find commission salespeople who (aesthetically) detest the products they are selling. However, I did find one wine salesman who admitted to me that he liked five-dollar bottles of wine just as much as the high-end wine that he was selling.

12. It is not only salespeople, of course, who use expensive products as social markers. Stanley Fish (1993) once skewered academics' pretensions in an essay on why so many academics drive Volvos.

13. I was struck by how much this monologue reminds me of dialogue in the television series *Mad Men*, which portrays people in the advertising industry selling emotions in order to sell product. While I could imagine several of the characters in *Mad Men* saying these very lines, this interview (one of the first in this project) occurred in March 2005, well before the debut of *Mad Men* in July 2007.

14. Veblen 2008 [1899].

Notes to Chapter 4

1. I thank my colleague Joe McLaughlin for a fascinating conversation that eventually led me back to Trilling's *The Liberal Imagination* and then to Henry James's *The Princess Casamassima* (1948 [1886]). Honoré de Balzac's *A Great Man of the Provinces in Paris* (1896) is another version of the trope. As Peggy McCormack points out in her book *The Rule of Money: Gender, Class, and Exchange Economics in the Fiction of Henry James*, "While metaphors far outnumber literal discussions about dollars and cents, both are so pervasive in James's writing that this economic language acquires a privileged status among his linguistic codes" (McCormack 1990, 1; see also Chandra 1981).

2. Another boundary crossing that is common fodder for exploration in literature is that between "old wealth" and "new money," as can be seen in novels ranging from F. Scott Fitzgerald's *The Great Gatsby* (2007 [1925]) through Tom Wolfe's *Bonfire of the Vanities* (1987). David Lodge's novel *Nice Work* (1990) is a terrific social satire based on a boundary crossing related to work. Enmeshed in this novel are trenchant observations about social class stereotyping, as Lodge describes how his characters are changed through the boundary crossing. Popular movies such as *Trading Places* (1983), in which a commodity trader and a homeless man switch places, make similar observations about social class boundary crossing and the larger nature/nurture debate.

3. Another interesting characteristic of fund raisers is that none whom I interviewed had consciously planned to become fund raisers. Many had short stints in other careers and then, as they put it, "found their way into fund raising." As one of my interviewees said, "I have never worked with, nor ever met, someone who had thought, 'I want to grow up to be a development professional.'"

4. I am grateful to the organization that allowed me to attend and participate fully in the fund-raising camp. It was an incredibly engaging, well-executed, and thorough training experience.

5. Zelizer 2005.

6. I am not sure that this ability "just comes naturally." I think what "naturally" really means here is that the person found it easy to do this because she is a friendly, outgoing person who likes to ask questions about other people and finds it easy to become interested in their lives.

7. In a more extreme version of this, the telephone solicitor calls and asks with mock sincerity, "How are you today?" usually making the recipient feel immediately cautious and on guard. The listener knows that this stranger cannot possibly care about the listener's well-being (particularly if the prospect can hear the noise of dozens of other solicitors in the "boiler room" asking dozens of others how they are feeling). In the fund-raising relationships I describe, the relationship is much more subtle and complex because there are genuine elements of friendship that develop in the relationship (which cannot happen in a one-time phone solicitation). Fund raisers often told me stories about attending the wedding of children of people whom they met while cultivating gifts. I should note that I did meet a small number of fund raisers who said they consciously avoided mixing "business" with "friendship" and would generally decline such invitations.

8. Early social exchange theorists made this very point—that every social exchange has some element of cost-benefit analysis and instrumental calculation (Homans 1958). Of course, if the theory is pushed to its limits, it becomes reductionist as it ignores noninstrumental aspects of relationships,

or it becomes tautological if it simply defines *everything* in cost-benefit terms. Paul Allison (1992) offers another alternative, suggesting that there are cultural selection pressures that produce altruism or, if you prefer, beneficence in certain situations. Georg Simmel (1971) in his writings on "gifts" noted the specialness of the first gift, as it is not given in exchange for a prior gift. However, one could even argue that at times a first gift is given with the expectation of a subsequent gift in return.

9. Scientific management is also known as "Taylorism" (after Frederick Winslow Taylor).
10. Weinstein 2009, 121.
11. See Winans 1984. Foster Winans has done a remarkable job recovering from this event, pursuing a life as a writer and a supporter of other writers, as well as lecturing about the lessons he learned from those early years.
12. For decision-making rules and their relationships to professions in a slightly different context, see Michele Lamont's *How Professors Think: Inside the Curious World of Academic Judgment* (2009), which examines scholarly evaluations across a wide array of academic disciplines.

Notes to Chapter 5

1. See Charles Dickens, *A Christmas Carol* (2007 [1843]).
2. Robin Leidner (1993) describes similar processes in her book *Fast Food, Fast Talk*. Perhaps the best description of the psychological manipulation that occurs in commission selling can be found in David Dorsey's *The Force* (1995), which describes a year with a Xerox sales team in Cleveland, Ohio. Dorsey has a finely tuned ear for the psychology behind a team of sales agents hustling to "move product" and the manipulation of emotion that occurs in sales occupations.
3. There has been an amazing proliferation in the notion that people will need at least one, if not two, million dollars to retire comfortably. Some people believe that this notion is trumpeted by the financial industry for self-serving reasons as well as altruistic ones. It is also interesting to contrast this widely accepted notion in the United States with the idea that in much of the world there is no concept of "retirement" at all, let alone one that can only be purchased with several million dollars. See Lee Eisenberg's *The Number: What Do You Need for the Rest of Your Life, and What Will It Cost?* (2006).
4. The vast majority of credit counselors I met were female. They often said they liked the career because it blended their interest in financial matters with their desire to help people. The only male credit counselor I interviewed had also come out of the banking field and had opened up his own consumer credit counseling service in New England.

5. Zelizer 1997, 166; see also 161–67.
6. In addition to interviewing debt and credit counselors, I was able to watch them interact informally with clients at their office. I also was able to observe several professional presentations given by counselors: one was a presentation to people about buying a home on a low to moderate income, and a second was on general financial literacy, checking and savings accounts, and the like. I accompanied another counselor to a presentation she gave at a roundtable discussion at the Federal Reserve Bank on creating programs for financial literacy in the K–12 curriculum. All these opportunities allowed me more time for informal conversation and observation of interactions. I decided not to intrude on actual counseling sessions, as I believed my presence at those would be disruptive, so instead I asked each counselor to describe typical counseling sessions and to show me the materials they used in counseling. Many, without prompting, began playacting as if I was the client, saying things like, "So, let's say you came in and had credit card debt and loans, and the creditors were hounding you. I would begin by talking with you about this, and then I would move on to showing you this budget diary and explaining how we would track your spending."
7. In a similar way, in Alcoholics Anonymous programs, recovering alcoholics are consistently reminded of the mantra "people, places, and things" as a way to be aware of what people, locations, and situations they should avoid, lest they lead to relapse. I once heard a recovering alcoholic respond to the "people, places, and things" slogan by quipping, "Okay, so now I have to avoid nouns?"
8. By this, I simply mean that Americans tend to view things more in individual terms than in terms of groups, social classes, or social structure.
9. The counselor, of course, does not see high-income individuals who have addictions but never end up in such bad financial shape that they visit a debt-counseling office. For a portrait of typical debtors in bankruptcy, see Sullivan, Westbrook, and Warren's *As We Forgive Our Debtors: Bankruptcy and Consumer Credit in America* (1999), which argues against the idea that debtors are spendthrifts.
10. Even the increase in the number of mentally ill homeless is caused in large part by a structural change: the disappearance of long-term institutional and residential care for the mentally ill. Since I interviewed some debt counselors before the major economic downturn that began with the bursting of the housing bubble and some others after that, I was able to notice some slight shifting in attitude. Counselors did report seeing more people who feared home foreclosure, and counselors were somewhat more likely to attribute that increase to national economic conditions, rather than to individual decisions, although some continued to describe it with such individualistic terms as "people getting in over their heads" or "buying a house they couldn't really afford."

11. I don't mean to imply that structural issues never arose in my interviews with debt counselors. Several of them, upon my probing, did say that clients' earning too little money from their jobs was a contributor to their indebtedness, but then they looked for an individualistic way out of the dilemma, by suggesting that the individual take on a second job or sell his or her belongings. Several mentioned, without probing, that the lack of health-care benefits puts people into debt when illness strikes. It almost seemed like these issues were too big to address for the debt counselors, or they did not have the wherewithal to address them; so this just represented the water in which their clients were swimming or, in many cases, drowning. Since debt counselors believed there was little they could do to alter the water, they grabbed for whatever life preservers they did have at their disposal.

Notes to Chapter 6

1. Randy Martin demonstrates the ubiquity of the market mentality in *Financialization of Daily Life* (2002).
2. Rohr 2001, 7.
3. Wuthnow 1994, 2.
4. Vincent Miller writes in his book *Consuming Religion: Christian Faith and Practice in a Consumer Culture*, "This is not a book about religion against consumer culture; it is a book about the fate of religion in consumer culture" (2003, 1). Much of the research in the sociology of religion leads to the view that religious clergy will exhibit a great variety of responses to social and political issues, so it is not a surprise that I found variation among respondents. After all, religious beliefs and practices related to money span the continuum from "ascetic poverty" to "prosperity theology." I think what did surprise me was how the same core issues related to money arose in the conversations, despite the variation in responses to it.
5. Englert 2006, 6. Englert describes one of the men this way: "Heiser was grateful for these gestures. It had been more than two years since he had a steady income, and he had become acutely aware of how he spent his money—a strange feeling for a forty-eight-year-old man who had worked his whole life. People might be spiritually dependent on him as a priest, but he would definitely be financially dependent on them" (273–74).
6. This priest might be an example of what Georg Simmel called "ascetic poverty" (1978 [1900], 251). Many priests, but not all, take a vow of poverty, depending on their particular religious order. However, individual lifestyles may vary quite a bit, from quite spare to fairly opulent, depending on one's circumstances. Most priests strive to "live simply," as they put it.

7. For this chapter, I interviewed Roman Catholic priests, Protestant ministers (both from mainline denominations and from large nondenominational megachurches, commonly defined as having over two thousand regular attendees), Muslim imams, and Jewish rabbis. Although all those I interviewed were from the Abrahamic religions, they represented a wide array of religious perspectives, including what might be considered conservative and liberal views. I interviewed Reconstructionist rabbis and orthodox rabbis; imams from black Muslim communities in Philadelphia as well as imams from the mainly white, upper-middle-class suburbs and one Sufi imam; and Roman Catholic priests and Protestant ministers from poor and wealthier parishes. As is true throughout this book, I am not choosing a representative sample but selecting individuals who might illustrate the variety of views on money. My goal was to include a wide array of working clergy in the largest denominations in the United States. A larger study with a random sample would be needed to ascertain whether clergy of different denominations think differently about money. Thus, I am careful in this chapter not to draw any conclusions about denominational differences in attitudes toward money. I did not interview religious leaders from non-Abrahamic traditions (e.g., the monastic Sangha—the Buddhist clergy made up of monks and nuns), as they have smaller representation in the United States. Buddhism's main precepts include a selflessness that militates against stinginess or hoarding and holds that wealth is impermanent and does not necessarily lead to happiness. On the other hand, if one is not a monk practicing simplicity, there is nothing inherent in Buddhism that derides wealth, as wealth could be viewed as the fruits of a positive karma. The more overarching concept is the Buddhist idea of a "right livelihood," which entails doing good for others if possible and certainly not doing harm to others (see Dalai Llama and Cutler 2003, 2009; Iyer 2008; Jinpa 2006). Similarly, in Hinduism, there is nothing that militates against wealth. Instead, working hard, gaining wealth, and supporting others is one of the four aims in life undertaken as part of a progression in Hinduism, and by the final step, one achieves a sense of balance, so that wealth for wealth's sake becomes relatively unimportant. There is some underlying sense, however, in both Hinduism and Buddhism that "enlightenment" of various types reduces the desire for large sums of money.

8. Durkheim 1915, 37. Durkheim made the point that there need not be anything inherent in an object that makes it either sacred or profane, yet he insisted that the two realms are conceived as separate in religious thought. In a different context, Eviatar Zerubavel, in his book *The Fine Line* (1991, 122), makes a strong case for the advantages of breaking free of what he calls "mental cages" created in part by overly dichotomized thinking.

9. Geertz 1973, 87. Fenella Cannell laments the lack of attention to Christianity among anthropologists, when she writes in *The Anthropology of Christianity*, "I would suggest that Christianity has functioned in some ways as 'the repressed' of anthropology over the period of the formation of the discipline" (2006, 4).

10. Matthew 19:24, Luke 18:25, and Mark 10:225 (New American Standard Bible).

11. Luke 12:34 and Matthew 6:21 (New American Standard Bible).

12. For example, in Stephen Ellingson's book *The Megachurch and the Mainline* (2007), we see significant variation even among Lutheran churches in the San Francisco Bay Area of California.

13. The time frame might actually extend to "eternity" within a religious framework that includes an afterlife. Interestingly, some economists include "afterlife consumption" as part of the utility function in measuring what it is that individuals gain from religion and how followers decide to allocate their time to church attendance. See, for example, Azzi and Ehrenberg (1975, 28). I thank Jared Peifer for pointing this out.

14. This holds true, at least, for secular financial advisors. The subset of financial advisors who use religious principles in guiding financial advice tend to adopt the "custodial view" of money. I thought it was interesting that those who solicit large donations from individuals would sometimes also take the view that since you cannot take money with you, it is better to put money to good use now. Here we have development and fund-raising professionals aligned with clergy in the view that money should be put to a good use now. Jared Peifer (2010) describes the similarities and differences between secular and religiously affiliated mutual funds.

15. *Zakat* is typically calculated at 10 percent of agricultural wealth and 2.5 percent of moveable property such as investments, jewelry, and other goods.

16. Anthropologist Bill Maurer writes in his intriguing book *Mutual Life, Limited: Islamic Banking, Alternative Currencies, Lateral Reason*, "Participants in the networks of alternative currencies and Islamic banking often believe that, by transforming the money-form, they will arrive at a transformation of the economy. Within both networks, there are those who interpret their activities with alternative monetary forms as a refusal or repudiation of the market. Others see it as a modification. And still others view it as a return, a going back to an imagined past, a time before the money-form and the commodity-form were equated" (2005, 88).

17. Criticism of the so-called prosperity theology was reflected in a 2008 request by Senator Charles Grassley for financial information from six well-known ministries, sometimes referred to in the media as the "Grassley Six." At the complete other end of the spectrum, Tom Beaudoin, in his book *Consuming Faith*, argues that what we buy should be a reflection of our religious beliefs, using the interesting term "economic spirituality" (2003, 20).

18. Note how different this stance is in comparison to some versions of the "Protestant ethic" that is used to venerate saving money. Although coming from a very different set of assumptions and goals, this religious stance mirrors the debate among economists and policymakers over whether it is better for the economy if people save more money or put money into circulation as consumers by spending money. No wonder people are confused about the best course of action, if there are both religious/moral disputes and economic/policy disagreements over the value of spending versus saving.

19. Bill Maurer in *Mutual Life, Limited* points out that the prohibition against *riba* and other forms of Islamic business contracts guide people toward more efficiency in transactions. In one of my favorite turns of phrase, Maurer describes this as "finding Posner in the Qur'an" (2005, 82).

20. Of course, this was probably the most important point made by sociologist Max Weber in *The Protestant Ethic and the Spirit of Capitalism* (1930). Weber argued that religious ideas played a major role in shaping capitalist development.

21. There are ways in which one can still provide money and be in accord with Islamic principles. For example, someone who gives money to a project can then take a stake or "interest" in the project rather than simply charging an interest rate. These sorts of accommodations seem to exist in all major religions, as religious leaders try to hold true to ancient practices and prohibitions in the modern world, and the accommodations extend well beyond financial issues. The controversy in Judaism over "Shabbat elevators" is another example of this kind of accommodation. Jews are not supposed to operate electric switches on Shabbat. The "Shabbat elevator" arose as an adaptation in skyscrapers in Israel. This elevator is automatically set to go to the top of a building and then to stop at every single floor, without any call buttons being pushed. If not for this elevator, it is hard to imagine how elderly people could get to the thirtieth floor of an apartment building (a structure that obviously did not exist when the original injunction was issued).

22. Not the entire prayer centers on financial issues; other couplets include things such as "Pray for the mourners. And for the mockers. Pray that we all may laugh together" and "Pray for the silenced and for the spin doctors. Pray that we all might speak our own truth with courage and love."

23. Note also that when Maimonides enumerated the forms of charity in the twelfth century, he listed helping people to be independent (e.g., by giving them work or giving them a grant that enables them to gain independence) as the highest level of charity.

24. I imagine this may also affect believers to some extent, but this study was not designed to look at the impact on followers of particular religious traditions.

25. This is not to say that a rabbi could not find out more about the amount each person gives to the synagogue. I am simply making the point that there is a

structure in place that allows rabbis to distance themselves from the specific finances of members.

26. In Germany, there is less separation of church and state than in the United States. As a result, teachers of religion in schools are often certified through the hierarchy of their religious organization (e.g., Catholic or Protestant). This has presented a problem for imams in Germany, as the decentralization of Islam does not provide an easy process for this certification process. This structural difference has made it difficult to incorporate teaching and training of Islam in Germany as well as made it difficult for mosques to qualify for state money (Hockenos 2010).

27. Clergy face an exceptionally acute "free-rider" problem, as described by economists. They rarely charge for anything, so someone can gain an amazing array of benefits without paying anything, while "free-riding" on the financial support of others. Since there are few mandatory fees (most contributions are considered voluntary for tax purposes, among other things), the free-rider issue can be significant. At the same time, many clergy operate in a paradigm in which they strongly believe in providing services to all and particularly to those who cannot afford them. One could argue, however, that what an economist calls a "free-rider" problem is actually the raison d'être for many religious organizations. As a result, both the uncertain revenue streams and the spiritual paradigm can box clergy in financially. Fortunately, the free-rider problem is often overcome by outpourings of generosity from those who are operating within this same spiritual or religious paradigm. A new field of academic inquiry called "Generosity Studies" or "The Science of Generosity" is engaging in research on some of these very issues.

28. Wuthnow 1997, 128.

29. Smith, Emerson, and Snell 2009, 32.

30. One or two mentioned that scandals involving televangelism have increased suspicions around money.

31. Here he is talking about the psychological concept of *transference*, described by Freud (1996), which refers to the redirection of (past) feelings onto another person. In the psychoanalytic setting, for example, an analysand might transfer his feelings for his father onto the analyst. In the example implied by the minister in this quotation, someone who has some unresolved past issues with money might transfer (sometimes unconscious) feelings onto another and see something in a situation that is not really happening (such as stealing money or not treating money properly, in this example).

32. Many clergy have access to a small amount of discretionary funds that they can use to help people in immediate and dire need. In some settings, individuals give donations to the clergyperson's discretionary fund; in other settings, an imam might use money from *zakat* donations. In some churches, priests or ministers are

sometimes given permission to use their "stole fees" for these purposes (the colloquialism "stole fee" comes from the fact that "when you put on the stole, you collect a fee," as suggested donations are given to a priest for performing a baptism, a wedding, or a funeral). Similar to the argument made by Zelizer in *The Social Meaning of Money* (1997), certain types of money can be earmarked as "discretionary money," and thereby more freedom is granted in how it is used.

33. Here he is referring to one of the founders of the Catholic Worker Movement, whose followers often lived and worked among the poor, taking direct action on their behalf.

34. Hyde 1979, xv. Anthropology has a well-developed understanding of the "gift economy," as it typifies many cultures studied by anthropologists. This literature emerged from Marcel Mauss's essay on the gift (2000 [1900]). Research suggests that gift giving is a key feature in many societies, can be an important mechanism of social solidarity, is threatened but not extinguished by a market economy, and can express power relations, particularly in asymmetrical gift-giving transactions (see, for example, Chiel 1988; Godbout 1998; Komter 2005; Osteen 2002; Vaughan 2007). Sociologists have been less likely to take up the issues introduced by Mauss, although Helmuth Berking's book *Sociology of Giving* (1999) is a notable exception. There has been a similar lack of attention to the phenomenon of "sharing" that occurs in many societies (an exception is the article by Russell Belk [2010] in the *Journal of Consumer Research*, which provides an excellent overview of the concept of sharing and an argument that it should not be subsumed under the concept of gift giving). Sociologists do have a more developed set of findings on exchange and reciprocity (Becker 1956; Blau 1964; Molm 2010).

35. Hyde 1979, 56.

36. In a recent ethnography, Jean-Sebastien Marcoux (2009) demonstrates how individuals may actually turn to the market for exchange specifically to avoid feelings of reciprocity and obligation.

37. Goodchild 2009, xi.

38. Robert Wuthnow in *The Crisis in the Churches* (1997) describes the difficulties Christian pastors face. Middle-class parishioners suffer from a significant time bind due to work and family demands. Combine this with the larger culture's promotion of the pursuit of self-interest, and you appreciate the challenges pastors face in communicating a message of stewardship.

Notes to Chapter 7

1. Although some employees at Cornell University participate in the program and have studied it, the Ithaca HOURS program did not emerge from the university but rather from local community activists.

2. Carruthers and Espeland 1998; Zelizer 2007.
3. Garson 2002.
4. Glover 1995, 30.
5. Simmel 1978 [1900], 198.
6. Simmel 1978 [1900], 212, 202.
7. Glover 1996, 5.
8. Glover 1996, 5.
9. Paul Glover said that he did some research that showed that while the local government was mandated to collect taxes in the form of money, it had some discretion in how it defined "money," which might allow the local government to pass a statute defining money as including Ithaca HOURS.
10. I do not want to imply that national currency does not carry meaning, because it certainly does (including carrying the very idea of fungibility), but instead I am suggesting that national-currency supporters often claim that money is devoid of political or social meaning in its essence and its creation. Ithaca HOURS are created to pursue a variety of social, community, and political goals, and their very usage is intended to promote certain ideals. This is why supporters emphatically insist that they are not creating a substitute currency for U.S. dollars but something distinctly different and laden with meaning. See also Peter North's book *Money and Liberation: The Micropolitics of the Alternative Currency Movement* (2007).
11. Bill Maurer, in *Mutual Life, Limited* (2005, 25), points out that proponents of Ithaca HOURS have even debated whether it is most appropriately called an alternative currency, a local currency, a community currency, or complementary currency. Each carries a different shade of meaning. See Collum 2011 for an overview of the many different motivations participants in alternative currency systems have and how motivation may affect participation.
12. Note, however, that even in many basic denary systems there can be coins (and occasionally paper money) that are not on the base-ten system—for example, the quarter (twenty-five-cent coin) in the U.S. system. It was really the absence of an equivalent of a one-dollar bill that made the Ithaca system particularly difficult as an adjunctive currency to the U.S. currency, and the one-tenth-hour bill has now resolved that issue. BerkShares, an alternative currency used in the Berkshires area of the United States, follows a denary system similar to U.S. currency.
13. Alternative currency systems also seem to catch on among intentional or alternative communities. So, for example, some of the new experiments in sustainable agriculture have also chosen to use their own currencies to facilitate bartering of locally grown produce for services such as painting or gardening. Since many of these communities engage laborers who get some of the produce

in exchange for their work, it makes good sense to use a local currency to track and facilitate exchange. One example of an intentional community using a local exchange is Dancing Rabbit Ecovillage in northeastern Missouri.

14. Although unusual, there are other "pay what you want" businesses. The most common seem to be among restaurants, but there is also a taxi driver in Vermont who allows passengers to pay what they want for a cab ride.

15. Leonard 2010.

16. The Free Store did garner some publicity, including an article in the *New York Times*. I attempted to interview the "owner" of The Free Store (or would "creator" be a better term?), by leaving a letter for her at the store, but I never received a response. The Free Store in Williamsburg, Brooklyn, operated from 1999 to 2005. A successor store has since opened in another part of Brooklyn, under a large tent on a dirt lot on Walworth Street (Moynihan 2010). I am also aware of a similar store called the Free Shop in Berlin, as reported in the *Wall Street Journal* (Walker 2007, A1). This store seemed more utilitarian and less an art installation, as compared to the Brooklyn Free Store. The Berlin shop is run by a collective, one of whom was quoted in the *Wall Street Journal* article as saying, "It's totally free of the market logic that everything has a value in exchange" (Walker 2007, A14).

17. In the late 1940s and 1950s, the idea of the "soulful corporation" was made popular by the Managerialist School of academicians and business practitioners, which argued that modern corporations, owing to their dominant market share and financial strength, could be freed from the demands of profit maximization and thereby pursue the happiness of their workers (see, for example, Kaysen 1957 and Berle and Means 1982 [1949]. Intense foreign competition in the 1980s and beyond led to cost cutting and corporate takeovers designed to wring profits from these corporations, and these developments made the idea of the soulful corporation seem quaint, if not naïve. Gerald Davis (2009) offers a number of useful insights into the ways that elements of the global financial system pressured corporations to maximize shareholder return.

Notes to Chapter 8

1. I found it interesting that the etymology of the word *gasconade* comes from the description of people from the Gascony region bordered by the Pyrenees, who were reputed to be a very boastful people. So, although the term was likely a stereotype, its origin reflects a social belief in the connection between an individual trait and a culture.

2. Hansen and Movahedi (2010) make a similar point when they argue that it is a mistake to view greed as an individual psychological attribute that causes Wall

Street scandals. See Knorr-Cetina and Preda's edited collection *The Sociology of Financial Markets* (2005) for details on the structuring of market behavior.

3. This player had essentially quit playing poker and planned to go back to school for a graduate degree because he felt uncomfortable with the way he was becoming dissociated from the meaning of money and because of the loneliness he felt being a full-time player.

4. Brekhus 2008, 1059.

5. See Marx 1967 [1867]. Some scholars have gone so far as to argue that today consciousness and identity are formed more by consumption than by production (Ransome 2005). As Tom Bottomore and David Frisby argue in the introduction to their translation of Simmel's *The Philosophy of Money* (1978 [1900]), one of the things that distinguished Simmel's stance on money and finance from Marx's is that for Marx cultural phenomena such as commodity fetishism are a direct result of capitalism, whereas Simmel wanted to derive an aesthetics of money that was not entirely dependent on any particular form of economic relations. See also Frisby and Featherstone's edited book *Simmel on Culture* (1997).

6. I thank one of my anonymous reviewers for this important insight.

7. And they are not wrong about that, given that the American economy is largely a consumption-driven economy rather than a production- or savings-driven economy, with estimates putting consumption at about 70 percent of the overall U.S. economy.

8. Dorsey 1995, 220–21.

9. Simmel 1978 [1900], 312.

10. In a college course that I created at Temple University, titled "Money: Who Has It, Who Doesn't, and Why It Matters," I ask my students to imagine having unlimited money. Then I request that they consider how they would make their purchasing decisions throughout a typical day. They are often completely flummoxed by this exercise because they are so used to thinking in terms of scarcity and whether they can afford something or whether spending money on one item would give them more pleasure than spending the same money on something else. Most of my students have significant trouble imagining a world where scarcity and trade-off is not the primary criterion of their decision-making. After much prodding, my students usually then enter what I think of as a state of "hedonistic reverie," relishing in the dream of buying anything and everything they want. Continuing on in the discussion, some students eventually realize that they would need to develop a different standard for deciding whether to buy something—something like whether a purchase was "good" for them or whether giving money to a relative would be a wise thing to do (hints of a psychological measuring stick of some sort enters in) or whether it was "right" to spend money on a luxury item if others

needed the money to eat or were starving (hints of a moral measuring stick being developed).

11. Harvey 1990, 100.

12. This system contributes to people's difficulty in gauging value separate from price. How often do people look at a price tag and because of the high price come to believe the item is actually worth more than they had previously thought (or the reverse)?

13. This idea might also help explain why I have over one hundred rolls of paper towels stored in my basement. See Porter 2011 for an interesting discussion of how we arrive at prices.

14. See Menger 1892.

15. See also James Grant's 1992 book *Money of the Mind: Borrowing and Lending in America form the Civil War to Michael Milken* for an overview of the development of banking and credit (what Grant calls "democratizing credit"). Marieke de Goede, in her 2005 book *Virtue, Fortune, and Faith*, makes the argument that our current view of money and finance is itself a result of historical contestation over the meaning of money and over the respectability of the field of finance. As she writes at the beginning of her book, "I will argue that money, capital, and finance are not unmediated realities that can be taken as a starting point to academic inquiry but have been made possible through contested historical articulations and practices of valuation" (xv). She continues, "I have argued that the representation of financial history as a legend, in which the use of shells, the minting of coins, the invention of paper money, and the creation of credit are seen as logical, subsequent steps in monetary evolution, abstracts modern financial instruments from their political, and often violent, histories" (21).

16. Consider all the societal exhortations to put money to use. This has led to the widespread acceptance of the notion that the failure to invest money in some way is simply foolhardy.

17. Bloom 1996, 72.

18. Money is complicated further by its many and varied uses. Bloom (1996) describes at least eleven different major types of uses that have been stressed by researchers. In addition to serving as a medium of exchange, money also serves as a standard of value, so it can be used to store and retain value (of course, it can also lose value), and it can also serve to compare and measure the worth of one thing relative to another. We also know, though, that money has served ornamental functions in many societies. People collect and display attractive objects, and in modern society, money itself has become an object for display. Money has been inserted into our deepest social relationships, playing a role in marriage contracts, dowries, prenuptial agreements, and divorce settlements. Money has political meaning, ranging

from a measurement of the success of a society's political arrangements to its influence in the next electoral campaign. Money emerges out of, and shapes, internal and external trading relations with others. Money holds religious meaning, as all religions have important things to say about money. Money can serve as a marker of status, including giving people the sense that they have made it, or alternatively, not having enough money can be a source of constant worry and great anxiety. Baker and Jimerson (1992, 680) make a good case for a sociology of money that occupies a middle ground between anthropology and economics, which allows sociology to treat money as both the cause of social change and the consequence of social relationships.

19. Glover 1996, 102.
20. There are people who try to earn a living by building up the power of an avatar in a particular game and selling that character for money (i.e., a national currency). This suggests some interchangeability or an exchange rate between the online currency, which is earned through playing and allows one to create a more valuable character, and the national currency for which that character is then sold.
21. See Helft 2010. Popular games on the Facebook site are Farmville and Mafia Wars. Google reportedly has plans to turn credits into a microloan payment system. See also Kurtzman 1993.
22. One could imagine a future in which national currency becomes like gold during the era of the gold standard. National currency would mainly be kept by the Federal Reserve to back up virtual currency. Some people might even argue that this has already happened to some extent.
23. These observations should be thought of as particularly tentative ones in need of further study and confirmation.
24. Although income and wealth are obviously correlated, they are distinct measures. If a tithe was based on wealth, an extremely wealthy person would be asked to donate much more than if it were based on income.
25. Bellah et al. 1986
26. Sennett and Cobb 1973.
27. Barber 2007. See also Cohen 2003.
28. In this way, my argument dovetails with David Halle's finding that the working people he studied had three different but interrelated forms of consciousness: one formed through work, one formed through their residence and consumption, and one formed through national identity (Halle 1987).
29. Economists tend to use the term *desire* to refer to the degree to which an individual wants something due to the intrinsic qualities of that good or service, and they sometimes distinguish desires from *wants* or *needs*. I am simply pointing out that desires may not be individually based as much as they are socially

based, given the role of advertising, the extension of the availability of mass media, and the experiences that occur in social settings.

30. Crump 1981, 1; or as Forrest Gump might put it, "Money is what money does."
31. Crump 1992, 669.
32. This may be why the item that works best as money in a given society is often something that is useless as anything else. As Crump points out, this ensures that "there is no possible confusion as to whether or not any given object is money" (1981, 5).

Notes to the Methodological Appendix

1. Other sociologists who include a cognitive perspective in their research encounter similar challenges (Zerubavel 1991, 1997). Christena Nippert-Eng has developed many innovative ways to elicit the thought processes of her respondents, asking people, for example, to put lists of items into groupings and then asking why they grouped certain things together. She has also asked respondents to talk about what is currently in their wallet or in their purse and then discusses the meanings of those items to the respondent. She has also used observations (such as whether people display family photos on their desks) as indicators of how people think about work and home space (see Nippert-Eng 1996). I tried a few of these types of techniques, asking how much money people carried in their pockets or how often they visited an ATM machine, for example.
2. I thought of the idea for asking these basic questions when I recalled a scene from Tom Wolfe's *Bonfire of the Vanities*, written during the go-go years for bond traders in the 1980s. The lead character, Sherman McCoy—the self-styled "Master of the Universe"—is struggling to explain to his young daughter what a bond trader does for a living. Sherman's wife, who is angry at him for a suspected extramarital affair, steps into the conversation with this deflating explanation of what a bond trader does: "Daddy doesn't build roads or hospitals, and he doesn't help build them, but he does handle the *bonds* for the people who raise the money." "Bonds?" asks the young daughter, confused. "Yes. Just imagine that a bond is a slice of cake, and you didn't bake the cake, but every time you hand somebody a slice of the cake a tiny little bit comes off, like a little crumb, and you can keep that. . . . You have to imagine little crumbs, but a *lot* of little crumbs" (Wolfe 1987, 229; emphasis in original).
3. Arthur Frank (2010) makes a strong case for the importance of understanding stories. Examining the art and the mechanics of storytelling is one way of understanding the complexities of social phenomena.
4. See Meanwell, Wolfe, and Hallet 2008 for an overview of research on emotion work.

5. Disentangling the direction of causality is a major challenge, as I can only take a snapshot of a dynamic historical process in which the interaction of culture and structure is constant and ongoing. I tend to privilege structure producing culture, but in a dynamic workplace over time, it is obvious that the two are intertwined and operate in recursive fashion.

6. Paul DiMaggio (1994, 29) observes that when the field of economics moves toward considering the underlying bases of economic constructs such as "tastes" or "preferences," it tends to move toward the field of cognitive psychology rather than toward sociological or anthropological constructs of culture and identity. Moving in this direction is preferred because it fits better with the individualistic, as opposed to the communal, approach that underlies much of economic modeling. Since the publication of DiMaggio's article "Culture and Economy," there has been a rapid increase in neuroscientific-based approaches in cognitive psychology, based on brain imaging, and this has accelerated the tendency noted by DiMaggio. New brain-imaging techniques provide outcome measures that better fit into the microeconomic traditions of individual preference and taste (Knutson et al. 2007). Sociologists have not embraced brain-imaging techniques, although I am not certain there is any reason that they could not. For example, a sociologist could use a brain scan to see what part of the brain is activated when a social norm is broken, for example. While such a method could allow sociologists to produce physical evidence of the power of social norms, it does lead down a more individualistic explanatory pathway, and that may be why it has been less appealing to sociologists.

7. Geary 2011.

REFERENCES

Abolafia, Mitch. 1996. *Making Markets*. Cambridge: Harvard University Press.

Akerlof, George A., and Rachel E. Kranton. 2010. *Identity Economics: How Our Identities Shape Our Work, Wages, and Well-Being*. Princeton: Princeton University Press.

Allison, Paul D. 1992. "The Cultural Evolution of Beneficent Norms." *Social Forces* 71:279–301.

Azzi, Corry, and Ronald Ehrenberg. 1975. "Household Allocation of Time and Church Attendance." *Journal of Political Economy* 83:27–56.

Baker, Wayne E., and Jason B. Jimerson. 1992. "The Sociology of Money." *American Behavioral Scientist* 35:678–93.

Balzac, Honoré de. 1896. *A Great Man of the Provinces in Paris*. Boston: Roberts Brothers.

Barber, Benjamin. 2007. *Consumed: How Markets Corrupt Children, Infantilize Adults, and Swallow Children Whole*. New York: Norton.

Barley, Stephen, and Gideon Kunda. 2001. "Bringing Work Back In." *Organization Science* 12:76–95.

Baron, James, Michael Hannan, Greta Hsu, and Ozgecan Kocak. 2007. "In the Company of Women: Gender Inequality and the Logic of Bureaucracy in Start-Up Firms." *Work and Occupations* 34:35–66.

Baudrillard, Jean. 1975. *The Mirror of Production*. New York: Telos.

Beaudoin, Tom. 2003. *Consuming Faith: Integrating Who We Are with What We Buy*. Lanham, MD: Sheed & Ward.

Becker, Howard. 1956. *Man in Reciprocity*. New York: Praeger.

Belk, Russell. 2010. "Sharing." *Journal of Consumer Research* 36:715–34.

Bellah, Robert, Richard Madsen, William Sullivan, Ann Swidler, and Steven Tipton. 1986. *Habits of the Heart: Individualism and Commitment in American Life*. New York: Harper & Row.

Bellin, Andy. 2002. *Poker Nation: A High-Stakes, Low-Life Adventure into the Heart of Gambling Country*. New York: Perennial/HarperCollins.

Berking, Helmuth. 1999. *Sociology of Giving*. Thousand Oaks, CA: Sage.

Berle, Adolf, and Gardiner Means. 1982 [1949]. *The Modern Corporation and Private Property*. New York: William S. Hein.

Beunza, Daniel, and David Stark. 2004. "Tools of the Trade: The Socio-technology of Arbitrage in a Wall Street Trading Room." *Industrial and Corporate Change* 13:369–400.

———. 2005. "The Organization of Responsiveness: Innovation and Recovery in the Trading Rooms of Lower Manhattan." *Socio-Economic Review* 1:135–64.

———. 2010. "Models, Reflexivity and Systemic Risk: A Critique of Behavioral Finance." Working Papers Series, Social Science Research Network (SSRN), April. Available at http://www.ssrn.com/abstract=1285054.

Bielby, William , and James Baron. 1986. "Men and Women at Work: Sex Segregation and Statistical Discrimination." *American Journal of Sociology* 91:759–99.

Biggart, Nicole Woolsey. 1990. *Charismatic Capitalism*. Chicago: University of Chicago Press.

———. 2002. Preface to Nicole Woolsey Biggart, ed., *Readings in Economic Sociology*. Malden, MA: Blackwell.

Black, Fischer, and Myron Scholes. 1973. "The Pricing of Options and Corporate Liabilities." *Journal of Political Economy* 81:637–54.

Blau, Peter. 1964. *Exchange and Power in Social Life*. New York: Wiley.

Bloom, William. 1996. *Money, Heart, and Mind: Financial Well-Being for People and Planet*. New York: Kodansha.

Bok, Derek. 1993. *The Cost of Talent: How Executives and Professionals Are Paid and How It Affects America*. New York: Free Press.

Bourdieu, Pierre. 1977. "Cultural Reproduction and Social Reproduction." Pp. 487–510 in Jerome Karabel and A. H. Halsey, eds., *Power and Ideology in Education*. New York: Oxford University Press.

Brekhus, Wayne. 2008. "Trends in the Qualitative Study of Social Identities." *Sociology Compass* 2(3): 1059–78. DOI: 10.1111/j.1751-9020.2008.00107.x.

Brenner, Reuven, Gabrielle A. Brenner, and Aaron Brown. 2008. *A World of Chance: Betting on Religion, Games, Wall Street*. Cambridge: Cambridge University Press.

Brunson, Doyle. 1979. *Super System: A Course in Power Poker*. New York: Cardoza.

Burawoy, Michael. 1979. *Manufacturing Consent*. Chicago: University of Chicago Press.

Callon, Michel, and Koray Caliskan. 2005. "New and Old Directions in the Anthropology of Markets." Paper presented at the Wenner-Gren Foundation for Anthropological Research, New York, April.

Callon, Michel, Yuval Millo, and Fabian Muniesa, eds. 2007. *Market Devices*. Malden, MA: Blackwell.

Cannell, Fenella. 2006. Introduction to Fenella Cannell, ed., *The Anthropology of Christianity*. Durham: Duke University Press.

Carruthers, Bruce, and Wendy Nelson Espeland. 1998. "Money, Meaning and Morality." *American Behavioral Scientist* 41:1384–1408.

Chandra, A. K. 1981. "The Young Man from the Provinces." *Comparative Literature* 33:321–41.

Chase, Susan E. 1995. "Taking Narrative Seriously: Consequences for Method and Theory in Interview Studies." Pp. 1–26 in Ruthellen Josselson and Amia Lieblich, eds., *Interpreting Experience: The Narrative Study of Lives*, vol. 3. Thousand Oaks, CA: Sage.

Chiel, David. 1988. *The Gift Economy*. New York: Routledge.

Cohen, Lizabeth. 2003. *Republic: The Politics of Mass Consumption in Postwar America*. New York: Knopf.

Collom, Ed. 2011. "Motivations and Differential Participation in a Community Currency System: The Dynamics within a Local Social Movement Organization." *Sociological Forum* 26:144–68.

Connor, Steven. 1997. *Postmodernist Culture*. 2nd ed. Cambridge, MA: Blackwell.

Conrad, Mark. 2006. *The Business of Sports: A Primer for Journalists*. Mahwah, NJ: Erlbaum.

Craig, Michael. 2005. *The Professor, the Banker, and the Suicide King: Inside the Richest Poker Game of All Time*. New York: Warner Books.

Crump, Thomas. 1981. *The Phenomenon of Money*. London: Routledge & Kegan Paul.
———. 1992. "Money as a Ritual System." *American Behavioral Scientist* 35:669–777.

Dalai Llama, and Howard Cutler. 2003. *The Art of Happiness at Work*. New York: Riverhead Books.
———. 2009. *The Art of Happiness*. New York: Riverhead Books.

Davis, Gerald F. 2009. *Managed by the Markets: How Finance Has Reshaped America*. New York: Oxford University Press.

de Goede, Marieke. 2005. *Virtue, Fortune, and Faith: A Genealogy of Finance*. Minneapolis: University of Minnesota Press.

Derman, Emmanuel. 2004. *My Life as a Quant*. New York: Wiley.

Dickens, Charles. 2007 [1843]. *A Christmas Carol*. New York: Pocket Books.

DiMaggio, Paul. 1990. "Cultural Aspects of Economic Action and Organization." Pp. 113–36 in Roger Friedland and A. F. Robertson, eds., *Beyond the Marketplace: Rethinking Economy and Society*. New York: De Gruyter.
———. 1994. "Culture and Economy." Pp. 27–57 in Neil Smelser and Richard Swedberg, eds., *The Handbook of Economic Sociology*. New York and Princeton: Russell Sage Foundation and Princeton University Press.

Dorsey, David. 1995. *The Force*. New York: Ballantine Books.

Du Gay, Paul. 1996. *Consumption and Identity at Work*. London: Sage.

Durkheim, Émile. 1915. *The Elementary Forms of Religious Life*. London: Allen & Unwin.

Edwards, Paul, and Judy Wajcman. 2005. *The Politics of Working Life*. New York: Oxford University Press.

Eisenberg, Lee. 2006. *The Number: What Do You Need for the Rest of Your Life, and What Will It Cost?* New York: Free Press.

Eliade, Mercia. 1987. *The Sacred and the Profane: The Nature of Religion*. New York: Harcourt.

Ellingson, Stephen. 2007. *The Megachurch and the Mainline: Remaking Religious Tradition in the Twenty-First Century*. Chicago: University of Chicago Press.

Ellis, David. 2010. "Hedge Funds Are Making a Comeback." CNN.com, March 12. http://money.cnn.com/2010/03/11/news/companies/hedge_fund/index.htm.

Englert, Jonathan. 2006. *The Collar: A Year of Striving and Faith inside a Catholic Seminary*. Boston: Houghton Mifflin.

Erickson, Rebecca, and Amy Wharton. 1997. "Inauthenticity and Depression: Assessing the Consequences of Interactive Service Work." *Work and Occupations* 24:188–213.

Evans, James, Gideon Kunda, and Stephen R. Barley. 2003. "Beach Time, Bridge Time, and Billable Hours: The Temporal Structure of Technical Contracting." *Administrative Science Quarterly* 49:1–38.

Ferguson, Niall. 2009. *The Ascent of Money: A Financial History of the World*. New York: Penguin Books.

Fevre, Ralph. 2003. *The New Sociology of Economic Behaviour*. London: Sage.

Financial Crisis Inquiry Commission. 2011. *The Financial Crisis Inquiry Report: Final Report of the National Commission of the Causes of the Financial and Economic Crisis in the United States*. Washington, DC: PublicAffairs.

Fish, Stanley. 1993. "Ivory Tower Masochists." *Harper's*, September 1, 20–21.

Fitzgerald, F. Scott. 2007 [1925]. *The Great Gatsby*. New York: Penguin.

Flaherty, Michael G. 2010. *The Textures of Time: Agency and Temporal Experience*. Philadelphia: Temple University Press.

Frank, Arthur. 2010. *Letting Stories Breathe: A Socio-narratology*. Chicago: University of Chicago Press.

Fraser, Steve. 2008. *Wall Street: America's Dream Palace*. New Haven: Yale University Press.

Freud, Sigmund. 1996. "A Letter to Anna Freud." Translated by Michael Molner. *American Imago* 53:201–4.

Frisby, David, and Mike Featherstone, eds. 1997. *Simmel on Culture*. Thousand Oaks, CA: Sage.

Garson, Barbara. 2002. *Money Makes the World Go Round*. New York: Penguin.

Geary, James. 2011. *I Is an Other: The Secret Life of Metaphor and How It Shapes the Way We See the World*. New York: Harper.

Geertz, Clifford. 1973. *Interpretation of Cultures*. New York: Basic Books.

Gladwell, Malcolm. 2005. *Blink: The Power of Thinking without Thinking*. New York: Little, Brown.

Glover, Paul. 1995. "Grass Roots Economics." *In Context*, Summer, 30.

———. 1996. *Hometown Money: How to Enrich Your Community with Local Currency*. Ithaca, NY: Greenplanners.

Godbout, Jacques, with Alaine Caille. 1998. *The World of the Gift*. Montreal: McGill-Queen's University Press.

Goldberg, Herb, and Robert T. Lewis. 1978. *Money Madness: The Psychology of Saving, Spending, Loving and Hating Money*. New York: William Morrow.

Goodchild, Philip. 2009. *Theology of Money*. Durham: Duke University Press.

Goodman, Jordan E. 2006. *Master Your Money Type: Using Your Financial Personality to Create a Life of Wealth and Freedom*. New York: Warner Books.

Granovetter, Mark. 1985. "Economic Action and Social Structure: The Problem of Embeddedness." *American Journal of Sociology* 91:481–510.

———. 2002. "A Theoretical Agenda for Economic Sociology." Pp. 35–60 in Mauro Guillen, Randall Collins, Paula England and Marshall Meyer, eds., *The New Economic Sociology*. New York: Russell Sage Foundation.

Grant, James. 1992. *Money of the Mind: Borrowing and Lending in America from the Civil War to Michael Milken*. New York: Farrar, Straus & Giroux.

Groysberg, Boris. 2010. *Chasing Stars: The Myth of Talent and the Portability of Performance*. Princeton: Princeton University Press.

Gubrium, Jaber F., and James A. Holstein. 1995. "Biographical Work and the New Ethnography." Pp. 45–58 in Ruthellen Josselson and Amia Lieblich, eds., *Interpreting Experience: The Narrative Study of Lives*, vol. 3. Thousand Oaks, CA: Sage.

Halle, David. 1987. *America's Working Man: Work, Home, and Politics among Blue-Collar Property Owners*. Chicago: University of Chicago Press.

Hansen, Laura L., and Siamak Movahedi. 2010. "Wall Street Scandals: The Myth of Personal Greed." *Sociological Forum* 25:367–74.

Hardie, Iain, and Donald MacKenzie. 2006. "Assembling an Economic Actor: The *Agencement* of a Hedge Fund." Paper presented at the workshop "New Actors in a Financialized Economy and Implications for Varieties of Capitalism," Institute of Commonwealth Studies, London, May 11–12.

Harvey, David. 1990. *The Condition of Postmodernity*. Cambridge, MA: Blackwell.

Hayano, David M. 1982. *Poker Faces: The Life and Work of Professional Card Players*. Berkeley: University of California Press.

Healy, Kieran. 2002. "What's New for Culture in the New Economy?" *Journal of Arts, Management, Law and Society* 32:86–103.

Helft. Miguel. 2010. "New Money, Online Only." *New York Times*, September 23, B1.

Ho, Karen. 2009. *Liquidated: An Ethnography of Wall Street*. Durham: Duke University Press.

Hochschild, Arlie. 1979. "Emotion Work, Feeling Rules, and Social Structure." *American Journal of Sociology* 85:551–75.

Hockenos, Paul. 2010. "Educating Imams in Germany: The Battle for a European Islam." *Chronicle of Higher Education*, July 18. http://chronicle.com/article/Educating-Imams-in-Germany-/66282/.

Homans, George. 1958. "Social Behavior as Exchange." *American Journal of Sociology* 63:597–606.

Hughes, Everett C. 1958. *Men and Their Work*. Glencoe, IL: Free Press.

Humphreys, Michael, and Andrew D. Brown. 2002. "Narratives of Organizational Identity and Identification: A Case Study of Hegemony and Resistance." *Organization Studies* 23:421–47.

Hyde, Lewis. 1979. *The Gift: Imagination and the Erotic Life of Property*. New York: Random House.

Ingham, Geoffrey. 1996. "Money Is a Social Relation." *Review of Social Economy* 54:507–29.

———. 2001. "Fundamentals of a Theory of Money: Untangling Fine, Lapavitsas and Zelizer." *Economy and Society* 30:304–23.

Iyer, Pico. 2008. *The Open Road: The Global Journey of the Fourteenth Dalai Lama*. New York: Knopf.

Jacobs, Mark D., and Nancy Weiss Hanrahan, eds. 2006. *The Blackwell Companion to the Sociology of Culture*. Malden, MA: Blackwell.

James, Henry. 1948 [1886]. *The Princess Casamassima*. New York: Macmillan.

Jerry Maguire (film). 1996. TriStar Pictures.

Jinpa, Thupten. 2006. *Self, Reality and Reason in Tibetan Philosophy*. New York: Routledge.

Josselson, Ruthellen, and Amia Lieblich, eds. 1995. *Interpreting Experience: The Narrative Study of Lives*. Vol. 3. Thousand Oaks, CA: Sage.

Kadlec, Dan. 2009. "Will a Wall Streeter Win Big at the World Series of Poker?" Time.com, November 3. http://www.time.com/time/business/article/0,8599,1934041,00.html.

Kaysen, Carl. 1957. "The Social Significance of the Modern Corporation. *American Economic Review* 47:311–19.

Klebanow, Sheila, and Eugene L. Lowenkop, eds. 1991. *Money and Mind*. New York: Plenum.

Klontz, Brad, Sonya Britt, Jennifer Mentzer, and Ted Klontz. 2011. "Money Beliefs and Financial Behaviors: Development of the Klontz Money Script Inventory." *Journal of Financial Therapy* 2:1–22.

Knorr-Cetina, Karin, and Alex Preda, eds. 2005. *The Sociology of Financial Markets*. New York: Oxford University Press.

Knutson, Brian, Scott Rick, G. Elliott Wimmer, Drazen Prelec, and George Lowen-stein. 2007. "Neural Predictors of Purchases." *Neuron* 53:147–156.

Komter, Aafke E. 2005. *Social Solidarity and the Gift*. New York: Cambridge University Press.

Kurtzman, Joel. 1993. *The Death of Money: How the Electronic Economy Has Destabilized the World's Markets and Created Financial Chaos*. New York: Simon & Schuster.

Lamont, Michele. 2009. *How Professors Think: Inside the Curious World of Academic Judgment*. Cambridge: Harvard University Press.

Larson, Magali Sarfatti. 2006. "Professions as Disciplinary Cultures." Pp. 317–31 in Mark D. Jacobs and Nancy Weiss Hanrahan, eds., *The Blackwell Companion to the Sociology of Culture*. Malden, MA: Blackwell.

Lehrer, Jonah. 2009. *How We Decide*. New York: Houghton Mifflin Harcourt.

Leidner, Robin. 1993. *Fast Food, Fast Talk: Service Work and the Routinization of Everyday Life*. Berkeley: University of California Press.

Leonard, Christopher. 2010. "Serving Up Inherent Goodness." *Philadelphia Inquirer*, June 26, D1.

Lepinay, Vincent A. 2011. *Codes of Finance: Engineering Derivatives in a Global Bank*. Princeton: Princeton University Press.

Lewis, Michael. 1990. *Liar's Poker*. New York: Penguin.

———. 2010. *The Big Short: Inside the Doomsday Machine*. New York: Norton.

Lindsey, Richard R., and Barry Schachter. 2007. *How I Became a Quant: Insights from 25 of Wall Street's Elite*. Hoboken, NJ: Wiley.

Lodge, David. 1990. *Nice Work*. New York: Penguin.

Lowenstein, Roger. 2001. *When Genius Failed: The Rise and Fall of Long-Term Capital Management*. New York: Random House.

MacKenzie, Donald. 2006. *An Engine, Not a Camera: How Financial Models Shape Markets*. Cambridge: MIT Press.

MacKenzie, Donald, Fabien Muniesa, and Lucia Siu. 2007. *Do Economists Make Markets? On the Performativity of Markets*. Princeton: Princeton University Press.

Mallaby, Sebastian. 2010. *More Money than God: Hedge Funds and the Making of a New Elite*. New York: Penguin.

Mamet, David. 1994 [1984]. *Glengarry, Glen Ross*. New York: Grove.

Marcoux, Jean-Sebastien. 2009. "Escaping the Gift Economy." *Journal of Consumer Research* 36:671–85.

Martin, Randy. 2002. *Financialization of Daily Life*. Philadelphia: Temple University Press.

Marx, Karl. 1967 [1867]. *Capital*. Volume 1. New York: International Publishers.

Maurer, Bill. 2005. *Mutual Life, Limited: Islamic Banking, Alternative Currencies, Lateral Reason*. Princeton: Princeton University Press.

Mauss, Marcel. 2000 [1900]. *The Gift: The Form and Reason for the Exchange in Archaic Societies*. New York: Norton.

Maynes, Mary Jo, Jennifer Pierce, and Barbara Laslett. 2008. *Telling Stories: The Use of Personal Narratives in the Social Sciences and History*. Ithaca: Cornell University Press.

McCormack, Peggy. 1990. *The Rule of Money: Gender, Class, and Exchange Economics in the Fiction of Henry James*. Ann Arbor, MI: UMI Research Press.

McCrary, Stuart. 2002. *How to Create and Manage a Hedge Fund*. New York: Wiley.

———. 2005. *Hedge Fund Course*. New York: Wiley.

McManus, James. 2009. *Cowboys Full: The Story of Poker*. New York: Farrar, Straus & Giroux.

Meanwell, Emily, Joseph D. Wolfe, and Tim Hallett. 2008. "Old Paths and New Directions: Studying Emotions in the Workplace." *Sociology Compass* 2:537–59.

Menger, Karl. 1892. "On the Origin of Money. *Economic Journal* 2:239–55.

Miller, Arthur. 1996 [1949]. *Death of a Salesman*. New York: Penguin.

Miller, Vincent J. 2003. *Consuming Religion: Christian Faith and Practice in a Consumer Culture*. New York: Continuum.

Millo, Yuval, and Donald MacKenzie. 2007. "Building a Boundary Object: The Evolution of Financial Risk Management." Working Paper Series, Social Science Research Network (SSRN), November. Available at http://ssm.com/abstract=1031745.

Moeran, Brian. 2006. *Ethnography at Work*. New York: Berg.

Molm, Linda. 2010. "The Structure of Reciprocity." *Social Psychology Quarterly* 73:119–31.

Morris, Charles R. 2008. *The Two Trillion Dollar Meltdown: Easy Money, High Rollers, and the Great Credit Crash*. New York: PublicAffairs.

Moynihan, Colin. 2010. "In Brooklyn Store, Everything Is Always 100% Off." *New York Times*, August 16. http://www.nytimes.com/2010/08/16/nyregion/16free.html?--r=1&e,c=etal.

Nippert-Eng, Christena. 1996. *Home and Work: Negotiating Boundaries through Everyday Life*. Chicago: University of Chicago Press.

———. 2010. *Islands of Privacy*. Chicago: University of Chicago Press.

North, Peter. 2007. *Money and Liberation: The Micropolitics of the Alternative Currency Movement*. Minneapolis: University of Minnesota Press.

Osteen, Mark, ed. 2002. *The Question of the Gift*. New York: Routledge.

Partnoy, Frank. 1999. *Fiasco: The Inside Story of a Wall Street Trader*. New York: Penguin.

Peifer, Jared. 2010. "Morality in the Financial Market: A Look at Religiously Affiliated Mutual Funds." *Socio-Economic Review* 9:235–59.

Pesaran, Bijin, Matthew J. Nelson, and Richard A. Anderson. 2008. "Free Choice Activates a Decision Circuit between Frontal and Parietal Cortex." *Nature* 453:406–9.

Poggi, Gianfranco. 1993. *Money and the Modern Mind: Georg Simmel's Philosophy of Money*. Berkeley: University of California Press.

Porter, Eduardo. 2011. *The Price of Everything: Solving the Mystery of Why We Buy What We Do*. New York: Portfolio.

Portes, Alejandro. 2010. *Economic Sociology: A Systematic Inquiry*. Princeton: Princeton University Press.

Ransome, Paul. 2005. *Work, Consumption and Culture: Affluence and Social Change in the Twenty-First Century*. London: Sage.

Reskin, Barbara, and Patricia Roos. 1990. *Job Queues, Gender Queues: Explaining Women's Inroads into Male Occupations*. Philadelphia: Temple University Press.

Rohr, Richard, with John Feister. 2001. *Hope against Darkness: The Transforming Vision of Saint Frances in an Age of Anxiety*. Cincinnati: St. Anthony Messenger Press.

Sallaz, Jeffrey. 2009. *The Labor of Luck: Casino Capitalism in the United States and South Africa*. Berkeley: University of California Press.

Scannell, Kara, Deborah Solomon, and Gregory Zuckerman. 2006. "SEC Dealt Setback as Court Rejects Hedge-Fund Rule." *Wall Street Journal*, June 24–25, 1.

Schechtman, Marya. 1996. *The Constitution of Selves*. Ithaca: Cornell University Press.

Schiller, Robert J. 1990. "Speculative Prices and Popular Models." *Journal of Economic Perspectives* 4:55–65.

Sennett, Richard. 1998. *Corrosion of Character: The Personal Consequences of Work in the New Capitalism*. New York: Norton.

Sennett, Richard, and Jonathan Cobb. 1973. *The Hidden Injuries of Class*. New York: Vintage.

Siler, Kyle. 2009. "The Social and Psychological Challenges of Poker." *Journal of Gambling Studies* (electronic journal), December. DOI: 10.1007/s10899-009-9168-2.

Simmel, Georg. 1971. *On Individuality and Social Forms*. Edited by Donald N. Levine. Chicago: University of Chicago Press.

———. 1978 [1900]. *The Philosophy of Money*. Translated and with an introduction by Tom Bottomore and David Frisby. London: Routledge.

Smelser, Neil, and Richard Swedberg, eds. 1994. *The Handbook of Economic Sociology*. New York and Princeton: Russell Sage Foundation and Princeton University Press.

Smith, Adam. 1985 [1776]. *An Inquiry into the Nature and Causes of the Wealth of Nations*. New York: Random House.

Smith, Christian, Michael O. Emerson, and Patricia Snell. 2009. *Passing the Plate: Why American Christians Don't Give Away More Money*. New York: Oxford University Press.

Stewart, James B. 1992. *Den of Thieves*. New York: Touchstone Books.

Sullivan, Teresa, Jay Lawrence Westbrook, and Elizabeth Warren. 1999. *As We Forgive Our Debtors: Bankruptcy and Consumer Credit in America*. New York: Beard Books.

Swedberg, Richard. 2003. *Principles of Economic Sociology*. Princeton: Princeton University Press.

———. 2005. "Max Weber's Economic Sociology: The Centerpiece of *Economy and Society*?" Pp. 127–42 in Charles Camic, Philip S. Gorski, and David M. Trubek, eds., *Max Weber's "Economy and Society": A Critical Companion*. Stanford: Stanford University Press.

Swidler, Ann. 2001. *Talk of Love: How Culture Matters*. Chicago: University of Chicago Press.

Tett, Gillian. 2009. *Fool's Gold*. New York: Free Press.

Throsby, David. 2001. *Economics and Culture*. New York: Cambridge University Press.

Tomaskovic-Devey, Donald. 1993. *Gender and Racial Inequality at Work: The Sources and Consequences of Job Segregation*. Ithaca, NY: ILR.

Trading Places (film). 1983. Paramount Pictures.

Trilling, Lionel. 1979. "The Princess Casamassima." In *The Liberal Imagination*. New York: Harcourt.

Vaughan, Genevieve, ed. 2007. *Women and the Gift Economy*. Toronto: Inanna.

Veblen, Thorstein. 2008 [1899]. *The Theory of the Leisure Class*. New York: Oxford University Press.

Vila, Pablo. 2000. *Crossing Borders, Reinforcing Borders: Social Categories, Metaphors, and Narrative Identities on the U.S.-Mexico Frontier*. Austin: University of Texas Press.

Wachtel, Paul. 1983. *Poverty of Affluence: A Psychological Portrait of the American Way of Life*. New York: Free Press.

Walker, Marcus. 2007. "Dumpster Divers Go Mainstream in Thrifty Germany." *Wall Street Journal*, October 22.

Weber, Max. 1930. *The Protestant Ethic and the Spirit of Capitalism*. London: Allen & Unwin.

———. 1978. *Economy and Society*. Edited by Guenther Roth and Claus Wittich. Berkeley: University of California Press.

Weinstein, Stanley. 2009. *The Complete Guide to Fundraising Management*. New York: Wiley.

Weiss, Gary. 2006. *Wall Street versus America: The Rampant Greed and Dishonesty That Imperil Your Investments*. New York: Portfolio.

Wharton, Amy. 1993. "The Affective Consequences of Service Work: Managing Emotions on the Job." *Work and Occupations* 20:205–32.

Wilde, Oscar. 2004 [1891]. *The Picture of Dorian Gray*. New York: Barnes and Noble Classics.

Winans, R. Foster. 1984. *Trading Secrets: Seduction and Scandal at the Wall Street Journal*. New York: St. Martin's.

Wolfe, Tom. 1987. *Bonfire of the Vanities*. New York: Farrar, Straus & Giroux.

Wuthnow, Robert. 1994. *God and Mammon in America*. New York: Free Press.

———. 1997. *The Crisis in the Churches: Spiritual Malaise, Fiscal Woe*. New York: Oxford University Press.

Zelizer, Viviana. 1988. "Beyond the Polemics of the Market: Establishing a Theoretical and Empirical Agenda." *Sociological Forum* 3:614–34.

———. 1997. *The Social Meaning of Money: Pin Money, Paychecks, Poor Relief, and Other Currencies*. Princeton: Princeton University Press.

———. 2002. "Enter Culture." Pp. 101–25 in Mauro Guillen, Randall Collins, Paula England, and Marshall Meyer, eds., *The New Economic Sociology: Developments in an Emerging Field*. New York: Russell Sage Foundation.

———. 2005. *The Purchase of Intimacy*. Princeton: Princeton University Press.

———. 2007. "Money in Circuits." Paper presented at the annual meeting of the American Sociological Association, New York, August.

———. 2010. *Economic Lives: How Culture Shapes the Economy*. Princeton: Princeton University Press.

Zerubavel, Eviatar. 1991. *The Fine Line: Making Distinctions in Everyday Life*. New York: Free Press.

———. 1997. *Social Mindscapes: An Invitation to Cognitive Sociology*. Cambridge: Harvard University Press.

INDEX

ABOUT THE AUTHOR

Kevin J. Delaney is Professor of Sociology and Vice Dean for Faculty Affairs in the College of Liberal Arts at Temple University and author of *Strategic Bankruptcy* and *Public Dollars, Private Stadiums* (with Rick Eckstein).